STUDIES IN HIGHER EDUCATION
DISSERTATION SERIES

Edited by
Philip G. Altbach
Monan Professor of Higher Education
Lynch School of Education, Boston College

STUDIES IN HIGHER EDUCATION
PHILIP G. ALTBACH, General Editor

SAVING FOR COLLEGE AND THE TAX CODE
A New Spin on the "Who Pays for Higher Education" Debate
Andrew P. Roth

RESOURCE ALLOCATION IN PRIVATE RESEARCH UNIVERSITIES
Daniel Rodas

I PREFER TO TEACH
An International Comparison of Faculty Preferences for Teaching
James J.F. Forest

TENURE ON TRIAL
Case Studies of Change in Faculty Employment Policies
William T. Mallon

FROM HERE TO UNIVERSITY
Access, Mobility, and Resilience among Urban Latino Youth
Alexander Jun

SCHOLARSHIP UNBOUND
Kerry Ann O'Meara

TECHNOLOGY TRANSFER VIA UNIVERSITY-INDUSTRY RELATIONS
The Case of the Foreign High Technology Electronic Industry in Mexico's Silicon Valley
Maria Isabel Rivera Vargas

Tenure on Trial
Case Studies of Change in Faculty Employment Policies

William T. Mallon

LONDON AND NEW YORK

First published 2001 by RoutledgeFalmer

Published 2018 by Routledge
2 Park Square, Milton Park, Abingdon, Oxon OX14 4RN
52 Vanderbilt Avenue, New York, NY 10017

First issued in paperback 2018

Routledge is an imprint of the Taylor & Francis Group, an informa business

Copyright © 2001 by William T. Mallon

All rights reserved. No part of this book may be reprinted or reproduced or utilised in any form or by any electronic, mechanical, or other means, now known or hereafter invented, including photocopying and recording, or in any information storage or retrieval system, without permission in writing from the publishers.

Notice:
Product or corporate names may be trademarks or registered trademarks, and are used only for identification and explanation without intent to infringe.

Portions of chapters 1, 7, and 8 appear in modified form in "Why is Tenure One College's Problem and Another's Solution" in The Questions of Tenure, ed. Richard P. Chait. Cambridge: Harvard University Press, © 2002 by the President and Fellows of Harvard College. Reprinted by permission.

Library of Congress Cataloging-in-Publication Data

Cataloging-in-publication data for this book is available from the Library of Congress.

ISBN 13: 978-1-138-98864-4 (pbk)
ISBN 13: 978-0-415-93219-6 (hbk)

Contents

CHAPTER 1
Introduction   3

CHAPTER 2
Tenure and Contract Systems: An Overview   15

CHAPTER 3
Scott College   45

CHAPTER 4
Rowlette College   69

CHAPTER 5
Lakeview College   97

CHAPTER 6
Accomac College   125

CHAPTER 7
How Did these Colleges Move in Opposite Directions?   151

CHAPTER 8
Conclusions   173

Appendix: Research Design and Methodology 187

References 209

Index 219

Tenure on Trial

CHAPTER 1
Introduction

ACADEMIC TENURE HAS BEEN CALLED A "THIRD RAIL" (MACGRATH, 1997) and the "abortion issue" of the academy (Chait, 1997). Even a cursory examination of professional publications, *The Chronicle of Higher Education*, or the op-ed pages of the nation's newspapers explains why. Discussions about tenure are more often impassioned arguments than empirical analyses. One way partisans "prove" their case for or against tenure is by speculating about what would happen if colleges were to abolish tenure. Two examples from the vast array of literature will suffice. One critic of tenure argued that "the replacement of lifetime tenure with fixed-term contracts would, at one stroke, restore accountability, while potentially freeing the vast untapped energies of the academy. . . ." (Sykes, 1988, p.258). Conversely, many tenure stalwarts have claimed that an institution that relinquishes tenure could not attract top-notch recruits, thus severely impairing the quality of faculty (e.g., Cotter, 1996; Finkin, 1996).

Two problems arise with these assertions. First, both sets of claims, until now, have been speculative. Proponents and opponents of tenure alike have been inattentive to the colleges that have actually done what pundits have only pondered. A number of institutions of higher education have abolished tenure, while others have pursued the opposite path, eliminating contracts and instituting tenure. Do the conventional arguments for and against tenure apply at these colleges? How and why did institutions with tenure eliminate a practice so deeply embedded in higher education? How and why did institutions with contracts adopt a policy so touted by tenure's critics? This book addresses these questions with data rather than assumptions and anecdotes.

Second, the typical litany of benefits and drawbacks to both tenure and contract systems tend to be rationally based. A rational model posits that college and university leaders would examine tenure and the alternatives and then logically choose the appropriate employment system based on a dispassionate cost-benefit analysis. Thus, advocates of change have argued that contract systems are better than tenure because they more readily enable adjustments to the labor force and ensure greater performance accountability. Conversely, champions of conventional practice have maintained that tenure is superior to contracts because, among other reasons, the one-time, up-or-out evaluation process guarantees more rigorous reviews than periodic contract renewals. This attention to the rational strengths and weaknesses of both policies ignores important symbolic and ambiguous properties of tenure, and the nonrational ways that colleges sometimes undergo organizational change. This book explores these shifts toward and away from tenure using several nonrational theories of organizational change as a framework.

A (VERY) BRIEF OVERVIEW OF FACULTY EMPLOYMENT POLICIES

There are two prevalent forms of faculty personnel policy.[1] Academic tenure, the most common, is defined as:

> an arrangement under which faculty appointments ... are continuous until [voluntary] retirement ... , subject to dismissal for adequate cause or unavoidable termination on account of financial exigency or change of institutional program. (Commission on Academic Tenure, 1973, p. 256)

Term contracts at institutions without tenure have one main attribute: appointments are for a specific period of time. Furthermore, at most institutions with contracts, the contracts are renewable without any up-or-out stipulation and contract length often varies based on seniority or length of service (Chait & Trower, 1997).

Of these two "pure" types of faculty employment policies, tenure systems are, by far, the norm in higher education. Conventional wisdom, supported by recent survey data, suggests all but a tiny fraction of four-year colleges offer tenure systems. Therefore, tenure "does convey an aura of legitimacy and at least the appearance of an institution respectful of academic tradition" (Chait & Ford, 1982, p. 65). Because tenure is the preferred system of faculty employment and a hallmark characteristic of higher education (Adams, 1974; Cotter, 1996; Iffland, 1998; National Center

---

[1]. A small number of institutions offer "hybrid" personnel policies, in which faculty choose whether to be on a tenure or non-tenure track (Chait & Trower, 1997).

for Education Statistics, 1996), a college shifting from tenure to contracts moves away from the professional norms of higher education.

WHY IS TENURE ON THE TABLE?

At the dawn of the 21st century, institutions of higher education in the United States are under increasingly intense pressure to improve quality, bolster productivity, contain costs, and modify employment systems (e.g. Immerwahr, 1999; Levine, 1997b). Shifts in demographics, advances in technology, and changes in the economy and labor markets have transformed the ways in which Americans produce, use, and rely on information and knowledge. Colleges and universities face a strong imperative to respond to these pressures because they are on the forefront of knowledge production and dissemination.

With escalating energy and urgency, critics and supporters alike are calling for higher education to rethink areas such as student learning, pricing and financial aid, access and equity, faculty roles and rewards, and community relations. Some calls for change in the late 1980s and early 1990s were quite shrill; the vituperations in books like *Profscam* by Charles Sykes (1988), *Tenured Radicals* by Roger Kimball (1990), and *Killing the Spirit* by Page Smith (1990) condemned many of the policies and practices of higher education. Op-ed pieces and commentaries in newspapers and magazines appear with regular frequency urging reform and overhaul (e.g, Carlin, 1999; Cottle, 1998; Los Angeles Times, 1999; St. Louis Post-Dispatch, 1999; Sowell, 1998; Tully, 1995). In addition, many inside higher education have recently raised concerns about the future of American colleges and universities (Bok, 1992; Breneman, 1993; Kennedy, 1997; Levine, 1997a; Levine, 2000; O'Brien, 1998; *Policy Perspectives*, 1994, 1996). Commentators have argued that higher education should not simply tinker at the edges, but fundamentally revamp how it educates students, employs faculty, and produces and distributes knowledge. The American Council on Education, for example, urged that colleges "alter the ways in which they think about and perform their basic functions of teaching, research, and service" and asserted that institutions must "transform" themselves to remain relevant to society (Eckel, Hill, & Green, 1998, p. 3).

Of the many potential areas for change, faculty appointment policies are among the most frequent targets for modification or overhaul (Aigner, 1998; Austin & Rice, 1998; Chait, 1995; Greenberg, 1997; Guskin, 1996; Immerwahr, 1999; Leslie, 1998). Most commentators have targeted their criticisms at traditional academic tenure, suggesting that it will have to be altered to accommodate changes in the broader society (Breneman, 1997; Chait, 1995; Levine, 1997b; Tierney, 1998b). For example, Tierney (1998b) summarized:

Tenure, as we have known it, needs to change in order to keep pace with new social, intellectual, and economic contexts, as do all organizational structures. We ought not to reify a structure—tenure—and assume it is a belief that cannot change; we also should not take a belief—academic freedom—and assume that it can be supported without a structure. Protecting academic freedom as the bedrock of the academy is imperative if we are to remain intellectually curious, competitive, and free. But tenure as we have known it will not be particularly functional for the changing circumstances of the twenty-first century. (p. 59)

PRESSURES TO CHANGE

If it is true, as Tierney suggests, that academic employment policies need to change to "keep pace with new social, intellectual, and economic contexts," what are these contexts? At least three new pressure points propel academic leaders to re-examine conventional faculty employment policies:

1. Pressure from market forces

Universities and colleges face mounting pressure to increase faculty productivity and accountability and to reduce costs. Some of these sources, such as state and federal government, have been with higher education for a long time; the cries for reform have simply gotten louder (Wellman, 2001). But, significantly, there is a new source of pressure at hand: for-profit competition. In 1997, one investment company predicted considerable growth in the for-profit sector:

> The already overburdened publicly funded higher-education system is likely to continue to create opportunities for proprietary, degree-granting education companies that are more keenly focused on client services . . . , rationalizing costs, and effective marketing. With no private or public institution enjoying a significant market share, . . . the opportunity for sizable, for-profit, nationwide service providers to emerge is substantial. (Lehman Brothers, 1997, p. 64)

This opportunity for growth was realized. By 2000, scores of for-profit companies had entered the higher education market: Argosy Education Group, Apollo Group, Capella University, Career Education Group, DeVry, Harcourt, ITT Educational Services, Jones International, Sylvan, and Whitman Education, to name a few. Moreover, a number of non-profit and public universities created for-profit operating units: Cornell, Columbia, New York University, Temple, and University of Maryland University College. This trend affects the faculty appointment policies of traditional higher education because these proprietary institutions—and

Introduction

even the university spin-offs—do not embrace the typical qualities of mainstream colleges and universities. Most notably, faculty members employed by these organizations are usually part-time, do not have tenure, and often do not have control over the curriculum that they teach. These characteristics have made traditional faculty wary of the for-profit sector's growth in popularity (Carr, 1999, 2000; Leatherman, 1998).

2. Organizational restructuring

Downsizing, outsourcing, and underemployment are common in today's economy, with significant restructuring having already occurred in health care, business, and government. Cappelli, et al. (1997) predicted that a contingent workforce—part-time, temporary, and contract—will be "part of the more permanent change in employment relations in the future" (p. 7). Boyett and Snyder (1998) further projected that, if trends continue,

> Many Americans—by some estimates as much as half of the workforce—will be contingent workers. . . . Meanwhile, the other half of the workforce will be employed in full-time permanent jobs where they will be expected to behave as continuously adaptive, self-developing team players in exchange for the benefits of career employment. (p. 5)

In this new employment paradigm, some state legislators, college trustees, and members of the public are calling for modifications to faculty employment practices in the academy for many of the same reasons that health care, government, and the private sector went through downsizing: to contain and lower costs and redirect scarce resources. Furthermore, critics are attacking academic tenure because they perceive tenure to afford lifetime employment, which—if true—would privilege the professoriate at a time when many workers in society have no such security.

3. Dissatisfaction with changes in faculty appointments

A third source for the increased interest in and scrutiny of both tenure and contract systems comes from the dissatisfaction within the academy with the growth of part-time and non-tenure-track faculty. The proportion of part-time faculty members increased from 22% to 41% between 1970 and 1995 (National Center for Education Statistics, 1998); according to one source, "perhaps as few as 38% to 40% of all faculty appointments made in recent years are 'traditional' in the sense of being full-time and either tenured or tenurable" (Schuster, 1998). According to a report issued in December 2000, non-tenure-track instructors and graduate assistants account for the majority of instructional staff in the humanities and social sciences (Coalition on the Academic Workforce, 2000). These alterations have produced an outcry from faculty members, graduate students, and disciplinary associations to increase the number of full-time tenure-track appointments. For example, the American Mathematical Society denounced the trend of colleges to hire unemployed Ph.D.'s on a part-time basis, and called for a reversal of the practice (Chronicle of Higher Education, 1994). Further criticism came during the soft job markets in the mid- to late-1990s. In the sciences, for example, the job market was so poor that only one-third of new Ph.D.s found positions in academe (Cage, 1995). In the late 1990s, graduate-student groups decried professional organizations for not taking a strong stand against the increase in part-time and non-tenure-track faculty appointments (Leatherman & Wilson, 1998).

THE SCOPE OF THIS BOOK

Given this context of market pressures, organizational restructuring, and shifting faculty employment trends, there is much speculation in the higher education literature about the future direction of faculty appointment policies. To the extent that colleges and universities have responded to these demands, most institutions have *modified* or *altered* their existing employment policies. "Where elimination of tenure is not considered a viable option, less drastic modifications to traditional tenure systems have been enacted or are under active consideration" (Trower, 1996b, p. 1). For example, at the end of the 1990s, post-tenure review for public college faculty members was underway in more than 30 states (Licata, 1998). Twenty-four percent of 280 institutions in a recent survey have or were about to create long-term non-tenure-track appointments (Trower, 1996b).

Only a few four-year colleges or universities, however, have completely overhauled their policies by either relinquishing tenure and instituting term contracts or eliminating term contracts and embracing tenure. Through the course of research for this book, I identified 23 such institutions: eight that instituted tenure and 15 that removed tenure. These colleges are profiled in Table 1.1 and 1.2. Institutional names have been masked to assure anonymity of the four sites in this study.

Introduction

Table 1.1. Institutional characteristics of colleges that shifted from contracts to tenure

	Year of Change	Control	Number of students	Source of identification
1	1991	Religious	1,300	*Academe*
2	mid-1980s	Religious	2,400	Harvard Project on Faculty Appointments
3	1984–85	Public	3,200	*Academe*
4	1997	Independent	8,000	*Chronicle of Higher Education*
5	1993	Public	1,500	Harvard Project on Faculty Appointments
6	1989	Public	2,200	Harvard Project on Faculty Appointments
7	Unknown	Religious	1,300	Harvard Project on Faculty Appointments
8	1996	Independent	2,300	Harvard Project on Faculty Appointments

Table 1.2. Institutional characteristics of colleges that shifted from tenure to contracts

	Year of Change	Control	Number of students	Source of identification
1	1982	Independent	4,700	Harvard Project on Faculty Appointments
2	1994	Independent	400	*Chronicle of Higher Education*
3	1993	Independent	1,500	*Chronicle of Higher Education*
4	1979	Religious	4,100	Harvard Project on Faculty Appointments
5	1974	Independent	1,300	Harvard Project on Faculty Appointments
6	1982	Religious	2,100	Harvard Project on Faculty Appointments
7	mid 1990s	Independent	4,200	*Chronicle of Higher Education*
8	1979	Religious	3,900	Harvard Project on Faculty Appointments
9	1982	Independent	750	*Academe*
10	1986	Independent	800	Harvard Project on Faculty Appointments
11	Unknown	Independent	1,200	Harvard Project on Faculty Appointments
12	mid 1980s	Religious	800	Harvard Project on Faculty Appointments
13	1991	Independent	860	Harvard Project on Faculty Appointments
14	1979	Independent	1,400	*Academe*
15	1983	Independent	1,900	*Academe*

In this book, I profile four of these institutions: two colleges that abolished tenure and two others that moved from tenure to term contracts; in other words, two sets of colleges that have moved in opposite directions. I analyze how these institutions undergo what is arguably among the most significant overhauls a college can make. This book, then, focuses on two important gaps in the literature: (1) the scant empirical research on academic tenure, and (2) the relevance of organizational change theories to shifts toward or away from academic tenure.

Proponents and opponents of tenure tend to rely on assertion rather than research. For example, advocates of tenure are quick to highlight their envisioned negative consequences of removing tenure: institutions will be unable to recruit and retain qualified faculty, autocratic administrators will exclude faculty from decision-making, and academic freedom will be violated. Conversely, opponents assert that eliminating tenure will lead to better teaching, more productivity, removal of deadwood faculty, and greater accountability. Whether these forecasted outcomes have actually come to pass has previously been unexplored. While one study examined the modification of a tenure system (Wolf, 1980), no research has focused on colleges that completely relinquished tenure. Similarly, the research on non-tenure contract institutions has largely considered colleges that were *founded* without tenure (Chait & Ford, 1982; Chait & Trower, 1997; Trower, 1996a), not those that *changed* to contracts.

The point of the book is not to take sides or to marshal evidence in support of employment system or the other. Rather, this exploration provides data on how and why colleges made these significant and momentous shifts in policy and to inject conclusions based on evidence rather than on conjecture.

The second problem this study addresses is the appropriateness and relevance of particular organizational theories in higher education to the process of basic changes in faculty appointment policies. Several scholars have asserted that, because of higher education's organizational uniqueness, major changes of policy or strategy in colleges and universities are more difficult to accomplish than in other types of organizations (Birnbaum, 1988; Kerr and Glade, 1986), and that organizational theories drawn from the corporate sector do not adequately illuminate the peculiarities of higher education (Peterson, 1985; Seymour, 1988; Weick, 1982). Despite these admonitions, many writers have applied organizational change theories developed in other settings to higher education, including the rational model (Chaffee, 1983; Hardy, 1988; Hoverland, McInturff & Rohne, 1986); institutionalism (Gates, 1997); political and power theories (Baldridge, 1971; Baldridge, et al., 1978); paradigm-shifting models (Simsek and Louis, 1994); and strong-leader framework (Fisher 1984; Fisher, Tack & Wheeler, 1988; Jones, 1977). However, only loosely coupled systems theories (Cohen & March, 1974, 1986; Weick, 1976, 1984) were primarily generated from education settings.[2]

The empirical research on loose coupling in higher education has focused mostly on large, multi-unit research universities. For example, Cohen & March (1986) include "a disproportionate number of wealthy and large schools" in their study (p. 238). Equally important, their theory of organized anarchy studied higher education during a time of organizational growth and expansion.

---

2. These theories have different names—garbage can model, organized anarchy or loose-coupling—but they share enough fundamental characteristics (which will be addressed in detail in chapter two) to be grouped together.

Introduction

Although the development of loosely coupled theories relied predominately on research universities in a specific historical time frame, the model is widely applied to *all* types of institutions in both scholarly and popular higher education literature (Lutz, 1982; Peterson, 1985). In fact, because loose coupling has been applied so often to higher education settings, it is often considered the "normative model" of organizational change in universities (Lutz, 1982, p. 653). Despite this profession-wide appropriation of the loosely coupled model, researchers have not examined whether the model applies equally to very different types of higher education institutions. Furthermore, as Simsek and Louis (1994) noted, loosely coupled models "are descriptive of the historical phase in which universities enjoyed prosperous growth that was facilitated by . . . a highly decentralized structure" (p. 689). It is unclear whether the loosely coupled model applies to institutions that are not in an expansion-and-growth mode.

Because of the prevalence of the loosely coupled model of organizational change in the higher education literature, I investigate in this book whether there is congruence between the *theory* of organizational change under the loosely coupled model and the *practice* of organizational change at four institutions, none of which is a research university, that reworked their faculty appointment policies.

RESEARCH PROPOSITIONS

What will this research demonstrate? Based on my understanding of the issues surrounding academic tenure and guided by previous research on organizational change, I developed three propositions:

First, for colleges that institute tenure, the process of organizational change is marked by the involvement of many participants in the decision-making and change process. The president is one voice among many who contributes to the change in policy. Faculty members are active participants. "Who's in charge" of the organizational change process is unclear and, at times, contested. The goals and outcomes of the change in faculty appointment policy are not agreed upon by participants.

Second, for colleges that implement term contracts, the process of organizational change is tightly coupled. The change process is directed and controlled by a limited number of participants "from the top," especially the board of trustees and the president. The president has a clear line of authority to implement the policy shift. Faculty are comparatively excluded from the decision-making and organizational change process. The change leaders clearly tie the results of the shift in policy to intended goals.

Third, the theories of loosely coupled systems apply to the process of organizational change when institutions move toward tenure—that is, when the type of change embraces the values that higher education deems important and exemplary. Since tenure is the common policy of faculty employment, the loosely coupled model of change applies to the process of change to tenure. Conversely, the loosely coupled model of change does not apply to colleges that moved from tenure to contracts.

METHODS

A complete discussion of research methodology can be found in the appendix. To summarize, I used multi-site case study methods because this study focuses on explanatory questions (Yin, 1994) and complex, contemporary processes that are hard to control and quantify (Merriam, 1988). My analysis called for a case study method because "interpretative case studies . . . are used . . . to illustrate, support, or challenge theoretical assumptions held prior to data gathering" (Merriam, 1988, pp. 27–28).

Unit of Analysis

In this study, the unit of analysis—"what my case is and where my case leaves off" (Miles & Huberman, 1994)—is limited to two aspects of change. First, I studied the process of change *in faculty appointment policy* at each institution. I was not studying the nature of *all* decision-making processes but rather just the bounded territory of this one change in faculty employment practices. Second, I narrowed the *magnitude of change* to whole-scale reversals in faculty personnel policy. I did not examine colleges that only modified—but did not abandon—existing tenure or contract systems. Instead, I focused exclusively on institutions that substituted one policy for the other. Therefore, throughout this book, when I discuss "change in faculty employment policy," I refer to the substitution of tenure for contracts or contracts for tenure and not to smaller-scale alterations or modifications of existing policies.

Sample

Four research sites for this study were appropriate because the total universe of four-year colleges that have changed faculty appointment policies is small (see Table 1.1 and 1.2) and access may have been difficult at a larger number, especially those that made the alteration in policy many years ago. I used a criteria-sampling technique to identify the four case sites. I reviewed all known institutions that changed their faculty employment policies from a system of contracts to tenure or from tenure to contracts, and identified the following criteria of importance (Patton, 1990): (1) the change occurred at a single institution and not through the merging of two colleges; (2) the institution fundamentally changed its faculty appointment policy "recently;" (3) the institution granted me access; and (4) the presi-

Introduction

dents and most institutional leaders (e.g. vice president for academic affairs, key faculty members, and board of trustees leaders) were accessible to be interviewed. More information on the site selection process is detailed in the appendix.

Data Collection

Interviews from key informants were the primary method of data collection in this study. I used several methods to identify key informants.

- I used a primary informant (as identified by the president) to identify other key informants, such as the chief academic officer, other vice presidents, deans, key faculty members, and board of trustees members who were instrumental in the change process.
- To further expand the informant base, I used a snowballing or chain technique (Patton, 1990; Bogdan and Bilken, 1992) for locating "information-rich key informants" by asking "Who knows a lot about this process? Who should I talk to?" (Patton, 1990, p. 176).
- To offset key informant biases (Maxwell 1996), I reviewed institutional documents (faculty senate minutes, student newspaper articles, and other documents) to identify other informants, particularly those who might have opposed the change in policy and who would not be identified by the primary informant or through the snowballing technique.

I used a focused interview approach—a set of structured, open-ended questions—to elicit comments on particular topics (Yin, 1994). I also collected data through written documentation—faculty handbooks, memoranda and speeches (from presidents and faculty leaders), meeting minutes, and institutional reports—which provided a means of triangulating interviews (Patton, 1990).

A ROADMAP TO THIS BOOK

If readers are new to the topic of tenure and term contracts, chapter two provides a comprehensive overview to the typical litany of advantages and disadvantages offered by proponents and opponents of the two employment systems. This chapter considers the following question: what rationales would one expect to hear in support of the decision to end or institute tenure? Chapter two also provides an introduction to various theories of organizational change that will be used elsewhere in the book.

The following four chapters profile the research sites—Scott College, Rowlette College, Lakeview College, and Accomac College. Each chapter tracks historical influences, identifies prominent characteristics, examines important constituencies, and analyzes the process of change.

Chapter seven compares the four cases thematically: how were the two sets of colleges similar and how were they different? The reader will find that the four colleges share similar backgrounds yet diverged in their aspirations. Presidential leadership, or lack thereof, was an important influence. Most important, chapter seven explores the symbolic purposes of the change process.

Finally, chapter eight offers some additional, and surprising, findings and offers implications for practice—practical advice that administrators, faculty, trustees, and other policy makers should consider when revamping their own employment policies.

ACKNOWLEDGMENTS

This book grew out of my doctoral dissertation at the Harvard Graduate School of Education. The research discussed herein was conducted under the auspices of the Harvard Project on Faculty Appointments with generous support from the Pew Charitable Trusts. As anyone who has ever written a doctoral thesis knows well, the act of writing a dissertation is by no means a singular endeavor. I acknowledge many people for their assistance, encouragement, and support. Dick Chait, my mentor, doctoral advisor, and committee chair, offered prompt, insightful, and detailed feedback on every aspect of this book. Jim Honan and Stacy Blake-Beard also made this a far better piece of work because of their guidance.

Others who provided feedback, suggestions, and support include Matt Hartley, Joel Vargas, Michal Kurlaender, Alixe Callen, Dave Ferrero, Tim Lannon, Peter Eckel, and Judy McLaughlin. Cathy Trower deserves a special note of gratitude for her encouragement, laughter, and use of her personal library.

My thanks also go to the faculty, administrators, and trustees at Accomac, Lakeview, Rowlette, and Scott colleges who participated in this research project.

Finally, I gratefully acknowledge the support of my wife, Debbie, and family—Dad, Lan, John, Kristen, Bob, Alanna, Kyle, Brett, and Jayna—who have supported me over the years in immeasurable ways.

CHAPTER 2

Tenure and Contract Systems: An Overview

WHY WOULD A COLLEGE OVERHAUL ITS BASIC FACULTY APPOINTment policy? What rationales would one expect to hear in support of the decision to end or institute tenure? How do institutions that embark on such a fundamental shift in policy achieve their goals? These questions presume a familiarity with what tenure is, what its alternatives are, and what arguments are offered for and against the various systems. Because this book is also about how colleges undergo change, it also presumes knowledge about various theories of organizational change. This chapter reviews the literature pertinent to faculty employment policies (tenure and contract systems) and organizational change theories. It is divided into three sections:

- An overview of faculty appointment policies in higher education, highlighting the prevalence of tenure systems in the academy and the infrequency of term contracts as the primary basis for faculty employment.
- An examination of *the reasons* for change in faculty employment policies. Because there is scant literature on the change process from tenure to contracts or contracts to tenure, this section concentrates on the arguments that advocates of change *might* muster. I will examine rationales surrounding academic freedom, job security, campus governance, and other areas of concern.
- A review of *the process* of change, exploring the literature on organizational theories that have been applied to higher education settings with particular attention to the theory of loose coupling.

AN OVERVIEW OF FACULTY EMPLOYMENT POLICIES AND PRACTICES

As defined by the *1940 Statement of Principles on Academic Freedom and Tenure* of the American Association of University Professors, tenure is an arrangement under which faculty have "permanent or continuous [appointments]" in which "their service should be terminated only for adequate cause, except in the case of [voluntary] retirement for age, or under extraordinary circumstances because of financial exigencies" (AAUP, 1995, p. 4).

The tenure system in the United States had its origins in Germany. Academic freedom had two meanings in the German higher education systems: *Lernfreiheit* and *Lehrfreiheit* (Hofstadter & Metzger, 1955). *Lernfreiheit* denoted freedom in the learning environment, and referred primarily to students' freedom from administrative and curricular rules and regulations. *Lehrfreiheit* meant "that the university professor was free to examine bodies of evidence and to report his findings in lecture or published form—that he enjoyed freedom of teaching and freedom of inquiry" (Hofstadter & Metzger, 1955, p. 387). When American academics adapted the German concept of academic freedom to their own institutional contexts, the connotation of *Lernfreiheit* was dissociated from the definition of academic freedom (Hofstadter & Metzger, 1955). Hence, the authors of the 1915 report of the American Association of University Professors wrote, "the freedom which is the subject of this report is that of the teacher" (AAUP, 1915, p. 20).

Eighteen full professors at Johns Hopkins University prompted the formation of the AAUP in 1915 after many years of concern about the security of their profession (Metzger, 1973). In addition, "for many years—intensely since the controversy over evolution in the 1870s—professors had sought 'academic freedom'—immunity from matters of expression and belief" (Metzger, 1973, p. 136). As it has developed, tenure serves two primary and interrelated goals: to ensure academic freedom and to provide economic security (AAUP, 1940).

According to the most recent survey data, virtually all research universities, public doctorate-granting institutions, and public four-year colleges offer tenure, and only 88 of 573 private four-year liberal arts colleges do not offer tenure (National Center for Education Statistics, 1996).[1] Many writers consider tenure to be a hallmark characteristic of higher education. Historically, tenure has been called an "inviolable principle" of the acade-

---

1. "Even though the estimates indicate that 100 percent of public research, private research, public doctoral, and public comprehensive institutions had tenure systems for their permanent full-time instructional faculty and staff, the reader is reminded that the estimates . . . are derived from a sample and are subject to sampling error and nonresponse" (National Center for Education Statistics, 1996).

my (Adams, 1974), highly significant "to the quality of a first-rate university" (Brewster, 1972), and one of higher education's core, defining elements (Cotter, 1998; Iffland, 1998).

At institutions without tenure, contracts tend to have the following attributes: appointments are for a specific period of time, the contracts are renewable at the college's option without any "up-or-out" stipulation, and contract length often varies based on seniority or length of service (Chait & Trower, 1997). Institutions that do not offer a tenure system and rely solely on term contracts are a rare breed in American higher education, generally regarded as outside the mainstream. As Chait and Trower (1997) have noted, most institutions with term contracts are relatively small, not well endowed, and, thus, financially fragile.

Most literature on academic employment focuses on tenure rather than contracts, perhaps not surprisingly since tenure is nearly ubiquitous in higher education. Moreover, the vast majority of literature is anecdotal and opinion-based. There are some empirical studies in areas such as the economics of tenure (Radner & Kuh, 1977); productivity (Ashcraft, 1983; Holley, 1977; Orpen, 1982; Tien & Blackburn, 1993; Trower, 1996a); the effects of tenure on junior faculty (Austin & Rice, 1998; Trower, 1996a); the effects of tenure on women (Finkel & Olswang, 1994); and academic freedom (Keith, 1997). But the preponderance of literature is not empirically based.

The "how" and "why" of change from one faculty employment policy to another is an area that particularly lacks empirical study. Commentators offer a host of hunches about the reasons for abandoning or instituting tenure, but without research on these issues, the hypotheses about changes to faculty appointment policies must be gleaned indirectly from the literature. The next section examines speculation about the "how" and "why" of change from tenure to contracts or contracts to tenure.

STRENGTHS AND WEAKNESSES OF TENURE AND CONTRACTS

This section reviews the substantive reasons that *may* influence institutions to move one way or the other. If institutions approach the decision to change in a rational way, then *presumably*, the following arguments may be raised during the course of campus conversations about change. It is *not* my intent to *evaluate* the strengths and weaknesses of these assertions. Rather, in the following pages, I will *report* what those arguments may be for change in personnel policy.

Academic Freedom

Academic freedom is the hallmark of the tenure system in the United States. Colleges changing from contracts to tenure or from tenure to contracts might be faced with concerns over the protection of academic freedom. The following rationales in the area of academic freedom may be offered by proponents of the two employment systems.

Assertion: Tenure Ensures Academic Freedom

The 1940 AAUP Statement defined academic freedom in three arenas: (1) full freedom in research and in publication of results; (2) freedom in the classroom in discussing subject matter; and (3) freedom from institutional censorship or discipline to speak and write extramurally (AAUP, 1940). Writers, both historical and contemporary, have contended that academic freedom is tenure's most important objective (Adams, 1974; Benjamin, 1995, 1998; Brown and Kurland, 1990; Carr, 1972; Chemerinsky, 1998; Commission on Academic Tenure, 1973; Cotter, 1996; Finkin, 1996; Grunig, 1996; Iffland, 1998; Tierney, 1998c, 1998d). Academic freedom—and thus tenure—is necessary for the uninhibited development of the truth and the open exchange of knowledge and ideas. Professors must be unconstrained by both external forces (legislators, trustees, alumni, and the public) and internal coercion from colleagues and administrators. Kingman Brewster, Jr. (1972), the late president of Yale University, wrote:

> If a university is alive and productive it is a place where colleagues are in constant dialogue; defending their latest intellectual enthusiasm, attacking the contrary views of others.... It is vital that this contest be uninhibited by fear of reprisal. (Brewster, 1972, p. 382–83)

By granting tenure, academic institutions permit scholars to pursue the long-term search for knowledge (Adams, 1974), unlike the corporate arena, which usually demands short-term and practical benefits to the time and money invested in research. Tenure guarantees "the freedom to follow untried trails and to explore the frontiers of knowledge without fear of dismissal before the task can be finished" (Adams, 1974, p. 123).

Cotter (1996) also asserted that, because of academic freedom, tenure encourages creativity among faculty. Tenure liberates faculty from the orthodoxies of their discipline, from their colleagues' viewpoints, and from the college administration. They can think in new ways, test theories held as sacrosanct, and flourish uninhibited by the fears of retaliation. In addition, academic freedom provides for the common good. Adams (1974) and Finkin (1996) argued that tenure was, in fact, designed foremost to serve the public good. The 1915 AAUP General Report of the Committee on Academic Freedom and Academic Tenure explicated this benefit:

> [One of the functions] of the modern university is to develop experts for the use of the community. . . . The scholar must be absolutely free not only to pursue his investigations but to declare the results of his researches, no matter where they may lead him or to what extent they may come into conflict with accepted opinion. To be of use to the legislator or the administrator, he must enjoy their complete confidence in the disinterestedness of his conclusions.
>
> The responsibility of the university as a whole is to the community at large, and any restriction upon the freedom of the instructor is bound to react injuriously upon the efficiency and the *morale* of the institution, and therefore ultimately upon the interests of the community. (AAUP, 1915, pp. 28–29. Italics in original.)

In addition to protecting the rights of tenured faculty members and serving the public good, proponents have also claimed that the tenure system assures freedom on campus for nontenured instructors. The Commission on Academic Tenure in Higher Education (1973), for example, alleged that "tenure creates an atmosphere favorable to academic freedom for all [faculty on campus]—the nontenured as well as the tenured—because the tenured faculty form an independent body capable of vigilant action to protect the freedom of their nontenured colleagues" (1973, p. 15).

Finally, supporters have proclaimed that no other means or method—including the First Amendment guarantee of free speech—protects academic freedom adequately. Chemerinsky (1998) argued that the protection of faculty members' research, teaching, or extramural speech would not be adequately safeguarded with grievance procedures in long-term contracts or in the legal action in the courts, in part because faculty, not the institution, would bear the initial burden of proof. He concluded that "no alternative yet described is likely to succeed in providing both the procedural and the substantive protections accorded by tenure" (Chemerinsky, 1998, pp. 640–41).

Counter-Assertion: Tenure Does Not Fully Protect Academic Freedom

Despite the claims that tenure is the best and only way to ensure academic freedom, many commentators have declared that tenure does not protect the academic freedom of many faculty (Austin & Rice, 1998; Carr, 1972; Greenberg, 1997; Grunig, 1996; Keith, 1997). Tenure creates a system of haves and have-nots in which "senior professors with structured employment contracts control the texture of academic life so that those who do not conform will find themselves in jeopardy" (Tierney, 1998b, p. 10). In the early 1970s, Carr alleged that senior faculty with political agendas "use[d] their tenured posts of authority to deny academic freedom, through a kind of reverse McCarthyism, to students, untenured junior colleagues, or young job-seeking Ph.D.s who do not share their social and political prejudices" (Carr, 1972, p. 121). Much more recently, Keith (1997) found that college teachers viewed nontenured faculty as having considerably less academic freedom than tenured professors. Austin and Rice (1998) uncovered similar results in their qualitative study of early career faculty and graduate students:

> Academic freedom is compromised by the very system established to protect it. In some cases, rather than protecting the freedom of faculty to pursue ideas that seem most promising to them, the tenure system is leading faculty to choose topics based on the speed with which those topics can be addressed or on the degree to which the topics are likely to be attractive to more senior colleagues who sit on the tenure and promotion committees. (Austin & Rice, 1998, p. 748)

Commentators have argued that junior faculty are risk-adverse because they lack academic freedom (Carr, 1972; Tierney, 1998b). "Tenure is meant to facilitate the development of knowledge via novel inquiry and exploration free from external pressures. However, tenure processes may instead result in uniformity, timidity, and conservatism among junior faculty" (Wolfe, et al, 1996, p. 222).

Assertion: Contracts Do Not Adequately Protect Academic Freedom

In addition to identifying tenure as an guarantor of academic freedom, writers have also evaluated the sufficiency of contract systems to protect academic freedom. The Commission on Academic Tenure in Higher Education (1973) asserted that "[it] is simply not proven" that due-process procedures in contract systems would assure academic freedom for professors; rather the Commission declared that, under contract systems, "academic freedom is not adequately protected" (p. 19).

Chemerinsky (1998) contended that grievance procedures in long-term contracts do not provide the same protection afforded under traditional tenure in two ways. In his review of the language used to protect academic freedom in long-term contracts, Chemerinsky found that the language was vague in many areas and did not offer the *substantive* protections that tenure does. In addition, he asserted that, from a *procedural* perspective, faculty members on multi-year, fixed, or rolling contracts might be less likely to take unpopular positions with their colleagues or administrators if they know that their employment is not certain.

Counter-Assertion: Contract Systems Do Protect Academic Freedom

Several researchers and commentators have contradicted Chemerinsky's assertion regarding academic freedom on campuses with contracts. For example, Jane Jervis (1995), president of Evergreen State University, an institution without tenure, offered anecdotal evidence that faculty on her campus are "more cussedly outspoken, more highly innovative, and more dedicated to students than faculty at most institutions" (1995, p. 22). In a study of 70 faculty members at five private universities, Keith (1997) reported that 77 percent of responding faculty thought that academic freedom would be moderately to completely protected at their institutions if tenure was eliminated. Trower's study (1996a) of junior faculty on the tenure-track, off the tenure-track, and at institutions without tenure found that academic freedom is *enhanced* in contract systems and that junior faculty on campuses without tenure feel less constrained than tenure-track faculty. In their study of five institutions without traditional tenure systems, Chait and Trower (1997) found similar situations: "junior faculty did not perceive or experience any threats to academic freedom from more senior colleagues, a criticism commonly registered by untenured faculty elsewhere" (p. 12). These institutions pride themselves on the fact that they extend academic freedom to all faculty. Chait and Trower cautioned, however, that "faculty confidence rests upon honorable institutional behavior to date.... Contract systems depend upon a mix of procedural safeguards, policy statements, *and* tradition, trust, and goodwill." (pp. 13, 24).

Summary of Academic Freedom and Faculty Employment Policy

Several empirical studies have determined that academic freedom does exist on campuses without tenure (Chait & Trower, 1997; Keith, 1997; Trower, 1996a). However, as Chait and Trower (1997) noted, academic freedom at colleges with contracts rests upon the good will of administrators and good relations between faculty and administration. Despite this empirical evidence to the contrary, most commentators maintain that tenure *is* necessary for academic freedom. Therefore, change agents rallying for tenure might be expected to advance the argument that academic freedom is not adequately protected under a contract system.

Job Security

The second objective for tenure, as stipulated in the 1940 AAUP statement, is to provide economic security for the profession. Many commentators have noted benefits and drawbacks associated with job security; colleges changing faculty personnel policies might encounter arguments on each side.

Assertion: Tenure Provides Job Security To Attract Talent

Tenure provides "a sufficient degree of economic security to make the profession attractive to men and women of ability" (AAUP, 1940, p. 49). Radner and Kuh (1977) identified tenure as a compensating wage differential that offsets higher salaries in industry, the professions, and the corporate sector. By providing job security through tenure, the academy is able to recruit the intellectually gifted (Finkin, 1996), and thus ensures quality among its faculty ranks (Brewster, 1972). In fact, some writers have professed that tenure enables colleges and universities to recruit the nation's best and brightest young people who would pursue different careers if the academy did not offer job security (Cotter, 1996; Iffland, 1998).

Counter-Assertion: Tenure Preserves Lifelong Employment Regardless Of Circumstance

Many analysts have insisted that the job security and protection afforded under the tenure system have several deleterious effects that constrain institutions.

1. Tenure reduces institutional flexibility.

Observers often criticize tenure's inflexibility (Chait & Ford, 1982; Greenberg, 1997; Grunig, 1996; Tierney, 1998b; Wilke, 1979). Because tenure requires that institutions make lifelong commitments to faculty members, and because the standards for dismissal are so stringent, colleges and universities have little ability to reduce their labor force in times of fiscal hardships or to change curricular offerings to meet changing market demands. Radner and Kuh (1977) explained this concern in economic terms:

> From the point of view of the academic employer, tenure acts as a constraint on labor force adjustment in the face of changing enrollment demand. In particular, when enrollment becomes stable it limits the institution to two main sources of attrition [to] create places for new hires: retirement and nonrenewal of contracts for nontenured faculty. (Radner & Kuh, 1977, p. 2–3).

2. Tenure permits individual goals to trump institutional objectives.

Another criticism holds that tenure fosters only individual faculty goals to the neglect of institutional goals (Aigner, 1998; Carr, 1972; Chait, 1995; Chait & Ford, 1982). Tenure assures teachers and researchers substantial leeway and employment security to pursue their own interests, regardless of whether those interests conform to institutional parameters. Presumably, if faculty didn't have the security of tenure, they would be more likely to conform their interests with those of the institution.

Therefore, the argument goes, tenure hinders administrators and trustees from enacting institutional objectives. A common example of this problem is manifested in undergraduate teaching. Administrators have little ability to command tenured faculty to teach better or to spend more time with undergraduates.

    3. Tenure protects "deadwood."

Detractors also charge that tenure protects unproductive faculty from sanctions or dismissal. Because procedures for dismissal are so convoluted and complex, tenured professors who are poor teachers or incompetent researchers are virtually impossible to fire (Aigner, 1998; Commission on Academic Tenure, 1973; Tierney, 1998b). While, in theory, tenured faculty can be removed for poor performance, in practice such professors are rarely dismissed because of cumbersome litigation and political costs (Mooney, 1994; Shulman, 1974; Trachtenberg, 1996). Bowen and Schuster (1986) wrote:

> The procedures for ridding the profession of misfits are so arduous and so embarrassing that few administrators are willing to take the time of themselves and the faculty to prosecute the cases. The procedures take on the flavor of a trial for murder. (Bowen and Schuster, 1986, p. 243)

    4. Tenure and job security are anachronistic.

Cappelli, et al. (1997) noted that, by the end of the 1980s, job loss among professional and white-collar workers was higher than among hourly workers; they predicted downsizing to be "part of a more permanent change in employment relations" in the future (p. 7). In this context, Chait (1995) and Leslie (1998) maintained that the idea of economic security in academe seems anachronistic. Leslie decried the problems that tenure causes *within* the academy:

> On one hand, few will openly acknowledge that tenure in its traditional form may be a relic of past battles that no longer serves its original purpose.... On the other hand, the academic community is willing to employ substitute, temporary, and part-time faculty—faculty not eligible for tenure—on a proportionately massive scale, thereby tacitly acknowledging that the enterprise really cannot afford to do its business under the traditional constraints of the tenure system. The reality appears to be that tenure as commonly implemented has become too expensive and too rigid. (p. 654)

Chait (1995) elucidated the public relations quagmire that lifetime employment security creates for higher education with its *external* constituencies:

> Even the most sympathetic supporters of higher education will be hard-pressed to defend lifetime appointments that are virtually impervious to dis-

missal irrespective of economic conditions, revenue shortfalls, or market demand. Juxtaposed against pervasive corporate cutbacks, especially of white-collar workers, permanent employment for professors stands in sharp relief and presents a formidable public-relations challenge. (p. 3)

Assertion: Contracts Provide Greater Institutional Flexibility And Incentives Than Tenure

Some writers have maintained that contract systems would rectify the problems associated with tenure's lifelong job security. The reasoning is as follows:

1. Contract systems permit greater flexibility by allowing for labor force adjustment.

In theory, contract systems allow institutions to increase or decrease the size of their faculty or reallocate positions if needed for financial reasons, changes in market demands, or enrollment fluctuations (Commission on Academic Tenure, 1973). Chait and Trower (1997) determined that most colleges with contracts regard their flexibility as "an important hedge and a valuable last resort to protect economically brittle, tuition-dependent colleges against catastrophic losses in enrollment and related financial hardships" (p. 9).

2. Contracts provide an incentive for good performance, emphasize professional development, and encourage innovation and cooperation.

It is asserted that term contracts keep professors on their toes. With the knowledge that their performance will be regularly reviewed, faculty members under contract have an obvious incentive to remain effective as teachers and scholars (Commission on Academic Tenure, 1973). Moreover, Trower (1996a) found that junior faculty at institutions without tenure

> believe that innovation is enhanced with contract systems for several reasons[,] including: (1) greater faculty participation and collegiality because of the absence of status differentials, 2) fewer tensions like those created by competitive, up-or-out decisions, 3) greater academic freedom, and 4) an atmosphere of continuous improvement, as evidenced in ongoing assessment of faculty performance. They believe that contract systems allow for greater flexibility for experimentation on the part of faculty members, which tends to lead to increased innovation. (p. 237)

Finally, Chait and Trower (1997) stated that some faculty members at contract colleges view such systems as producing more collaboration and less competition among their colleagues. "Faculty regarded contract systems as 'more humane' and an approach that has enabled newer faculty to be 'a lot calmer' and to work at a 'nice steady level'" (p. 18).

Counter-Assertion: Contracts Do Not Offer Greater Flexibility

In contrast to the alleged benefits to contract systems over traditional tenure, several researchers have provided evidence that the anticipated personnel flexibility provided by contracts is largely unrealized. Contrary to the belief that contracts are a more responsive personnel policy than tenure, researchers (Chait & Ford, 1982; Chait & Trower, 1997; Trower, 1996a) found that contract colleges do not attain greater flexibility. According to Trower (1996a), two contract colleges in her study had extremely high renewal rates: in 26 years, Evergreen State College renewed 96% of its contracts and, in 18 years, Hampshire College reappointed 84% of its contract faculty. Trower concluded

> Theoretically, contracts permit greater flexibility in institutional planning, budgeting, and program development by allowing expansion, contraction, and modification to the faculty to meet institutional circumstances. In practice, however, this benefit appears to be largely unrealized. While contract systems do permit greater flexibility, institutions without tenure, like their counterparts with tenure, tend to hire part-time faculty for these purposes. (pp. 240–41)

Chait and Trower (1997) came to a similar judgment: "Contract systems, *in practice,* mirror tenure systems on the dimension of economic security" (p. 6). They offer four possible reasons for the lack of turnover on contract campuses:

1. The tight employment market has impeded mobility among academics.
2. The campuses in their study did not adopt contract systems to foster involuntary turnover.
3. The threat of litigation complicates dismissal for cause.[2]
4. The dismissal of a professor, even one with a poor record of performance, has very high political costs. (Chait & Trower, 1997, pp. 7–8)

Jervis (1995) confirmed these various findings in her reflections as president of Evergreen State College when she stated, "my ideal academy [would use] a group of short-term faculty to respond to short-term curricular needs and provide institutional flexibility for financial exigency. Their insecurity is inextricably linked to the security of the long-term faculty" (p. 23).

---

2. This same charge also is made against tenure systems (Shulman, 1974), as noted on p. 23.

Writers have concluded that there is little actual difference between contract and tenure systems in terms of economic security. Chait and Trower determined that "while contract systems differ from tenure systems in theory, they operate quite similarly in practice" (p. 10). Grunig (1996) reported that colleges without tenure end up with "pseudo-tenure" (p. 5).

Additionally, contract systems do not necessarily promote alignment between individual and institutional goals. Critics disparage the tenure system for its apparent propensity to discourage faculty's alignment with institutional goals. The belief that faculty under contract systems would be more responsive to institutional goals than tenured faculty, however, does not appear to be true. Chait and Ford (1982) discovered that

> irrespective of particular personnel policies, the very nature of the profession militates against "team play" and bureaucratic conformity. After all, most colleges and universities actively encourage open debate and vigorous dissent, even about institutional goals. . . . Neither a tenure system nor a term contract system inherently promotes greater harmony between individual agendas and long-range institutional goals. (p. 53)

Summary of Job Security and Faculty Employment Policies

Researchers have found that many of the criticisms leveled against tenure in the area of economic security also apply at colleges with contract systems. Contract colleges offer as much—if not more—job security as tenure colleges; contract colleges have higher rates of reappointment than the success rate for probationary faculty at institutions with tenure. These institutions, however, preserve the "last-resort" ability to lay off faculty in severe financial crisis to an easier extent than do tenure colleges.

Proponents of contract systems might cite flexibility as a reason for moving from tenure to contracts; they might argue that an institution's financial situation warrants having a more flexible faculty personnel policy than tenure affords. They also might insist that contracts would provide institutions with more flexibility in faculty turnover and reappointment, despite evidence to the contrary.

According to the literature, proponents might argue that the job security associated with tenure will make their institution more attractive to potential faculty members. They also might endorse tenure because they discover that contracts offer no more institutional flexibility than does tenure; therefore, they might submit, why not have a tenure system, which is more accepted and mainstream in American higher education.

Shared Governance: a corollary to academic freedom and job security

Because tenure protects academic freedom and job security, supporters contend that tenured faculty enjoy other benefits, namely, the ability to participate more fully in campus governance and to counterbalance administrative power in decision-making. Writers have offered divergent ideas about the degree to which tenure and contracts systems provide power to faculty members in institutional decision-making.

Assertion: Tenure gives faculty more power in campus governance

According to the AAUP, "the protection of the academic freedom of faculty members in addressing issues of institutional governance is a prerequisite for the practice of governance unhampered by fear of retribution" (AAUP, 1995, p. 186). Therefore, at campuses with tenure, faculty have the confidence to criticize administrative decision-making or policies without worry of vengeful administrators. In higher education, "grounds for thinking an institutional policy desirable or undesirable must be heard and assessed if the community is to have confidence that its policies are appropriate" (AAUP, 1995, p. 188). The association claims that tenure affords faculty members this vital voice. Without tenure, faculty could be at the mercy of autocratic administrators who squash faculty criticism and dissent through sanctions or dismissal.

Counter-Assertion: Contract systems eliminate distinctions between junior and senior faculty and permit junior faculty greater participation in college governance.

Unlike traditional tenure systems, which create distinctions between tenured and nontenured faculty, contract systems remove those differences and support collegiality. Chait and Trower (1997) argued that contract systems level the playing field between junior and senior faculty members in campus governance and faculty issues. Trower (1996a) declared:

> Contract systems may foster greater participation of junior faculty members in campus governance and institutional decision-making, and may enhance collegiality among all faculty members. Junior faculty at institutions without tenure do not feel like "junior" faculty. These faculty feel that they are on an even keel with senior colleagues, that their opinions are respected, and that there are no class distinctions. These faculty say that there are no "haves" and "have-nots" on the faculty. (p. 236)

Summary of Shared Governance

The literature purports that tenured faculty can openly criticize administrators, thereby giving tenured faculty power and influence in institutional decision-making. Champions of tenure might contend that a move toward tenure would benefit (1) faculty, because they would gain influence and participation in campus governance, and (2) the institution, under the theory that greater employee participation enhances productivity, effectiveness, and morale.

Change agents abandoning tenure might offer as a rationale the desire to level the playing field among junior and senior faculty members' ability to participate in campus decision-making. More nefariously, a president or board may eliminate tenure because they want to limit or exclude faculty from participating in the governance system.

Other areas of concern with tenure and contracts

Researchers and commentators have marshaled several other arguments that could be invoked to support change in faculty employment policies. First, critics have exchanged accusations about the effects of each employment system on quality. Some have claimed that contracts reduce teacher quality (Commission on Academic Tenure, 1973; Finkin, 1996; Jervis, 1997; Machlup, 1964), while others have posited that tenure discourages teaching effectiveness (Premeaux & Mondy, 1996; Leslie, 1998; Tierney, 1998a). Second, writers have charged that tenure impairs the professional experience of junior faculty and contract colleges enhance their work conditions (Austin & Rice, 1998; Wolf, et al., 1996). Third, evidence has suggested that performance reviews at contract colleges consume too much time to be effective (Chait & Ford, 1982; Chait & Trower, 1997). Finally, writers have asserted that contract colleges suffer from a lack of legitimacy because their employment systems are outside the norms of American higher education (Chait & Trower, 1997). I will examine each of these areas in greater detail.

Assertion: Tenure ensures quality and productivity

Some have argued that tenure ensures quality through its rigorous and strenuous review and evaluation procedures (Commission on Academic Tenure, 1973; Finkin, 1996; Machlup, 1964). If a college offers tenure to a faculty member, his or her colleagues and the administration have decided that the individual merits a long-term commitment, possibly 30–40 years. Therefore, the institution wants to ensure that only the "most qualified" candidates obtain tenure. Tierney (1998a) argued that tenure also guards against decreasing quality. He claimed that the growing cadre of part-time instructors, adjuncts, and teaching assistants are less effective instructors than tenured professors; therefore, having a core group of tenured faculty mitigates against the declining quality of undergraduate teaching.

Many researchers and observers have stated that tenure has, at worst, a neutral effect and, at best, a positive effect on faculty productivity.[3] Through his observations as president of Colby College, Cotter (1996) noted that tenured faculty are more productive than nontenured faculty. Habecker (1981), Grunig (1996), and Chait (1995) found in reviews of the literature that tenure does not diminish productivity. Other studies show little change in faculty productivity in pre- and post-tenure periods (Ashcraft, 1983; Lewis, 1980; Orpen, 1982; Tien & Blackburn, 1993).[4]

Related Assertion: Contract systems lower the quality of faculty

Because contracts do not require a one-time "up-or-out" decision about the quality of a faculty member's teaching and scholarship, critics have emphasized that contract systems permit professors with marginal performance records to remain at the institution. For example, Machlup (1964) hypothesized that quality would decline at institutions without tenure because faculty and administrators take the one-time tenure decision more seriously than contract renewals that occur every three to five years. He argued that deficient teachers would more readily be allowed to stay at colleges with contracts until the next performance review, a pattern that would repeat itself until the instructor ended up with "tenure by courtesy" (p. 114). Chait and Ford (1982) highlighted one college's task force that determined "the most striking and worrisome conclusion is that the contract system and other reappointment policies and procedures have the overall impact of lowering the quality of the faculty" (p. 20). Chait and Trower (1997) and Jervis (1995) voiced the same concern. Jervis noted that at Evergreen

---

3. Observers and researchers do not have a common definition of faculty "productivity." As Trower (1996a) noted, productivity measures generally have been limited to the quantity of publications and not the quality of research. None of the studies cited here discussed teaching and service productivity.
4. This is not to say, however, that all researchers agree that tenure has either a neutral or positive effect on productivity. One empirical study found that productivity decreases with the awarding of tenure (Holley, 1977). Several researchers have noted that the evidence does not support a definitive conclusion about the relationship between tenure and productivity or between contract systems and productivity (Chait & Ford, 1982; Trower, 1996a).

State College, "because there is not a high-threshold evaluative decision point, some faculty members have become automatically 'tenured,' when perhaps they ought not to be" (p. 25).

Assertion: Tenure hurts teaching

In theory, most institutions place weight on both teaching and research in the tenure-review process. In practice, colleges and universities often place heavier importance on research and publication than on teaching and student contact. One study found that administrators and faculty agree that "tenure does not help promote teaching excellence, and in fact it may actually hinder [it]" (Premeaux & Mondy, 1996, p. 27). Tenure is too unidimensional for a multidimensional job (Leslie, 1998). It encourages "output creep," the move away from teaching toward research (Leslie, 1998; Tierney, 1998b). Tenure impairs teaching because the institutional culture that has developed through the tenure system screens out teaching skills (Tierney, 1998b). Donald Kennedy, former president of Stanford University, decried that "young faculty . . . are regularly urged by their advocates to concentrate on research and, if necessary, skimp on teaching" (Kennedy, 1997, p. 30). Similarly, a guide for new professors at Indiana University stated:

> [Tenure-track faculty members'] evaluation is based on research, teaching, and service. In a research-oriented (publish-or-perish) university, research must be the primary evaluation criterion. Hence, I advise you to be a good teacher, but not to the point where devotion to teaching will seriously interfere with your research. (Indiana University Computer Science Department, 1993)

Assertion: Tenure creates a culture stressful and harmful to junior faculty

Several studies have examined the effects of tenure on probationary faculty and nontenurable faculty. Austin and Rice (1998) found that new faculty received unclear and conflicting messages about expectations, worried about tenure time lines, had difficulty maintaining balance in their lives because of tenure requirements, received insufficient feedback and evaluation, and had little sense of community. Their investigation led Austin and Rice to conclude:

> In its present form, the tenure system is leading early career faculty to replace their idealism, energy, and willingness to address the various missions of the academy—including teaching and public service—with tension, anxiety, and limited views of the kind of work and contributions they can make.

Similarly, Wolfe, et al. (1996) found in their preliminary study of business school faculty that the tenure process promotes conformity and timidity among junior faculty.

Assertion: Performance reviews under contract systems are overly time consuming

Researchers have noted that performance reviews in contract systems can consume huge amounts of time for administrators and faculty. In their study of three institutions without tenure, Chait and Ford (1982) discovered that "faculty and staff alike complained persistently about the effort required and the work load generated by the contract system. . . . The contract system, as practiced at these colleges, would [not] work in a larger environment" (p. 59). Fifteen years later, Chait and Trower (1997) reached a similar conclusion:

> . . . faculty feel constantly beset by the need to prepare a massive dossier or to assess colleagues' ponderous portfolios. The process has been characterized as "enormously labor intensive," "tedious at best," "a bureaucratic nightmare," "a tremendous amount of paperwork," and "a pain in the butt." The burdens on academic administrators are no less onerous: scrutinizing mammoth folders, writing evaluations, participating in review committee meetings, meeting one-on-one with faculty, and sending follow-up letters. (p. 21)

McPherson and Winston (1993) summarized the problems inherent in reviewing senior faculty members: "given the logic of the academic employment structure, it is far from obvious that intensive hierarchical efforts to evaluate and motivate senior faculty in fact make much sense. Monitoring worker performance is an expensive activity, and it may itself have a negative impact on morale" (p. 125).

Assertion: Contract colleges suffer from a lack of prestige

As noted earlier, tenure systems are the preferred system of faculty employment in higher education. For the institution, a tenure system demonstrates a mainstream approach to faculty employment and academic tradition. Some faculty at contract colleges report a lack of status in the profession and a concern that they do not hold the "common currency" in higher education (Chait & Trower, 1997, p. 19).

Summary of Other Areas of Concern

In shifting from contracts to tenure, proponents may contend that tenure ensures faculty quality; the rigors of the tenure system assure the capabilities of teachers who receive lifetime job security. They may also have convinced colleagues that the time and effort needed for performance evaluations was prohibitive and that a tenure review process will reduce those inefficiencies. Finally, they may have persuaded the institution that tenure signals normality, legitimacy, and acceptance of the mainstream in American higher education.

Advocates to eliminate tenure may insist that contracts will aid the development of junior faculty on campus or perhaps mend a detrimental rift between junior and senior members. They also may contend that a contract system places more emphasis on teaching and less importance on research. Finally, they may promote the notion of contracts as outside "the norm" as a way to make a statement of bold action, innovation, and willingness to disrupt the status quo.

So Why Would a College Change Faculty Employment Policies?

The literature reviewed in this section provides a number of reasons for change from either tenure to contracts or contracts to tenure. Advocates of tenure may argue to abandon contracts and embrace tenure because:

- The institution as a whole or constituents of the institution fear threats to academic freedom. For example, a breach of academic freedom might prompt faculty to demand greater protection through tenure.
- Advocates propose that tenured faculty members will be afforded a greater role in campus governance and decision making.
- The institution realizes that contracts afford no more flexibility than tenure in promoting faculty turnover, and require substantial amounts of institutional time and resources for faculty evaluations.
- Advocates believe tenure will increase the quality of the faculty.
- The job security inherent in tenure systems is attractive to prospective faculty.
- The institution wants to be considered part of the mainstream of higher education.

Proponents of contracts might argue to shift from tenure to contracts because:

- The institution views the tenure system as harming relations between junior and senior faculty members, or because junior faculty lack an equal role in campus governance as their senior colleagues.

- The institution wants to focus on ongoing and continuous professional development rather than a one-time up-or-out personnel decision.
- The institution perceives that contracts will provide greater flexibility in budgeting, planning, or downsizing.
- Reframing personnel policy may permit faculty and administrators to place more emphasis on institutional priorities.
- The institution wants to do something innovative and radical.

Each of these reasons helps to answer the question I posed at the beginning of this chapter: Why would an institution change either toward or away from tenure? Two observations seem appropriate. First, there is a need for further investigation of institutions that have actually undergone such change to determine if these reasons were, in fact, determinative or if other arguments or circumstances were more influential.

Second, each of the reasons for change posited in this section is based on *rational* reasons for change. There is a clear implication of cause and effect. However, it is quite possible that shifts toward or away from tenure occurred for reasons largely unrelated to the benefits and drawbacks of a particular employment policy. Therefore, in the next section, I will review the various organizational change theories that may offer alternative explanations and processes of change.

ORGANIZATIONAL CHANGE THEORIES

Numerous organizational change theories suggest ways in which higher education institutions undergo large-scale change. This section focuses on organizational change models that have been applied to higher education, examining how change in faculty employment policies might occur under each model.

The Rational Model

The rational model of organizations—sometimes called the rational-legal, rational-bureaucratic, or classical management model—takes a deliberate, purposeful view of organizational behavior. Influenced greatly by Taylor (1911) and Weber (1947), rational systems posit a view of change that is centralized, with clear goals and outcomes. In rational organizations, "goals are *specific* to the extent that they are explicit, are clearly defined, and provide unambiguous criteria for selecting among alternative activities.... The cooperation among participants is 'conscious' and 'deliberate'; the structure of relations is made explicit" (Scott, 1992, p. 23). Rationality has a specific meaning in this model, referring to the extent to which a series of actions is organized in such a way as to lead to predetermined goals with maximum efficiency. Thus, rationality refers not to the selection of goals but to their implementation. (Scott, 1992, p. 30)

Studies using the rational model in higher education have found it has limited use (Chaffee, 1983; Hardy, 1988). Baldridge and Deal (1983) summarized:

> As the experience of changing organizations began to accumulate, it soon became apparent that people and organizations are not very rational—or at least they operate from a logic very different from that of theorists and administrators. Efforts to clarify goals produced more confusion, and results never seemed to follow from the activities designed to produce them. (p. 7)

Nevertheless, many management books and articles still incorporate this rational framework. The rational approach, according to Chaffee (1983), is popular "because a greater value has been placed on order and logic than on chaos and intuition in Western culture. The rational approach is inherent in the economic theory of the firm, in the scientific method, and in prepackaged management tools" (p. 11). Furthermore, as Weick (1976) noted, "people tend to overrationalize their activities and to attribute greater meaning, predictability, and coupling among them than in fact they have" (p. 9).

One might expect, using a rational framework, that administrators would offer a clear set of policy objectives and an explicit explanation of cause and effect in changing faculty appointment policies. Using a rational model, the campus community could ascertain the goals and consequences of the change and leaders would judge the outcome by specific criteria (Hardy, 1988). The rational model dictates a change process that is centralized, administratively directed, and logical.

The Political Model

The development of a political model of higher education is most closely associated with J. Victor Baldridge (1971, 1978), who developed the political framework of organizational change based on an in-depth case study of New York University. The framework drew from preexisting research in other settings such as conflict theory, community power studies, and research on interest groups (Baldridge, 1971). Under the political model, a college or university operates in the following manner:

> A complex social structure generates multiple pressures, many forms of power and pressure impinge on the decision makers, a legislative stage trans-

lates these pressures into policy, and a policy execution phase finally generates feedback into the form of new conflicts. (Baldridge, 1971, p. 24)

Baldridge (1971) identified five key stages of decision-making in the political model. First, a *social structure* exists in which divergent interest groups wrestling for power and influence lead to conflict. In this model, conflict is natural and expected. Second, there is a process of *interest articulation*, in which various groups make their views known. Third, a *legislative phase* occurs where a governance body debates and negotiates various policy proposals. Fourth, a compromise stage (*formulation of policy*) is reached when the legislative body enacts a final proposal. The final stage in Baldridge's framework is the *execution of policy* stage, in which "the resulting policy is turned over to bureaucrats for routine execution" (Baldridge, 1971, p. 24). This model is built on six assumptions about organizations in higher education:

1. Inactivity prevails—most people most of the time are uninterested in policy formation.
2. Fluid participation—people's involvement in policy development is episodic, so that only a small number of individuals govern most decision.
3. Fragmented interest groups exist.
4. Conflict is normal.
5. Authority is limited—administrators must negotiate with interest groups to build support for policy initiatives.
6. External interest groups are important. (Baldridge, et al, 1978, pp. 35–36)

The political model originated from only one case study at a large, urban university. Commentators subsequently criticized it for overestimating the importance of political processes, ignoring various types and sizes of higher education institutions, underplaying the importance of environmental factors, and focusing on episodic rather than long-term decision-making characteristics (Baldridge, et al., 1978).

Under a political model, change in faculty appointment policies would be dominated by various interest groups (trustees, administrators, and faculty being the obvious three) asserting power and influence to preserve, institute, or abolish tenure. One would expect a highly contentious process of change marked by open, public disagreements about problems and solutions. One would also expect the final policy to be a compromise of the divergent values of the various groups in the process.

The Collegial Model

The collegial model of higher education, influenced by Millett (1962) and Goodman (1962), is not so much an organizational change theory as a view of life in academe. Although there is little empirical research on the collegial "model" as an organizational theory per se, I include it here because of the widespread belief that the collegial framework explains how colleges and universities are supposed to work. Birnbaum (1988) presented a succinct summary of organizational life in a collegium:

> The hierarchical structure and rational administrative procedures seen at many institutions, which emphasize precision and efficiency in decision making, are absent [in a collegial model]. Instead, because all members have equal standing, there is an emphasis on thoroughness and deliberation. It often takes a long time to reach major decisions. . . . . Decisions are ultimately to be made by consensus, and not by fiat, so everyone must have an opportunity to speak and to consider carefully the views of colleagues. Certainly, some members are more influential and persuasive than others . . . [but] real consensus . . . arises when open discussion is possible and expected, when participants feel that they have had a fair chance to state their position and to influence the outcome, and when people are comfortable about supporting the chosen alternative even if it was not their first view. . . . (Birnbaum, 1988, pp. 88–89)

In a "purebred" collegial institution, one would expect that change in faculty appointment policies is reached by consensus after extensive deliberations. While a collegial model may fit well the deliberative nature of a faculty group (for example, in a highly functional faculty senate or a department comprised of well-natured colleagues), some have argued that this model does not address the contentious interactions among different groups. For example, Baldridge, et al. (1978) noted that the collegial model does not account for conflict in an institution. They asserted that "the collegial literature often confuses *descriptive* and *normative* enterprises . . . Frequently, the discussions of collegium are more a lament for paradise lost than a description of present reality" (Baldridge, et al., 1978, emphasis in original).

Institutional Isomorphism

Institutional isomorphism asserts that organizations change to become more like other organizations. According to DiMaggio and Powell (1991), "organizational change[s] occur as a result of processes that make organizations more similar without necessarily making them more efficient. . . . Once a field becomes well established . . . there is an inexorable push toward homogenization" (p. 64). This theory posits that rationalism does not take into account the environmental factors on an organization: "in the long run, organizational actors making rational decisions construct around themselves an environment that constrains their ability to change further in later years" (DiMaggio and Powell, 1991, p. 65). Isomorphism is a constraining process that forces one organization to resemble other organizations with the same set of environmental conditions. Organizations change because of three isomorphic pressures: (1) they are *coerced* by other organizations upon which they are dependent, (2) they *mimic* other organizations when goals are vague and environmental factors are uncertain, and (3) they abide by *norms of professionalization* (DiMaggio & Powell, 1991).

Institutional isomorphism was developed principally from primary and secondary school settings (Meyer, 1975; Meyer & Rowan, 1978; Rowan, 1982). At least one study applied the institutional isomorphism framework to higher education (Gates, 1997). Gates found that all three isomorphic elements (coercive, mimetic, and normative) were present in his study of university retrenchment. He concluded that "the institutional model provides a sound tool for discerning the preferences and behaviors of both administrators and faculty engaged in retrenchment" (Gates, 1997, p. 273). It is possible to speculate that institutions of higher education adopt tenure systems for two reasons under the institutional isomorphism theory: (1) because they want to be like other highly regarded institutions (mimetic isomorphism), which have tenure systems, and (2) because faculty members, who abide by the norms of professionalization, demand tenure systems because non-tenure colleges are considered outside the norm in the academy. Institutions abandoning a tenure system might want to mimic other professional organizations outside academe that do not have a tenure-equivalent (e.g. "We want to run more like a business").

The Strong Leader Model

Theories of leadership are plentiful, and leadership, in part, accounts for the operation of an organization. Some writers (Fisher, 1984; Fisher, Tack & Wheeler, 1988), however, have professed that the leader of the organization has such strong influence and power that, in effect, "the organization IS the leader" (Fisher, Tack & Wheeler, 1988, p. 40. Emphasis in original.) If that premise is accepted, then, an exploration of this model is appropriate because this leadership theory is also an organizational theory. An organization changes depending on how the leader wants it to change.

In opposition to a collegial model, strong leader theory suggests that presidents of colleges and universities change the organization by "making bold decisions, taking risks, and sometimes moving against the prevailing winds" (Fisher, Tack & Wheeler, 1988, p. 70). Strong leaders do not rely on consensus, and they remain aloof and distant from colleagues (Fisher, 1984).

Fisher (1984) based his theory on French and Raven's five-fold topology (1959) of power that leaders use to accomplish goals (and affect change). *Coercive power*, the least desirable type, uses threats and punishments to force followers into compliance. *Reward power* uses rewards and recognition to achieve goals. *Legitimate power* gives the leader power based on common norms of the group. *Expert power* is based on the leader's authority and knowledge of a subject. Finally, *charismatic power* is derived from the admiration of followers. Fisher (1984) claimed the charismatic power is the most effective of the five types. He asserted that, if a leader is charismatic,

> People simply want to agree with and to follow charismatic leaders, often twisting logic to agree with a leader's position. Followers will even defend a charismatic leader when he or she is not present, and will take strong exception to those who are unfairly critical of the leaders. People who follow charismatic leaders are convinced that things will get better.... (Fisher, 1984, p. 40)

One other study of higher education argued for an approach similar to the Fisher framework of decision making and change in colleges and universities. Based on a study of five institutions, Jones (1977) found that a shared governance model "has not been practiced on any wide scale in American higher education" (p. 88). He suggested a model of presidential leadership, in which organizational change rests with "the authority and responsibility of the president to decide" (Jones, 1977, p. 90).

Under the Strong Leader Model, change in faculty employment policies would occur because the president of the institution imposes his or her desire to institute change. Constituent groups (trustees and faculty) would agree to the change because of the president's coercive, rewarding, legitimate, expert, or charismatic power.

The Paradigm-Shifting Model

Recently there have been a number of frameworks of organizational change based on Thomas Kuhn's analysis of scientific revolutions (1970). Kuhn believed that scientific progress, while slow and steady for long periods of time, is punctuated by radical revolutionary leaps of knowledge. Social scientists have appropriated Kuhn's framework to organizational theory. In a "paradigm-shifting" organizational model, institutions typically pursue small, adaptive changes. But large-scale, revolutionary change can occur during certain periods; this process can be explained in a five-phase framework (Simsek & Louis, 1994):

1. *Normalcy*: This period is characterized by adaptive organizational activities and a slow pace of change. It is assumed that a particular paradigm has established dominance in guiding the organizational activities and imposing a set of tacit organizational knowledge as reference to those activities. . . .
2. *Confronting Anomalies*: Anomalies can result either from facing unresolved puzzles or from sudden changes occurring within and outside the organization. In order to view problems as anomalies, they must provide certain stimuli within the organization for an extended period. . . .
3. *Crisis*: If organizations experience anomalies . . . over a long period of time, they may trigger the beginning of a crisis period in which the organization's paradigm is questioned. Members begin to look for new ways of thinking which either spring from within their own sector, or are transferred from paradigms available in other organizational industries or sectors. A new leader is often seen as a catalyst to solve the crisis.
4. *Selection*: During the crisis period, the competition between available, but largely untested, paradigms is intense. . . .The selective mechanism for preferring one paradigm over others is access to power and influence. . . .
5. *Renewed Normalcy*: As a new paradigm becomes dominant, a new wave of enthusiasm appears in the organization. . . . (Simsek & Louis, 1994, pp. 675–76)

Simsek and Louis's study (1994) of organizational planning at a large public university found that "the paradigm shift model based largely on Kuhn's theory fits our data well" (p. 687). While this theory has been applied to organizational studies in other sectors, Simsek and Louis's research is the only example of a paradigm-shifting model used in a higher education study.

Using the Paradigm-Shifting Model, change in faculty appointment policies would occur in a discontinuous, radical fashion precipitated by long-brewing crisis. Institutions eliminating tenure might look outside of academe for a new "paradigm" of employment practices; colleges instituting tenure might look to the predominant tenure "paradigm" within the academy. The Paradigm-Shifting Model suggests that, once the new employment policy is in place, a new period of normalcy envelops the campus, implying that the old paradigm has been rejected as an appropriate model.

Loosely Couple Systems Models

Models that operate under loose coupling include those articulated by Cohen and March (1974, 1986) and Weick (1976, 1984), although each theorist has a different name for his model. Weick (1976) first applied "loose coupling" to educational settings while Cohen and March described university organization as an "organized anarchy" and the decision-making process at universities as a "garbage can" (1974). Despite the differences in these theories, they share a number of commonalities that permit them to be classified together. For simplicity's sake, I will refer to the theories under the umbrella of loose coupling.

In a loosely coupled system, according to Weick, connections between organizational elements may be "circumscribed, infrequent, weak in [their] mutual effects, unimportant, and/or slow to respond" (1976, p. 3). Loose coupling exists if A affects B

> 1) suddenly (rather than continuously), 2) occasionally (rather than constantly), 3) negligibly (rather than significantly), 4) indirectly (rather than directly), and 5) eventually (rather than immediately). (Weick, 1984, p. 380)

The loosely coupled nature of colleges and universities "makes it difficult to use administrative processes to affect change" (Birnbaum, 1988, p. 40). When change is necessary, "upper-level participants tend to respond to disruptions of ongoing activities or to improve selected activities through subtle interventions, rather than to engage in dramatic attempts to radically change institutional functioning" (Birnbaum, 1988, p. 196). These theorists specifically focus on four different elements in the process of organizational change:

1. *Leaders*. Leaders are more symbolic than significant; they have limited ability to institute broad, institution-wide change.

Cohen and March (1986) asserted that "the president's role [in decision-making is] more commonly sporadic and symbolic than significant.... The president has modest control over the events of college life" (p. 2). According to this model, it is unlikely that the president of institution could "order" a top-down overhaul of faculty appointment policies. If leaders promote organizational change, they tend to focus on incremental changes that are confined to subsystems (Weick, 1976).

2. *Participants*. The "multicephalous" characteristic of higher education makes it difficult to coordinate and control change.

Scott (1992) called loosely coupled systems "multicephalous" because many "heads" make decisions. Birnbaum (1988) argued that, because faculty are involved in decision making through the shared governance structure, "the authority of various constituencies to participate in or make decisions is often unclear and frequently contested" (p. 28). This model suggests, therefore, that decision making is decentralized and authority is diffuse. It would be difficult for participants to agree on what needs to change, why change is necessary, how to proceed, and who is in charge of implementation.

3. *The connection among goals, processes, and outcomes.* Decision making is nonrational and nonlinear.

Under the model of organizational change suggested by these theorists, the reasons and processes of change are not always rational or tied to clear objectives and goals. Universities, as organizational garbage cans, are "a collection of choices looking for problems, issues and feelings looking for decision situations in which they might be aired, solutions looking for issues to which they might be the answer, and decision makers looking for work" (Cohen & March, 1986, p. 81). In this nonrational organizational structure, Cohen and March asserted, an important feature of the decision-making process "is the partial decoupling of problems and choices. Although we think of decision making as a process for solving problems, that is often not what happens" (p. 90). Participants in a change process are unlikely to agree on linkages between cause and effect (Weick, 1984). The loosely coupled model of change suggests a decision-making process that is potentially unrelated to problems and unconnected with outcomes. This nonrational process might manifest itself in the decision to change faculty employment policies in interesting ways. For example, one researcher suggested that "when the consequences of an action are ambiguous, the stated *intentions* of the action serve as surrogates for the consequences" (Salancik as referenced in Weick, 1976, p. 8).

4. *Magnitude of change*: Loose coupling supports small, incremental change rather than radical, revolutionary change.

Loosely coupled systems focus on continuous adaptation but have less tolerance for fundamental overhaul. "If a major change needs to be introduced into a school, that change is more likely to occur quickly when the system is tight than when it is loose. Large-scale change is seldom needed in a loosely coupled system that continually updates itself. But if such a change is needed, it is difficult to design it and diffuse it" (Weick, 1982, p. 674). It is unlikely in a loosely coupled institution that transformation—change that is deep and pervasive (Eckel, Hill, & Green, 1998)—could or would need to occur.

According to the loosely coupled theory, change in faculty employment policies, whatever the direction and nature of the change, would occur slowly and incrementally. Many campus constituents would be involved in the decision-making process; the president would be only one voice among many. Participants might not agree to the reasons for change or its intended outcomes. Furthermore, it would be difficult to determine if goals had been met.

Although there was a strong focus on research universities in the development of loosely coupled theory, the model is widely applied to all types of institutions in both scholarly and popular higher education literature (Lutz, 1982; Peterson, 1985). Many studies and essays invoke the loosely coupled model, either explicitly or implicitly (Butler & Davis, 1992; Cannon & Lonsdale, 1987; Clugston, 1986; DiBiasio & Ecker, 1982; Emmert, 1998; Gerber, 1997; Kuh, 1993; Lutz & Lutz, 1988; Penrod & Dolence, 1991; Richardson & Skinner, 1990; Rutherford, Fleming & Mathias, 1985; Whalen, 1995). For example, Emmert (1998) implicitly embraced a loosely coupled model when he asserted that change in higher education must occur "in the context of diffused authority ... must accommodate the decentralized authority structures of universities ... [and] needs to occur in more modest steps and at multiple levels" (pp. 8, 9). Richardson and Skinner (1990) declared that all "colleges and universities are loosely coupled organizations" (p. 492). In fact, because loose coupling has been applied so often to higher education settings, it is often considered the "normative model" of organizational change in universities (Lutz, 1982, p. 653).

Despite this profession-wide appropriation of the loosely coupled model, it is not at all clear that the loosely coupled theory should be the "normative model" of organizations and organizational change in higher education. There are several reasons for such caution:

- First, researchers have not examined whether the model applies to different types of higher education institutions. Most often, organizational studies focus on research universities: Gumport's study on program reduction (1993), Hanna's research on affirmative action for women faculty (1988), and Twombly's investigation on the selection of deans (1992), for example, all engage the loosely coupled or organized anarchy theories to some degree by focusing solely on university settings. While many studies have been conducted on small colleges, organizational theory research focusing on these institutions is rare. Hammond's transitional political governance model (1981) is the only organizational theory derived from a study of small colleges. No research has specifically investigated the appropriateness of the loosely coupled model on smaller institutions.
- Furthermore, it is unclear whether the loosely coupled model applies to institutions that are not in an expansion-and-growth mode. Weick (1984) noted that the loosely coupled model of organizational change is "less harmful" to wealthy, expanding institutions than

cash-poor ones. He elaborates: "a rich family can use its food budget to experiment with nutrition in food purchases and can discard the failures, but poor families cannot afford this hit-or-miss strategy. As resources diminish, a series of expensive partial successes from incremental changes made to collect insights may ensure total failure" (Weick, 1984, p. 390). This caveat about the loosely coupled change model has important implications in the current environment of higher education. Unlike the 1960s and early 1970s, when student populations were booming and resources were plentiful, the last decade has been marked by downsizing, cost containment, and heightened accountability. It is not clear than *any* college or university these days has the slack resources to experiment with "food purchases" and to "discard the failures."
- Finally, it is unclear whether the loosely coupled models of change are appropriate to describe all types of decision-making. The elimination of tenure is a process that goes against the norms of higher education and may occur to the dismay of faculty. The introduction of tenure embraces the prevailing standards of faculty employment and would likely be supported by faculty. Researchers have not investigated whether the loosely coupled models applies equally to policy changes that go in opposite directions, one embracing and the other rejecting the normative model of faculty appointment and professionalization.

Because the loosely coupled/organized anarchy models have been developed from education settings, and because scholars have argued that theory must be developed from the area under study to be effective (Cannon & Lonsdale, 1987), I will use loose coupling as the conceptual framework for the research described in this book.

CHAPTER SUMMARY

This chapter demonstrated the following:

- Academic tenure is the modal system of faculty employment in American higher education. Tenure is "the norm." Term contracts are rare and institutions that employ faculty only by contracts are considered outside the mainstream of academe.
- Pundits and researchers have offered rationales for possible reasons of change in faculty employment policies toward or away from tenure. However, there is not research that proves or disproves these speculations. Furthermore, there has not been research that investigates how institutions undergo the process of change to faculty employment policies.

- Many different organizational theories have been applied to higher education, including rationalism, the political model, the collegial model, strong leader model, institutional isomorphism, the paradigm-shifting model, and loose coupling. Only loosely coupled systems theories were primarily generated from higher education settings.
- Despite the strong focus on research universities in the development of loosely coupled theories, the model is widely applied to all types of institutions in both scholarly and popular higher education literature. However, researchers have not examined whether the model applies to different types of higher education institutions and different types of policy changes.

CHAPTER 3
Scott College

THIS BOOK EXPLORES THE QUESTIONS OF HOW AND WHY COLLEGES added or abolished tenure by telling the stories of change at two sets of colleges: Scott College and Rowlette College, which altered their faculty employment policies from tenure to term contracts, and Accomac College and Lakeview College, which shifted from contracts to tenure.[1]

This chapter is about Scott College, which moved from contracts to tenure. The next three chapters take the other institutions in turn. Each of these chapters are arranged in a similar fashion, focusing on the college's history, prominent characteristics, important constituencies, the process of change in faculty employment policies, reasons for the overhaul in policy, and an analysis of the process of change.

SCOTT COLLEGE

Scott College, an independent, private institution of 1,500 students, stopped offering tenure in 1993. Those faculty members already tenured retained that status, but all tenure-track and new faculty were placed on multi-year contracts after a six-year probationary period of one-year contracts.

A SHORT HISTORY

As a four-year institution, Scott College is comparatively new. A missionary petitioned the state Synod of the Presbyterian Church in 1905 to open

---

1. The names of the institution, individuals, and place locations in this book are pseudonyms.

a primary school for "those of both sexes who are deserving, but yet financially unable to secure an education above the free school. The purpose should be to make the school a self-sustaining 'family' by requiring all students to spend a portion of their time in various duties assigned to them . . ." (College Catalog, p. 3). The state granted the Synod a charter in 1906 for the Scott School "to undertake the task of providing the boys and girls of the [region] with an education." In its first year, the school enrolled 180 students, including 36 boarders.

Scott School operated as a primary school and then a high school until 1956, when it received accreditation as a two-year junior college. The format changed again in 1964, when a four-year liberal arts curriculum replaced the two-year format. The college earned preliminary accreditation in 1965 and full accreditation in 1971. Although the institution evolved into a four-year baccalaureate college, in some ways it retained the feeling of a secondary school. The first academic dean, for example, was a former school superintendent. According to a faculty member, "Even by the late 1970s, many of the faculty had been hired out of a secondary education mode. A lot of faculty weren't traditional academics; they would never have been faculty members at a four-year college otherwise."

From 1921 until 1981, the school-then-college had only two presidents, each of whom served 30 years. The second of these individuals, Shaun Daily, was considered the college's "founding" president by many on campus. Health problems forced Daily to resign in 1981. Said one observer, "in the eyes of most people, he had stayed too long." Daily recovered from his poor health and installed himself as chairman of the board of trustees. Observers attribute the rapid turnover in the four subsequent presidents between 1981 and 1988 to Daily's micro-management as board chair. The first president to succeed Daily lasted ten months. An interim president took over, followed by another president who remained four years. This president, a trustee recalled, "was a young administrator. There was a holdover from Dr. Daily, still trying to run the institution. With Daily trying to run the school, it was difficult for [the new president] to do anything except side with the faculty. So faculty had, for the first time, a president who would at least listen to them."

Another interim president followed for a year in 1987. Trustees were "weary with the turnover," although faculty describe this period as a time of "tremendous influence. The faculty had been quite powerful and the administration very deferential to faculty." Terrence Kelly, the incumbent at the time of this research, assumed the presidency in 1988.

In 1990, at Kelly's request, the board of trustees changed the institution's name from Scott School to Scott College. According to 1998 figures, the college enrolled 1,563 students, 65 percent of whom came from in-state or the nearest border state. The full-time faculty numbered 86 and the student-faculty ratio was 14:1. According to an analysis of the faculty listing in the college catalog, 58 percent of the faculty held doctorates and 12 percent were alumni of the college.

PROMINENT CHARACTERISTICS

During my site visit to Scott College, I immediately observed two aspects of the physical landscape that later proved to be important characteristics in the story of institutional change: the college's trim campus, an indicator of its financial position, and its street names, an indicator of the importance of mission.

Wealth

Most colleges without tenure are financially brittle (Chait & Trower, 1997). Conventional wisdom suggests that these are small, unheralded places with limited resources and tight budgets. If this is true, then Scott College is clearly an exception to the rule.

Located several miles from a small tourist city, in a landscape of rolling hills, one-lane highways, cows, and crops, Scott College did not *look* poor. Its grand "Gates of Opportunity" led to neatly manicured lawns, patches of tulips blazoned in reds and golds, and blooming red-bud trees. Well-maintained, if nondescript, buildings surrounded an artificial lake, complete with a fountain and floating swan house. The bells of the chapel tolled every quarter-hour.

The well-heeled appearance of the campus is, in fact, a reliable indicator of the college's financial position. Its approximately $200 million endowment ranks among the top 150 in the country, similar in size to Franklin and Marshall, Davidson, Colby, and Union colleges. It recently received a bequest of $10 million—a gift of record size. It is regularly cited in *U.S. News & World Report*, *Money Magazine*, and *Barron's* as a "best-buy" or top regional liberal arts college.

Mission

My second observation of Scott College was the street signs. As I drove through the Gates of Opportunity, I intersected Academic Avenue. Proceeding down Opportunity Avenue, I crossed Patriotic Place, Vocational Way, Spiritual Street, and Cultural Court. Beyond was Lake Honor. This college wanted to make its mission transparent to the most casual observers. As suggested by its street names, the college's five-fold aims and objectives, as stated in the Catalog, are:

1. Academic Growth, "advanced by helping a quality student body put together past, present, and future knowledge into an ongoing, usable system."
2. Vocational Growth. "Vocational growth is encouraged by giving students the opportunity to experience the dignity and worth of work in their lives through employment in productive industries and services on campus."
3. Spiritual Growth, "fostered by establishing a Christian community on campus that unites administration, faculty, students, and staff. This is enhanced by formal study of Christianity through classes in the literature and religious teachings of the Bible in addition to courses in religion, ethics, and philosophy."
4. Patriotic Growth, "promoted in a climate where loyalty to American institutions, ideas, and obligations is based on the knowledge and understanding of United States history and government."
5. Cultural Growth, "cultivated in a social environment which gives students the opportunity to experience the joy of participation in and observation of an abundance of enriching life experiences."

Two other symbols of the college's mission were prominently displayed on an expanse of lawn between the library and chapel: a replica of the Liberty Bell—at this college, a reminder of patriotism—and a plaque of the Ten Commandments.

The religious milieu at Scott College is particularly strong. The college has an explicit religious component to student and faculty life. The board of trustees emphasized this religious character when, in 1968, it passed a resolution that "[Scott College] shall always maintain as one of its prime objectives the promotion of the cause of Christ and His Kingdom and the maintenance of high academic standards within the context of a Christian environment" (College Catalog, p. 26). That commitment was evident in the late 1990s: the college catalog informs students that "community worship is an integral part of life on our Christian college campus. Therefore, a reasonable participation in chapel services and various other campus Christian life activities is considered a student's responsibility and privilege. . . . Christian convocations are held several times each semester to intentionally present the gospel of Jesus Christ in a culturally relevant way. Attendance at a certain number of these convocations is required of all full-time students" (p. 26). The college requires active participation in Christian worship among its faculty, too. Among the areas in which faculty are evaluated, "a faculty member should demonstrate a Christian commitment by church membership and attendance, and by a commitment to the spiritual dimension of life on campus" (*Faculty Handbook 1996*, p. 8).

The religious tone of the institution affects the composition of faculty. As one faculty member said, "there's a certain philosophy that you sign on to here." A colleague emphasized, "this is a conservative environment. You don't find the liberal, heterogeneous population among the faculty." The president also highlighted the importance of the spiritual mission in regard to faculty: "[Scott College] has parameters. It makes a religious statement . . . although one tends to be marginalized for taking one's faith seriously. But we take that seriously here, and we operate within a broad values system. Therefore, we're interested in hiring people who buy into that mission."

The strong, mission-driven characteristic of Scott College comes from the top. President Kelly is particularly fervent about his "calling." With his voice as energized as a preacher in the pulpit, he proclaimed, "To me, this is more than a job. I'm going to carry out the mission of the school, and *anything* that gets in my way is going to have to stand aside, because that mission is *bigger* than me, and it's bigger than everyone else around here, and it's worthy."

IMPORTANT CONSTITUENCIES

The process of change in faculty employment policy at Scott College involved three constituencies: the board of trustees, the faculty, and the administration, primarily the president.

The Board of Trustees

Faculty, administrators, and a trustee described the 21–member self-perpetuating board of trustees as "typical" for private higher education, comprised "mostly of business people." Indeed, 18 of 21 current board members are individuals from business or the professions. One is a philanthropist and two are "retired educators" (including a former vice president of the college). An administrator noted that "there is no sympathy for tenure among them." According to a current board member, his colleagues thought that "tenure is automatically something evil . . . The original idea of getting rid of tenure came from the board." Two board members were particularly vociferous in their contempt for the policy (although my informant would not name them).

Not surprisingly, faculty felt removed from and wary of the trustees. A former faculty member called the board "anti-intellectual." With no regular faculty representation on the board, the two groups had little official interaction. One faculty member recalled making a presentation at a trustees' dinner but, "nothing like sitting at board meetings, no."

Faculty

Several characteristics of the faculty are evident from the case description thus far: faculty described themselves as politically conservative and homogeneous and, until recently, many came from a secondary-school or nontraditional mode. Most professors seemed reluctant to assert the traditional faculty role in issues of power and governance:

> "You know the rules, you abide by them."
> "Most people don't want to rock the boat."
> "People are reluctant to make waves."
> "I wouldn't want to be perceived as a troublemaker."

It is unclear if faculty willfully embrace this role or if they are forced to accept it. Both scenarios are likely. Several faculty members indicated that they have no interest in such matters; one said, "the majority of people . . . believe in management, believe in authority of position. They believe their job is one of a professor and not one of making those major decisions, making administrative decisions. There are a lot of faculty who don't want to spend their time doing those kinds of things." Others expressed a more cynical acceptance of their role: "Faculty do whatever they have to do to keep their jobs." Another colleague said, "You just expect to be told how it's going to be and, if you don't like it, there's the front gate."

With little voice in the management of the institution, faculty reported that other factors drew them to and keep them at Scott College. Said one, "We have faculty who have grown up in this area, who were students here, who love the institution. They want to remain." Another professor indicated that it is "a quality of life issue," referring to the good schools, country atmosphere, and religious character of the college. Yet another said:

> A lot of people like small colleges, like liberal arts colleges. A lot of people just want to teach, they don't want to do research. A lot of people want family environments, they want Christian environments . . . So I think you have to say, "Will my career flourish here? How much do I really want to be part of all that other stuff? If I want a place to raise my family that's a great area, then I'll be here." I truly love this place. It provides a lot of students an opportunity who don't have money to get an education. You've got such nice students. . . . In those ways, it's really nice. I've been at the University of Iowa and taught there—150 papers to grade, not knowing students' names—I didn't want that. It's nice to be in this environment, to know the students.
>
> *Is it a trade-off?*
>
> Yes, it is. It's a quality of life issue, and it's an individual issue. I have three boys and I was responsible for raising them and I thought to myself, "Where else do I want to be but someplace that's supportive of that environment?" So, in my case, I said, "People can tell me what to do."

President Kelly

Kelly worked at two small private colleges—as a professor of biology for six years and a president for 11 years—before arriving at Scott. He was, an observer noted, a "different animal" than his short-lived predecessors. One board member described him as "about as strong an administrator as I've ever known. . . . [He] determined that 'you're going to do things my way or we're not going to do them.'" Faculty members concurred with this analysis: "Terrence Kelly makes the decisions," said one faculty member. Others called his style top-down, hierarchical, and autocratic. After Kelly arrived, a professor opined, "it became more of a dictatorship then. It's the way the college is run now." This is a characterization with which Kelly does not disagree: "I guess I'm a dictator, but I'm a benevolent one."

Kelly said that he had a mandate from the board upon arriving in 1988:

> The board was unhappy over the financial management, they were unhappy over the kinds of students admitted here, they were unhappy over some of the philosophical rumblings coming out of the faculty. They were basically unhappy, almost desperate.
> *How quickly were you able to come up with a plan of what to do?*
> I already had a plan.
> *Even before you were in office?*
> Yes. Yes. . . . At my first board meeting, I asked the board to pass a resolution to bring expenses in line with revenues. I got them to abolish the mandatory summer session and change the financial aid system. Then, I went out and made these changes.

Kelly made other dramatic changes in his first two years: changing the school's name, instituting fees for room and board, and tightening student work requirements.[2]

CHANGE AFFECTING FACULTY

Under Kelly' administration, there were alterations to several areas of faculty work life: changes in governance, faculty evaluation, and faculty employment policy.

Changes in Governance

Kelly mandated two modifications in faculty organization and governance. First, in 1989, he established six academic divisions to replace 23 departments in order to streamline the number of direct-reports to the academic

---

2. Students at Scott College work on campus in lieu of paying tuition.

dean. Second, in 1991, he asked the board to pass a resolution that mandated a revision to faculty governance. The existing faculty governance system was a faculty-wide group that met monthly with its own elected officers. "The meetings were sometimes contentious," said one faculty member. This system was unacceptable to Kelly because:

> I think the dean is the chief academic officer who should be in charge of the faculty. You cannot put them in charge of themselves. . . . All I cared about was who is in charge. When I came here, I remember that the dean was given so many minutes to address the faculty at faculty meetings. I about had a stroke when I heard that. Who's running this college anyway? The dean can have all the time he wants . . .
>
> Shared governance was a problem and it had been shared too much. . . . If the president and the dean are capable people, they won't let that happen. Faculty members should have a proper role . . .
>
> I see the role of faculty more traditionally than at a lot of places. I think they should teach young people. That's what I think they should do. They shouldn't be running the college.

With a penchant for clear administrative authority and a "chain of command," Kelly "simply said that the governance system was going to change because I was not going to delegate it down to a self-appointed chair [of the faculty]." In December 1991, an eight-member faculty committee began work with the dean and president for an acceptable replacement to the old system. In September 1992, the Academic Council replaced the previous faculty organization.

The dean of the college chaired the new Academic Council, composed of the division chairs, who were appointed by the administration; a member of each division, elected by faculty; and the chairs of three committees. Faculty reaction to the change in governance was mixed. One, who declared the all-faculty government a "disaster," said, "I don't think it was a big concern." Others were less supportive and interpreted the change as a reduction in faculty power. One professor said "[Kelly] no longer wanted elected faculty officers. I think a lot of democratic processes went *phhhtt—*." Another indicated that when the faculty ceased meeting as a whole, it was difficult to assert unified positions: "the faculty was divided."

History of Faculty Tenure and Evaluation

Scott College had a very informal, nearly automatic process of granting tenure to faculty for several decades. Long-time faculty members told stories of receiving tenure via the phone, memo, or in person:

- After my fourth year, I went to the dean's office to pick up my new contract. I told the dean, "I'm supposed to get tenure this year." So,

the dean picked up the phone and told his secretary, "Sandra, Steve gets tenure this year."
- I got tenure after I'd been here seven years. I didn't "do" anything.
- I called the dean on the phone and I said, "Look, I want tenure. I've been here six years, I've finished my master's, I'm working on my Ph.D. There's no reason why I shouldn't have it." He said, "Write me a letter about why you think you should have tenure." I wrote him a letter, and I got tenure.
- I didn't do anything. It appeared on my contract one year.
- I got called to the dean's office—I don't know how long I had been here—and was simply told I was going to get tenure. There was no committee, no application, no process. Evaluation had been done solely by the dean at that time.

As a result of the informal tenuring process, some faculty at Scott were tenured who, in the eyes of their colleagues and later administrators, should not have been. A faculty member decried, "tenure had been so easy to get, [it] had created some monsters. And we're still dealing with some of them because they are tenured and, as you know, it's very, very difficult to get rid of a tenured faculty member."

In subsequent years, the tenure process became more codified and formalized. In 1982, a faculty handbook committee wrote tenure and promotion guidelines. Several years later, an up-or-out policy was implemented. The tenure-granting process began to resemble more traditional tenure policies, although "it was less than perfect," according to one faculty member. For example, a professor who was reviewed for tenure in the mid-1980s explained, "there was a committee of three people, one from the department, one of my choice, and one who was the dean's appointment. There weren't many guidelines about what to include in my file. There wasn't a formalized student evaluation system, but I had done my own."

The New Evaluation System

In October 1991, the administration and board took another step to create a more sophisticated evaluation process. The board directed the administration and faculty to implement an evaluation system, "which shall include tenure review." A 13-member faculty committee developed a proposal over the course of a year, with the Academic Council passing the proposal in April, 1993, by a 10–4 vote. The board of trustees accepted the proposal the same spring. The new evaluation system created a Faculty Evaluation Committee, composed of a representative from each of the six divisions selected by the administration, and chaired by the non-voting academic dean. The new evaluation system required all faculty, tenured and nontenured, to be reviewed by the committee on a six-year rotational basis.

The members of the committee were appointed by the administration, not elected by their peers. An evaluation committee member explained that "we were just called and told that we were on the committee. None of us wanted to do it—who likes to evaluate their peers? It's almost like a life sentence."

Change in Faculty Employment Policy

When Kelly became president in 1988, academic tenure was already an issue with the board. One long-time faculty member indicated that the board had been concerned with tenure for 10 or 15 years prior to Kelly's arrival, a claim verified by a trustee:

> *The board considered the elimination of tenure before Kelly arrived?*
> A long, long time before that.
> *What took them so long to act?*
> The college was in a building state during the many years with Dr. Daily as president. Tenure wasn't a big talking point, but as time went on, it became more and more of a talking point.

During the presidential selection process, Kelly made it clear that he was unsupportive of tenure. A faculty member of the selection committee recalled that Kelly was "very upfront" about his disdain for the policy. At that time, he was president of another college that did not offer tenure and "philosophically, I certainly was comfortable with the trustees' attitude [of opposing tenure]." Kelly concluded that tenure was a lifetime contract that had been abused in higher education. "I've always believed people should be retained based on their productivity. I don't like dealing with people who think they can't be held accountable." After he was offered the presidency at Scott, Kelly learned from the chairman of the board, "if I would agree, tenure would be gone before I got inside the gate. My response was 'well, I don't mind making that decision but I'd rather make it from a position of strength', and I didn't think that was the way to go."

In October, 1993, two years after the new evaluation system has been installed, Kelly proposed, and the board embraced, a motion to eliminate tenure. Kelly described the process:

> The board passed a resolution indicating the policy of tenure was being discontinued. It took a majority vote [of the board.] I did not go back to the faculty and ask them to vote as to whether they wanted me to ask the board to discontinue tenure. I am not naïve and stupid to be in office all this while. Why do that? If people perceive they're giving something up, they don't want to do it, whether it's tenure or something else. So, I didn't do that. And I was harshly criticized because I didn't *ask* the faculty. Well, I don't *report* to the

faculty for one thing. My duty is to recommend what's in the interest of the college. So, I just did it.
During the board meeting, was there any dissent? Were there factions that said, "Maybe we shouldn't do this"?
No.

The dean of the college notified the faculty as a group in a meeting in November 1993. Tenured faculty members retained that status while those on the tenure-track and all new hires were placed in a multi-year contract system.

Reaction Among Faculty and External Groups

Faculty reaction was not uniform. First, faculty differed in their preparedness for this announcement. One professed complete surprise:

> It was just like, "Bang!" Here it is.
> *Did people see that coming?*
> There had been rumors, but we never thought this particular president would do it. We never thought it would happen. It happened very fast and quickly early in Dr. Kelly's tenure as president, and it caught people by surprise.

Other faculty expressed an opposite view: "It didn't happen overnight. I don't think [faculty] were surprised. I think they were expecting it by that time."

Second, faculty differed in their level of support for the decision. A group of 10–15 tenured faculty members were vocal in their anger and disappointment—writing editorials to the local newspaper, speaking with the higher education press, and contacting the AAUP.[3] One faculty member noted that, in the aftermath, "there was a lot of unhappiness and a lot of talk. There were a lot of unhappy people and many of them still are, although many of them either have retired or gone somewhere else."

Media reports made the college's actions known to the wider higher education community. Faculty groups at one state-supported college and one private institution passed resolutions condemning the board and the president. The state affiliate of the AAUP printed an article in its newsletter comparing Scott College to Jonestown, the infamous suicide cult led by Jim Jones. Kelly angrily denounced such a comparison, charging, "That was part of a big campaign to get rid of me, which of course didn't work. In fact, I think it strengthened my position. The majority of the faculty here wanted nothing to do with it."

---

3. Several interviewees reported that the national AAUP declined to pursue the case.

Of those I interviewed, most professors corroborated that view. Faculty who were less demonstrative about the decision indicated that "the majority of faculty had the feeling that it didn't really make any difference. I don't think the majority of the faculty were opposed to it or really cared. If we do our jobs, we're not going to get thrown out the window." Another commented, "Since I wasn't affected by the removal of tenure [because I maintained my tenure status], it didn't disturb me a whole lot." One professor cautioned that faculty's lack of protest and demonstration was indicative of the campus culture. Many faculty were comfortable with administrative decision making in any realm. "[They] do whatever they're told to do.... I think they like it here. They're secure here. Some are graduates of the institution. They're going to do whatever they have to do to keep their jobs." Another professor indicated that faculty were already beaten down from losing battles on other issues, such as the change in governance: "I think people were stunned. It was one more thing that was happening to us. People went back into their own holes around campus and haven't come out."

The Link Among Governance, Evaluation, and Tenure

The changes in governance, evaluation, and tenure all occurred in a relatively short period of time between 1991 and 1993. Several faculty and administrators have noted that these different elements were linked with the common purposes of increasing faculty accountability to the administration and decreasing faculty power in decision making. One professor indicated that "it was an evolving process, changing the whole structure of the faculty beneath the dean and making people more accountable for their actions." Another said, "I think, when Dr. Kelly came here, he had all those things in mind and meticulously went about them. He did it in small steps over the five years and tenure was probably the ultimate one. But I think it was a master plan from the very beginning." The president agreed that changes in the governance system, evaluation, and faculty employment policy were part of a power struggle:

> We had a power struggle here. I think the board thought people were hiding from accountability because they had tenure. Some [faculty] were outright hostile to the institution... I guess it was a struggle for the heart and soul of [Scott College]. So there was a struggle, and it came down to power. That's reflected in governance and it's reflected in the security that they think gives them license to do whatever they want. So, it's all changed...
>
> *You see the issue of changing the tenure policy as part of this ongoing power struggle—*
>
> To ensure accountability. To ensure accountability....

> *Were all these changes [in governance, evaluation, and employment policy] linked in some way?*
>
> They weren't linked in that they were part of the same motion. But, I'm the one sitting here, as you would perceive it, orchestrating all of this. It wouldn't have happened if I hadn't done it. Changing the governance system—that was also a signal that things were going to be done differently here and that there would be accountability.

In the president's view, "accountability" encompassed all three areas of governance, evaluation, and employment policy. The change in governance eliminated elections of faculty officers and gave the academic dean the authority to call faculty-wide meetings.[4] The more rigorous system of evaluation subjected *all* faculty, for the first time, to regular, formalized reviews by their peers and the administration. The removal of tenure was a capstone event in demanding accountability of faculty, the president argued, because they could no longer "hide" behind tenure and "do anything they want to do and not be responsible at all."

REASONS FOR THE OVERHAUL IN POLICY

Faculty and administrators identified several "problems" that the elimination of tenure was intended to solve:

Faculty accountability

Interviewees were nearly unanimous in asserting that the "problem" of accountability was "solved" by the elimination of tenure. Under an informal, automatic system, faculty received tenure without review of their qualifications or performance. Numerous faculty reported that some of these tenured professors became unproductive and irascible, failing in their most basic duties. One division chair explained that, when he chastised a professor for habitual tardiness to his class, the faculty member responded, "You can't do anything about it. I have tenure." Under this system of "non-evaluation," several faculty identified tenure as the problem. Professors commented:

- Some people semi-retired when they got tenure.
- I've been in too many situations where tenured faculty have been kept and they no longer do anything constructive and they no longer care about how they teach or how their students learn.

---

4. According the minutes of the Academic Council on September 17, 1992, meetings of the whole faculty, called Faculty Assemblies, "will be held on occasion during the semester.... [T]hese Faculty Assemblies will be considered required meetings. In order to miss one of these meetings a faculty member should have a Permission to be Absent filed with the office of the dean."

- We had some tenured people who simply were not carrying their weight.

Therefore, the abolition of tenure solved the problem, they argued, because tenure would no longer provide a protective shield against accountability and responsibility.

While most interviewees said that tenure was the cause of a lack of accountability, a few interviewees identified the lack of rigorous evaluation as the reason that there was "deadwood" on the faculty. The academic dean noted that tenure "had caused damage to this institution and, quite frankly, part of that was due to the way in which it had been handled. It had been mishandled at this institution." A professor lamented, "if we could have implemented [an] evaluation system 15 or 10 years ago, then maybe the tenure issue would not have been a problem.... I think the issue was that it was too easy to get tenure and we tenured people we shouldn't have." These comments point to faculty evaluation and rewards as concerns (which could have been a problem under any system of faculty employment), not of tenure *per se*.

Those that identified faculty accountability as the problem tended to be unclear or unsure about whether the solution was the elimination of tenure or, rather, other factors such as the more rigorous evaluation system or an early retirement package. A member of the evaluation committee noted that the removal of tenure "solved the problem down the road" because professors would no longer be awarded tenure. But more immediately, she observed, the new evaluation system only encouraged two tenured professors to retire after they received repeated negative responses on their evaluations—the evaluation system produced voluntary, not involuntary, turnover.[5] Another faculty member asserted, "the thing that solved more of the problem was an early retirement package . . . All of a sudden, people [who were not high-quality faculty members] are retiring. You're bringing in people fresh out of Ph.D. programs; they're bringing in new ideas. Academically, that's been the best thing that's happened to us."

The president viewed the solution as less direct and more symbolic. Eliminating tenure, he asserted, had a "halo effect." "Faculty think, 'if they can get rid of tenure, they can get rid of me.' It sends a signal that accountability is taken seriously."

---

5. Based on information provided by the dean's office, it does not appear that the contract system has been a mechanism for greater involuntary turnover. Between 1994 and 1999, 42 faculty underwent a post-tenure review or multi-year contract renewal review. Thirty-seven passed the review (88 percent) and five failed. Two of those five passed a second evaluation; two faculty members retired and one resigned after failing the review. Twelve junior faculty members underwent a multi-year contract evaluation (the equivalent of a tenure decision). Ten (83 percent) were awarded multi-year contracts. The two others remained on annual contracts (they were not dismissed).

Power

The president saw the elimination of tenure as part of a struggle over "what the school was going to be and who was going to run it." The abolition of tenure was one step in a series of measures, including revision of the governance structure, that transferred power from faculty to the president. Faculty reported that the president was an autocrat and a dictator who made decisions unilaterally. Kelly admitted an aversion to shared governance and saw the faculty's proper role in decision making as advisory. Kelly's rationale for the reduction in faculty influence and power was mission-driven:

> I'm responsible. Others who have ideas, they're not. They weren't named to this position. So, to me, it's a mission, it's a calling . . . I've been in about every controversy you can think of, but only because I was trying to restore the school to its historical mission and make the changes necessary to carry it out. Everything I touched caused controversy, but you would be hard-pressed to find a college that's more focused on its mission. It makes every honor roll and every piece of public recognition. Would it have happened if the school were being run by committees? Well, I know the answer to that and you do, too.

Symbolic reasons

The board's interest in making a brazen statement about their willingness to thwart the status quo was another reason for the elimination of tenure. The board would not have been swayed simply by arguments to improve the faculty evaluation system in order to increase accountability, according to the academic dean, because of the "mindset" of the trustees. "They were going to attack it." A professor expressed the belief that the president, too, wanted to make "a bold step." In other words, under this rationale, the problem was not simply poor evaluation, which had a substantive solution. Instead, the problem was tenure, which was symbolic of the mainstream higher education industry. The president and board wanted to send a signal to internal and external constituencies that they were capable of bold, aggressive leadership. They were willing to subvert the established norms of higher education. There is arguably no better way to make a statement of iconoclastic leadership in higher education than the removal of tenure.

Suppression of Dissent

Several faculty members said that abolishing tenure made it easier for the president to remove faculty members—both tenured and nontenured—with whom he disagreed. A professor speculated that removing tenure may have been a response to a group of faculty called "the Dirty Dozen," who actively opposed the president's reforms of governance and other changes. "The underlying reason," she reflected, "may have been that these people who were causing the problems were all tenured faculty." One former faculty member who was part of that group reported being told by the president that "no one is safe here."

There is not, however, a direct cause-effect relationship between the abolition of tenure and the president's ability to "get" faculty members he didn't like, since the "Dirty Dozen" were *tenured* faculty members. Abolishing tenure would not have had the *direct* result of giving the president power to summarily dismiss dissenting faculty members, since those tenured professors retained their protected status. More evident from faculty and administration interviews, however, is an *indirect* result—the creation of an atmosphere in which it became abundantly clear that the president had the upper hand in power and control. According to a tenured professor, once tenure was eliminated, "people feel reluctant to rock the boat too much. I think that's unfortunate because everyone needs to express their opinions . . . People are reluctant to make waves." A colleague declared:

> I think faculty feel like those who are vocal against the administration are reprimanded.
> *What would happen if a faculty member wrote a letter to the editor criticizing the president?*
> They would have a problem. "If you are so disgruntled, why don't you go someplace else?"
> *Even though his or her intention might be to improve the institution rather than malign it?*
> Right.

Presidential Experience

Kelly's previous presidency was at another college without tenure. "College presidents attempt to learn from their experience. They observe the consequences of actions and infer the structure of the world from those observations" (Cohen & March, 1986, p. 199). From his previous presidency, Kelly "learned" that the absence of tenure was better than its presence. "I came from a college that did not have tenure," he said, where he developed an opposition to tenure "because I saw it abused so much. It's especially inappropriate in small colleges like this." From his prior experience, then, Kelly "learned" that tenure limited accountability and impeded effective management. In his view of academic management, tenure was an obstacle that needed to be surmounted.

AN ANALYSIS OF THE PROCESS OF CHANGE

President Kelly is a dominating force at Scott College. His leadership style is contrary to the prevailing assumptions of leadership in higher education as expressed by Birnbaum (1988) and Green (1997), among others, which posit that presidents share power, have limited decision-making authority, and should rely on consensus and faculty input. Kelly exhibits none of these characteristics. He had an idea of how he wanted the college to change and he methodically achieved that goal. Over time, he reduced faculty influence in major decisions to a cursory, advisory role. The story of the change process at Scott College is one of power. The following section examines the circumstances and conditions that enabled Kelly to affect change.

Personal Characteristics of the Leader

Pfeffer (1981) maintained that one of the determinants of power in an organization is the personal characteristics of the leader. President Kelly's dominating personality is an important factor in the process of moving from tenure to contracts at Scott College. Some writers suggested that personal characteristics of presidential leaders can be so strong and powerful that, in effect, "the organization IS the leader" (Fisher, Tack & Wheeler, 1988, p. 40. Emphasis in original.) This theory posits that presidents of colleges and universities change organizations by "making bold decisions, taking risks, and sometimes moving against the prevailing winds" (Fisher, Tack & Wheeler, 1988, p. 70). Strong leaders do not rely on consensus, and they remain aloof and distant from colleagues (Fisher, 1984). Consistent with these ideas, many members of Scott College attributed the changes in policy to Kelly's bold, brash, even aggressive leadership. Tenure was eliminated, said one professor, because Kelly and the board wanted to take a "bold" step. Most certainly, Kelly's move to abolish tenure put him and the college at odds with the prevailing norm in higher education faculty employment policy.

Kelly exhibited several types of power that, combined, served as the catalyst for change. In Fisher's (1984) appropriation of French and Raven's (1959) five-fold framework of power, *coercive power*, the least desirable type, uses threats and punishments to force followers into compliance. Many interviewees suggested that, because faculty complied with the changes under the threat of retribution or dismissal, Kelly used coercive power to change the institution. For example, one professor said that dissidents would find their paycheck affected "so even those with tenure won't argue.... No raises for a couple of years—that gets your attention." Faculty and trustees also bestowed the president with *legitimate power*, which gives the leader power based on common norms of the group. Some faculty believed "in management . . . they believe their job is one of a professor and not one of making those major decisions." For these faculty, the shared norm is strong, administrative-driven decision making. For at least some members of Scott College, they believed that Kelly had the rightful role to move the organization in the way he saw fit. Finally, *charismatic power* is derived from the admiration of followers. Several interviewees expressed appreciation and respect for Kelly. One faculty member acclaimed, "I've grown to admire him. . . . He has a list of things he lives by. I don't think he cares if he goes up against the whole world if he thinks [his principles] are right." These various forms of power—coercive, legitimate, and charismatic—combined to imbue Kelly with a capacity to affect change. This interpretation supports Jones's conclusions (1977) that governance in smaller colleges rests with "the authority and responsibility of the president to decide" (Jones, 1977, p. 90).

Strong Mission

The college's clear five-fold mission, prominently displayed on its street signs, contributed to a culture of acceptance of power, restrictions on traditional faculty prerogatives, and unilateral decision making. As noted earlier, President Kelly adamantly proclaimed that "I'm going to carry out the mission of the school, and *anything* that gets in my way is going to have to stand aside, because that mission is *bigger* than me, and it's bigger than everyone else around here, and it's worthy." Many faculty seemed to agree with the importance of mission. One professor concluded, "A lot of people are really committed to the overall philosophy of the school. . . . Their commitment to the school was so strong" that, when tenure was abolished, even some of those that disagreed with the decision did not vocalize that sentiment. A colleague professed that, because of his commitment to the college's mission, "Even if they eliminated tenure completely [by stripping tenured faculty members of that status], I would have stayed, and I think most faculty would have, too."

Homogeneity of College Participants

Another condition that permitted the college to move from tenure to contracts was the similar values and background among members of the faculty, administration, and trustees. Interviewees reported that many professors were socially and politically conservative, respectful of the college's religious mission and culture, and, as alumni and long-time residents of the area, fiercely loyal to the college, characteristics that they shared with the president. Pfeffer (1981) postulated that a homogeneous set of participants in an organization can reduce conflict between groups and, thus, permit action to occur. Participants who are similar "with respect to their goals and preferences and in their beliefs about cause-effect relations" can be assembled "through selectively recruiting persons with very similar backgrounds and training, socialization of persons once they have been recruited into the organization, or the use of rewards or sanctions to produce at least the outward conformity to the dominant set of beliefs" (Pfeffer, 1981, p. 90). Each of these patterns of participant homogeneity is evident at Scott College:

Selectivity in recruitment

First, Scott selectively recruits faculty members. During the faculty search process, applicants must confirm in writing that they are willing to support and uphold the five-fold mission of the college. According to the academic dean, "People might not look at us when they consider our five-fold mission, a small teaching institution with a Christian commitment. Maybe they don't want to work in a place like that." The college is "interested in hiring people who buy into that mission" and, as a result, faculty say that "You don't find the liberal, heterogeneous population among the faculty."

Faculty also tend to come from similar academic backgrounds. Of those faculty with a Ph.D. or equivalent listed in the 1998–99 college catalog, 40 percent earned their doctorates at two public universities, one in-state and one located 100 miles from the Scott campus in a neighboring state. While the college does not seek out faculty only from these two institutions, one faculty member noted that geography contributes to the pro-management culture on campus: "this [region of the country] has a lot to do with it. For example, unionization was not welcomed by faculty. In 1979, a number of us tried to form an AAUP chapter. Only five or six signed up. . . . The faculty culture resisted unionizing. That's a common view in [this part of the country.]"

Socialization of members

Faculty also came to accept the power structure at Scott College through socialization once they arrived on campus. A professor reported:

> One faculty member in our division came from [a large research university]. He'll come into my office once in a while and say, "Is this really the way it's done?" And, I'll say, "Yeah, it's really the way it's done. This is how decisions are made." Sometimes, I think there's a little bit of a culture shock [for new faculty]. But, most of the time, they've made the decision to come here, they've made the decision to come to a smaller college, and they make it work. If they don't, they find another job and go.

This exchange is illustrative of one way in which long-standing professors encouraged new faculty members to accept the management style rather than resist, protest, or attempt to change the college's hierarchy and the president's power. By responding "this is how decisions are made," this professor underscored and tacitly endorsed the power differential between administrators and faculty. New faculty are socialized into the culture when they change their expectations: "they make it work."

Rewards and sanctions

Finally, conflict in the decision-making process at Scott College is reduced through rewards and sanctions. Faculty who accept the dominant culture are rewarded with job security and freedom to teach in the classroom. As one professor explained, "People are secure here as long as you do your job. . . . As far as my subject matter, I'm not restricted in what I teach." Another said, "As long as you do your job, you don't have anything to worry about." Those that attempt to subvert the system, however, find trouble. At the time when tenure was abolished, one division head told his faculty members, "Look, if we get irate, we're going to get our funds cut off. That's what he [President Kelly] would do." Another reported that those faculty members who were publicly critical of the president "either got fired or left." Those that remained "went back into their holes around campus," so that, to borrow Pfeffer's phrase, faculty displayed "at least outward conformity" with the autocracy.

Lack of Political Activity

Another factor that enabled the successful abolishment of tenure was the lack of political activity from the faculty as a whole. Political unrest of significant magnitude to unseat President Kelly or convince the trustees to reverse their position never materialized. A domineering leader, strong mission, and homogeneous constituents enabled power to be centralized at Scott College. When power is not distributed through an organization, political activity is also limited. Pfeffer (1981) compared decision making under centralized systems to countries run by dictators: "There is more political activity in democratic countries with relatively equal political parties than there is in countries which are run by strong dictators. When power is centralized, decisions are made and imposed by central authority. . . . [W]hen power is highly concentrated, the other participants in the system have little ability or motivation to engage in a contest for control . . ." (Pfeffer, 1981, p. 87). Pfeffer's language about the lack of *ability* and *motivation* is important in the Scott case. Faculty noted that, except for an attempt by a small number of faculty, "there wasn't a movement to overthrow the president" when tenure was eliminated. Faculty had already been stripped of the *ability* to meet as a group; they did not have sufficient political mechanisms to muster a counterattack. Also, lack of motivation was an important reason for limited political activity from faculty. The "fighters" on the faculty, said a professor, "were so beaten down [from struggles with the administration over governance] that no one was there to fight the battle."

President Kelly seemed cognizant of the importance of centralized power to limit political activity of other participants in the college. When he first became president, the board chair offered to eliminate tenure. Kelly declined the offer, explaining that he wanted to make the decision from "a position of strength." From 1988, when he became president, to 1993, when tenure was finally abolished, Kelly undertook a series of reforms that gave him more authority in decision making and reduced the faculty's voice in the affairs of the college; therefore, when tenure was removed, he did not encounter unmanageable political protest. Alternatively, if Kelly had agreed to the trustees' offer to abolish tenure before he arrived, he would have entered into an organization where power was much more decentralized and faculty were more capable of political activity.

Disruption in Faculty Communication

"Communication systems are power systems" (Barber, 1966, p. 65). Before the overhaul in its organization, the faculty met monthly. When the Academic Council replaced the faculty-wide organization in 1991, faculty lost their ability to meet as a group. As a result, faculty could no longer gauge opinions, formalize action, or mobilize support. "The whole faculty meetings had been taken away, so faculty had already been divided," said one professor. With the loss of that communication system, faculty lost power. The replacement system, the Academic Council, was a smaller body chaired by the academic dean—it was not a body of the faculty. Because some faculty members on the council are appointed by the administration, faculty reported that the council did not represent the diversity of viewpoints in the faculty as a whole.

Reducing the Importance of the Decision

Another circumstance that enabled the college to abolish tenure was the downplaying of the importance of the decision. Theories of organizational power stipulate that "critical decisions are labeled as being relatively unimportant in order to avoid the involvement and concern of organizational participants. . . . A related strategy involves taking a decision and breaking it into smaller pieces, each one of which is likely to appear to be less important for the organization" (Pfeffer, 1981, p. 92). These patterns are evident in the story of Scott College's elimination of tenure. First, the erosion of faculty authority and influence in decision making occurred in stages. The president mandated an overhaul to faculty governance, then to the evaluation system, then to tenure. A professor observed, "All these things were in the making . . . I think you saw small steps coming down, and those small steps meant less control for faculty." If changes to governance, evaluation, and employment policy happened at once, the small group of faculty dissidents may have had the energy and political capital to interfere with the president's plan. However, these alterations occurred incrementally, so that by the time the tenure decision was announced, the "alternative" faculty group was marginalized and unable to rally support for their cause.

Many faculty members and administrators interviewed for this study repeatedly stated that the abolition of tenure was not a monumental decision. The academic dean maintained that, "Among the majority of faculty, it was not a real do-or-die type of issue." One professor attributed their lackadaisical response to the fact that "it didn't affect us [who already had tenure]." Another said that tenured faculty "didn't have much to lose." It is possible that some of the individuals who expressed these beliefs were retrospectively interpreting their reaction to the decision, and that the passage of time may have dulled their distress. However, for a core group of faculty who were generally supportive of the president, their lack of involvement in the change process reflected their sincere conviction that they were not affected by the decision to eliminate tenure.

The Appearance of Involvement

Power theories account for symbolic rituals that render an appearance of shared power, even if there is no substantive sharing of power (Pfeffer, 1981). Pfeffer observed in another case that "even though the power clearly lay with the administration at the campus level, care was taken to provide the appearance of faculty involvement and faculty governance" (1981, p. 208). A similar situation occurred at Scott College. President Kelly simply could have unilaterally decided the structure of a new governance system. Instead, he asked the board to pass a resolution that required faculty and administration to devise a new faculty organization. He asserted, "I didn't care whether we had an academic council or a senate system. . . . I wouldn't have cared if they kept [all-faculty] meetings, but the dean was going to be the chair of it." These actions suggest an appearance of faculty involvement in the process and control over the outcome. By involving faculty in a process that was dictated to them, Kelly devised an appearance of shared input.

Several reasons exist for why faculty proposed a governance system that restricted faculty voice. First, because the administration handpicked the eight members of the faculty committee, commentators believed the committee was comfortable with implementing the president's wishes. "The faculty was a rubber stamp for whatever the administration wanted," said a faculty critic. Second, in situations where one group has more power than another, the "rule by anticipated reaction" tends to apply (Friedrich, 1937). This notion suggests that less powerful groups will take into account the reaction of the dominant group in formulating action. Therefore, if faculty were aware of President Kelly's abhorrence of shared governance, it is unlikely that they would have proposed a system that endowed faculty with much decision-making authority. As a result, the faculty governance committee proposed an organization with only an advisory role.

Institutionalization of Power

Finally, power theory suggests that the institutionalization of power was another condition that enabled tenure to be abolished at Scott College. Pfeffer (1981) stated:

> The tendency for ways of doing things in the organization, patterns of authority, and standard operating procedures . . . take on the status of objective social fact. Thus, instead of questioning the distribution of power, the making of certain decisions, or the following of certain rules of operation, these aspects of the organization become defined as part of the organization's culture and are seen and accepted by participants in the organization as a natural part of their membership in the particular social system." (pp. 298–99)

President Kelly's autocratic, top-down management style had persisted in the college since 1988. Interviewees reported that many of the faculty members that questioned the leadership and power distribution at the college left Scott for other teaching positions. The majority of those who remained supported Kelly's dictums. As new faculty replaced those that retired or resigned, they entered into a system where the existing balance of power was taken as "the status of objective social fact" (Pfeffer, 1981 p. 298). As a result, said one professor who was hired after tenure was abolished,

> Tenure is really not an issue.
> *Do people care about the tenure issue?*
> Not anymore.

CHAPTER SUMMARY

Other organizational theories also may contribute to the understanding of the change process in faculty employment policies at Scott College, but no other theory is as robust as power. Scott College abolished tenure because the president no longer wanted to offer it. Even though the board shared that sentiment for years before Kelly's arrival at the college, trustees were unable or unwilling to make the decision themselves without the leadership of a strong president. A combination of circumstances and events coalesced at Scott College, permitting the president and the board to eliminate tenure. Those conditions, as illustrated above, included Kelly's personal power characteristics; the college's strong mission, which encouraged loyalty to the institution despite attacks on traditional faculty roles; homogeneity of participants, which reduced conflict and friction; centralized power, which eliminated the ability and motivation to rebel; disruption of faculty communication, which prohibited unified action; reducing the importance of the tenure decision, which quelled dissent; the appearance of faculty involvement, which encouraged support; and the institutionalization of power, which solidified Kelly's sovereignty.

CHAPTER 4

Rowlette College

FACULTY EMPLOYMENT POLICY AT ROWLETTE COLLEGE, A SMALL, NON-sectarian, private institution, has evolved over 25 years from traditional tenure to multi-year contracts. Rowlette instituted tenure in 1966, began offering rolling contracts in addition to tenure in 1973, and moved to long-term contracts in 1986.

A SHORT HISTORY

Rowlette College, like Scott, is a relative newcomer in American higher education. Located in a small, rural community, Rowlette originally served the educational needs of returning veterans from World War II. The founding president realized that "large numbers of veterans . . . would be returning from service and their educational costs would be financed by the G.I. Bill" (Alumni magazine, 1997, p. 6). Rowlette College opened in 1946 with an enrollment of 67 men, one woman, and eight faculty. However, the college did not gain approval from the state to award baccalaureate degrees until 1949. College officials developed a three-year vocational program to meet the needs of the veterans, most in their mid-twenties and eager to start a career.

Almost immediately, the college was beset with financial difficulties. "By January 1947, [the president] was faced with $30,000 in bills and a promise of only $20,000 in payments due from the Veterans' Administration" (Alumni magazine, 1997, p. 8). A student enrolled in the first year commented, "I had to check [the local newspaper] every morning to make sure the college was still open!" (Alumni magazine, 1997, p. 7).

Rowlette's tenuous financial and academic position continued for years. The college was denied accreditation in 1954 because of its precarious finances, low standards for admission, insufficiently credentialed faculty, and deficient library holdings. Rowlette nearly closed several times in its early years because of poor finances. In the 1950s, items such as typewriters and unused textbooks were sold to raise cash. "At that time, the college was at an all-time low, with untrimmed shrubbery and unmowed grass" (Alumni magazine, 1997, p. 11). Rowlette continued down a path of financial hardship, suffering setbacks in 1973, 1984, and 1994. The college's lenders insisted that a Bank Special Operating Committee, composed of one trustee and two bankers, manage the affairs of the college after the 1973 crisis. This committee superceded the authority of the board of trustees; it met after each board meeting to review and approve the board's actions. The committee remained in place until 1989. According to a former president, the committee prohibited college leaders from taking stands; instead there was "a general atmosphere of decisions being tentative and tenuous" until they received "final" approval.

In the academic arena, the institution made progress in the 1960s. A four-year liberal arts curriculum replaced the three-year vocational program, although the college did not received full accreditation until 1967. A formal academic tenure policy was instituted in the 1966–67 academic year. A former administrator described this time as "years of rapid growth and development, of experimentation, of maturing and of success in achieving goals. . . . Many old-timers still refer [to this period] as the good years" (Alumni magazine, 1997, p. 15). During the 1970s, the college embarked on several innovative educational initiatives. Its January term program was one of the first in the country. Similarly, prior to the push for international experiences on most American college campuses, the college purchased in 1971 a British campus, where one-third of Rowlette students studied by 1973. (The January term was discontinued in 1983 and the British campus sold in 1996, both for financial reasons.)

In its 53 years, Rowlette has had 12 presidents, seven of whom served four years or less. At the time that this research was conducted, its 13th president was about to take office. According to 1998 statistics, the college enrolled 637 full-time students, 85 percent of whom came from out of state but within the region. Seventy-three percent of the 48 full-time faculty members had earned doctoral or terminal degrees, and the student-faculty ratio was 12:1. The college's endowment was $4.4 million.

PROMINENT CHARACTERISTICS
Financial Condition

My initial impressions of Scott and Rowlette colleges could not have been more different. Scott College was marked by blossoming flowers and impeccable grounds. In contrast, Rowlette's physical plant was faded and worn. The president's office in the main administration building displayed a tattered rug and a hodge-podge of old furniture. Paint peeled and a porch sagged at a building down the street. Its tiny $4.4 million endowment paled in comparison to Scott's $200 million endowment.

This is not to say that Rowlette College was wholly dilapidated. Indeed, it proudly displayed a spacious new student center in its admissions materials, and the warmth and vitality of its people was a welcomed respite from the chill of its mountainous clime. Nevertheless, the college exhibited evidence of deferred maintenance indicative of its financial straits. If Scott College defied the stereotype of financial unsteadiness at contract colleges, then Rowlette College embodied it. In each of its six decades of existence, the college has had financial difficulties. Most recently, Rowlette went through a retrenchment in 1994, marked by a 27 percent reduction of full-time faculty (both tenured and nontenured) and elimination of four academic majors. A former president said, "The college has never had long periods of stability—ten years at most. The institution doesn't have a long track record; there's been a lot of growing pains."

RELATED CHARACTERISTICS

Two other prominent characteristics emerged from Rowlette's shaky fiscal foundation. One was its steadfast focus on survival. Both interviews and written documentation evidence the college's tenacity. For example, during the financial crisis of 1973, faculty and staff were not paid from October to December. Despite the burden, however, employees remained loyal to the school. One current professor recalled that, of several hundred employees, only one resigned during the emergency: "Everyone hung around. The love for the institution was tremendous." The president's report to the board of trustees in April 1974 stated, "The fact that the College survived a near terminal case of fiscal cancer is exhilarating." A former administrator wrote: "Good leadership, community and regional support, and the dedication of faculty and alumni/ae . . . enabled the college to survive. The importance of these strengths is all the more impressive when we realize that at least five new and four older colleges in [the region] failed during the formative years of Rowlette College. . . . In each of its crises, the college has been blessed by a guardian angel that appeared at the right time" (Alumni magazine, 1997, pp. 6, 27).

The second characteristic arising from the college's financial history is the faculty's concern with compensation. Salaries have been *the* singular issue for faculty, more important than any of the changes in faculty employment policies. As far back as 1969, the Faculty Welfare Committee presented a "Five-Year Plan for Faculty Compensation" to the Board of Trustees. The report found that Rowlette College was among the lowest

5.8 percent of nearly 1,000 institutions in the 1968–69 AAUP survey on faculty compensation. The report to the board called for "the urgent need for improvement in professorial renumeration." Faculty, administrators, and trustees alike mentioned in interviews that faculty salaries typically prevailed as the most important issue of faculty work life. A trustee commented, "The huge issue for the board and with faculty is wages and benefits. Salaries are so low."

IMPORTANT CONSTITUENCIES

Like Scott College, Rowlette's process of change from traditional tenure to long-term contracts involved three constituencies: the board of trustees, the administration, and the faculty.

Board of Trustees

Rowlette College's board of trustees historically has consisted mainly of business people. In 1998, 16 of 19 trustees came from the corporate sector; two were in academic settings and one was in the nonprofit arena.[1] As a result, explained one trustee, "there are many who are deeply into the business scene. Tenure is not something that's popular in the business and commerce world. . . . The board is a commercial board; they don't understand it." A former administrator was more blunt in her assessment: "The board . . . was very opposed to tenure."

Both administrators and faculty named one trustee, Stephen Dravis, as very influential in the process of change in faculty employment policies. Dravis, who came onto the board in 1976, felt that "traditional tenure is out of the guild system of the middle ages. . . . Tenure is archaic." He believed that long-term contracts were a "more useful and reasonable approach for the institution and faculty" because they "protect both the institution and the individual." A former college administrator said, "Dravis was very much against tenure and was the formulator of many of the [changes to] the academic manual." Dravis noted that he "studied the [tenure] issue very carefully. I knew the head of the Association of Governing Boards and talked to him. I talked to experts on tenure, and read all the books and pamphlets." But Dravis admitted his interest in the topic was atypical: "Not too many trustees ever read [the faculty employment policy]. I did, I read it, but I was probably the only one."

---

1. This count excludes Rowlette's president, who is a member of the board.

Administration

Rowlette College had many leaders during the years of change in faculty employment policy. In the 33-year period from the inception of an academic tenure policy (in 1966) to the time that the research for this book was done (1999), Rowlette has had seven presidents and at least nine academic vice presidents. The result, according to faculty members, has been inconsistent policy-making and leadership. "It was like a revolving door," said one professor, "the administrators have been so erratic."

Long-time professors spoke passionately about their disdain for Paul Potrowski, president from 1973 to 1981. Potrowski had been academic vice president before the 1973 fiscal crisis. His controversial term as president began with the circumstances of his appointment. According to a former administrator:

> [The board] started a search for a new president and found out [the college] didn't have any money. Nobody knew that. At the end of [one of] the board meetings, Potrowski emerged and said, "I've just been appointed president. The search is off." So there was no search. . . . There were [faculty] who were outraged that he got the job and no one was asked anything about it.

Faculty members and administrators labeled Potrowski autocratic, confrontational, and totalitarian. A professor reminisced, "He moved the college from a collegial structure to a management structure. . . . Most faculty strongly disapproved of that approach and personally disliked Potrowski. He wasn't respected. . . . He rankled a lot of faculty." A history of the college stated:

> His methods of governance antagonized the faculty. His methods were more confrontational than collegial. He might surface an idea between two dissenting groups until it prevailed in one of the groups. At other times, he suggested ideas that, although not impossible, were highly impractical from the faculty's point of view. . . . Faculty opposing Potrowski marched in front of the administration building during the first week of his appointment. The pressures of his office at this time [during the 1973 financial crisis] required decisions for which there was neither adequate money nor time for faculty participation" (Alumni magazine, 1997, p. 20).

Since Potrowski's departure in 1981, Rowlette's presidents have been more respectful of faculty participation in decision-making, according to interviews. One of Potrowski's successors professed, "My approach was to take a professional attitude toward faculty—that academic freedom was essential and that we function within that framework." An academic vice president agreed, stating "I chose to work collegially," but noted that "there is not much formally in place to stop an autocratic administrator from taking over the [college]."

The autocratic president at Scott College dominated the administration during the process of change from tenure to contracts. Rowlette differed greatly. While Rowlette had an autocratic president for eight years, tenure was not a high-priority issue at that time; survival of the college was. Not until several years after Potrowski's departure did the college adopt a long-term contract system (in 1986). Instead of consistent, domineering leadership that marked the Scott College case, the story at Rowlette was one of considerable turnover in the administrative ranks during the evolution in policy.

Faculty

In the early days of Rowlette College, many faculty came from a high school background; one professor called the faculty in the 1960s "amateurish." As mentioned earlier, the college was denied accreditation for a number of years in part because not enough faculty had advanced graduate degrees. The environment began to change in the late 1960s when an academic dean instituted many elements of a liberal arts college, including an academic division structure and a tenure system, and began to hire new Ph.Ds.

Faculty described their propensity for an informal, collegial method of interaction. "Faculty perceived this college as a real academic community, one that didn't need to be bound by lots of academic procedures," said one professor. An administrator agreed; when he proposed a salary-equity plan, faculty balked. "They said they would rather if it were handled on a case-by-case basis. . . . The college operates on a personal model rather than on a policy model."

The faculty's influence in governance has varied during the history of the college. During Potrowski's presidency, faculty were often excluded from decision making. In 1974, a faction of the faculty moved to unionize because of their unhappiness with Potrowski's leadership. According to one professor, "Some faculty thought they couldn't negotiate with the administration with any sense of trust at all. This is why they were pushing for a union. . . . Faculty wanted a union because they thought there was a lot of manipulation going on by the administration." A colleague concurred: "A group of faculty who didn't have a lot of power saw this as an opportunity to displace those that did." This sentiment, however, was not universally shared within the faculty ranks; the union passed by only a one-vote margin. Said one professor who voted against the union: "I felt that the union wasn't the way to [get rid of administrators]. I thought the agenda was too confusing. . . . My feeling was that if your goal was to get someone fired, then you focus on that, and you worry about work conditions when you get rid of them." Interestingly, the union leaders were not motivated by job security issues. Said a professor, "I don't recall tenure coming up in [the union] discussions. The paradox is that the union movement didn't reflect concern about job security but about how decisions were made. No one's job was ever threatened by the administration during that time." The union existed for two years; faculty voted to de-authorize it in May, 1976—again, by a one-vote margin.[2]

Since the early 1980s, the faculty's role in governance and decision-making has increased. Faculty government is run in a town-meeting setting. All faculty can participate in the faculty organization, which meets monthly, chaired by an elected faculty member. One professor noted that "faculty have become increasingly more involved in governance." A colleague added, "Overall, this has been a faculty-driven college." A former administrator proclaimed, "When we had to retrench [in 1994,] it amazed me how faculty participated in that process. It wasn't the administration against the faculty. It was faculty standing by my side."

The faculty-trustees relationship has also evolved over time. In periods of fiscal crisis, relations were strained. In his memoirs, a former professor wrote,

> Back in the days of crisis [in 1951] . . . , we used to have joint meetings of faculty and trustees. I remember the long argument between [a trustee] and Mr. Clark, who was a biologist. We were discussing the lack of money and the two were down to swearing at each other, Clark cussing out [the board] for not coming up with money." (Alumni magazine, 1997, p.10)

One faculty member recalled that, by the 1970s, the board and faculty did not have much interaction: "The faculty didn't have much access to the board; the president kept the board insulated from faculty. Everything was filtered." Interviewees asserted that relations have improved since the 1980s. Faculty now have representation on the board; one faculty member is elected by his or her peers to attend the full board meetings. In addition, faculty representatives attend the meetings of various board committees.

Like their counterparts at Scott College, faculty at Rowlette were attracted to and remain at the college because of quality-of-life issues. A trustee speculated that "a lot of faculty like [the town and the region]. They like the environment. Tenure isn't what keeps them or makes them go." His beliefs were confirmed by a professor:

---

2. Faculty voted to de-authorized the union, according to a faculty member, because the union leadership "didn't seem to be achieving anything."

People stay here for a lot of reasons. It's beautiful, [and] people can hunt and fish [in the area]. You get a lot of authority at the college very early here. In a couple of years, you're chairing key committees; you don't have to wait until you're an old person. . . . So, I think it's quality of life. There are real things: very small classes, real relationships with students. I have students to my house all the time. You know families here. Everybody lives within a small radius.

THE PROCESS OF CHANGE IN FACULTY EMPLOYMENT POLICIES

I initially included Rowlette College in the list of institutions that changed from tenure to contracts based on a letter written in 1996 by the academic vice president, which stated, "The Board of Trustees eliminated tenure at Rowlette College in 1986, and introduced in its stead a system of long-term contracts." After my research began, however, I realized that the process of change from tenure to contracts did not occur in just this one year. Instead, the process evolved over several decades, culminating in 1986. This section describes that evolution.

The Original Tenure Policy

From the college's founding until the late 1960s, faculty were employed on one-year contracts. Little is known from institutional records about this system. References to a tenure system in the board of trustees' minutes appeared in 1966. The official "Faculty Personnel Policy," which described the tenure process, was entered into the board minutes in April 1967. The policy included many elements of a traditional tenure system, such as a seven-year probationary period of one-year contracts, a faculty committee charged with reviewing candidates for tenure, and the 1940 academic freedom statement of the AAUP.

The experiences of faculty members in the late 1960s, however, suggest that the provisions under the formal tenure policy were not always applied. First, despite the provisions for a tenure-review committee in the 1967 Faculty Personnel Policy, faculty earned tenure informally and easily. One professor noted that "tenure" appeared under the "comments" section in his annual contract in 1968; there was no application process or peer-review. A board member complained that the tenure process was virtually automatic: "It didn't have any standards except for the person being there five or six years."

Another discrepancy occurred with types of appointments. The Personnel Policy only included one type of appointment for new hires: an up-or-out tenure track. However, this was not the case in practice. One professor reported that he entered a non-tenure track: "I came here in

1969, fresh out of graduate school. There was a tenure system in place, but all the new hires in 1969 were not on a tenure-track." Since receiving accreditation in 1967, the college has always hired at least some faculty members on non-tenure-track appointments.

The Effects of Financial Crisis

At the time of the fiscal crisis in 1973, the board became concerned about the financial implications of tenure. A professor said:

> There had been quite a few [new faculty hired] in the late 60s, so tenure [cases] were going to be coming up [to the board for review.] The faculty had heard that the board took a rather jaundiced view of tenure and that they were not going to approve many [of the tenure candidates]. So, for most faculty, it appeared that the up-or-out situation was going to be an "out," regardless of merit. This sentiment deepened on the board with the fiscal crisis, since it would always be cheaper to hire new faculty than to support established faculty.

A trustee explained that tenure "became an issue because [it] cost the institution $1½ million [to tenure each professor]. It was an enormous expense for the college to incur." As a result of the financial emergency, both the board and faculty became preoccupied with the survival of the college. The board simply stopped reviewing candidates for tenure, and they indefinitely deferred action on those faculty members who had already applied for it. As a result, according to many interviewees, faculty members "got the message that tenure didn't exist." A professor declared, "many faculty were eligible for tenure, but they didn't apply because they knew the board wouldn't tenure anyone. They wouldn't make that long-term commitment."

According to faculty, the board's refusal to award tenure had little effect. Most faculty felt they had tenure in practice if not in policy:

> The board's position was that they never eliminated tenure, they just weren't going to grant it. It was on hold. They wouldn't entertain any applications. I thought that this was leading to the elimination of tenure.
> *How did faculty react to that?*
> They didn't see it as a big problem.
> *Why not?*
> It wasn't critical. It wasn't important. . . . It wasn't a gut issue. You didn't need tenure; you could stay here forever. So, tenure was secondary.

Faculty also did not protest the trustees' action because of the precarious financial condition of the college: "I don't think they could do anything about it because the college was in such bad shape. People weren't even getting salary checks for a long period of time." Tenure, at that point, was not at the forefront of people's minds. Said another professor, "Faculty didn't really seem interested in the issue. They were more preoccupied with the financial crises."

Once the board stopped entertaining tenure applications in 1973, some faculty found themselves in limbo: they had surpassed the seven-year probationary period without a tenure review. New faculty learned that, for all intents and purposes, tenure was not being granted. As a result, all nontenured faculty were on one-year appointments. Faculty were unhappy with this arrangement. Despite their assertions that job security as provided under a formal tenure system did not interest them, professors also indicated that they wanted some contractual assurance of employment beyond just one year. Therefore, the Faculty Welfare Committee and the academic vice president developed a three-year rolling contract system, which the board accepted for a trial period in 1973 and approved in 1975. "The rolling contract system was a faculty initiative," said a professor. "The faculty as a whole must have approved the plan, and I don't recall any fuss over it." The rolling-contract system did not displace tenure. Instead, said one administrator, the rolling system was "a stop-gap measure" to provide faculty a personnel policy with more stability than one-year contracts. Under this "revised" system, faculty could apply for tenure after six years but the policy had no up-or-out provision. By the time one professor came to the college in 1977, "most people were on rolling contracts."

No constituency at Rowlette—faculty, trustees, or administrators—sought to clarify the ambiguities of the faculty employment policy during this time. The college officially offered academic tenure, but few faculty members applied for it, and the board would not award it. Instead, at faculty initiative, three-year rolling contracts were implemented. Several reasons existed for this ambiguous situation. First, as noted above, during the 1970s, President Potrowski had antagonistic relationships with both faculty and trustees. It was during his presidency that faculty unionized for two years (1974–76). One former administrator observed that "there were a lot of conflicts and people were too concerned [with these conflicts] to make tenure a big issue." Second, ongoing financial difficulties meant that "the issue of tenure never got dealt with, even though it was supposed to be dealt with. There was this temporary arrangement [rolling contracts] but no pressure to do anything." Third, at least some faculty seemed indifferent to tenure and happy with rolling contracts. Said one:

> During the fiscal crisis (and we remained in a crisis-management mode for some years), the tenure issue was not a top priority. I don't know how typical I was, but . . . frankly, I never gave tenure a thought. . . . I think everyone

believed that the rolling contract system provided the faculty with as much job security as they were likely to enjoy. And everyone in principle seemed to subscribe to the notion that periodic review of all faculty in a teaching institution—where continued service should be based on excellent teaching—was preferable to a tenure system. Call us demented, but there were a number of us on the faculty who just couldn't have cared less about tenure.

During the 1970s, the board sporadically gave attention to faculty employment issues. Still dissatisfied with the tenure arrangement, in April 1977, the board directed the president to appoint a Task Force on Tenure (without specifying the composition of the committee) "to assist the Board in analyzing problems associated with the tenure system" (Board minutes, April 17, 1977). Board minutes do not include further references to the Task Force—it is unclear whether the president appointed the committee, if it reported back to the board, or if records of the Task Force's work were kept. However, in October 1978, the board formally imposed a two-year moratorium on tenure and directed the college to "seek means for development of a more satisfactory system of recognizing faculty service to the College which provides adequate security to the faculty member in the fashion other than Tenure."[3] (See Exhibit 4.1 on p. 95 for the text of the board's resolution.) At the same time, it denied tenure to five candidates (who remained on annual contracts). In 1978, Rowlette had 22 tenured faculty members. In 1973, 30 faculty were tenured. Attrition of tenured professors coupled with the board's policy to suspend tenure had significantly reduced the number of faculty with tenure.

In April 1980, the board extended the moratorium on tenure and introduced the idea of "continuing tenure in a form differing from the existing [format] in a way which will tighten and limit and make it denote extraordinary performance" (Board minutes, April 12, 1980). A month later, Trustee Dravis wrote the first draft of a new proposed tenure article, which stipulated that tenure would be independent of rank and salary and that "denial of tenure . . . shall not imply termination of the faculty member's relationship with the College" (Board minutes, May 19, 1980). Over a period of years, this draft was debated among faculty, administrators, and the board. It eventually was incorporated into the long-term contract policy in 1986.

---

3. It is possible that the Task Force on Tenure recommended the two-year moratorium. However, interviewees were unfamiliar with the group and its work. A faculty member who served as an administrator from 1977-79 said, "I don't recall that a task force on tenure was developed in the late 70s. . . . As a fellow administrator, you'd think I might have known of such a task force, if there was one." It is also possible that president never acted on the board's request, since the college was still struggling financially and President Potrowski and the board of trustees had an antagonistic relationship.

The Move to Long-term Contracts and "Honorary" Tenure

In October 1981, with Potrowksi vacating the presidency and the three-year rolling contracts and tenure system still both in place, the board mandated that the new president, Kenneth Schaefer, and the faculty develop a long-term contract and evaluation policy. Schaefer charged the Faculty Welfare Committee with the task. A committee member recalled, "My feeling was that the board was very unhappy with the [rolling] contract system. . . . I think the trustees were ready to go back to a one-year system again, and they certainly were ready to throw out tenure. No question." According to multiple sources, the board was dissatisfied with the lack of rigor in faculty evaluations under the rolling system. Some faculty and administrators shared that concern. A professor declared:

> [The board] may have felt that [the rolling-contract system] was trapping the college into sustaining faculty who might not have survived an up-or-out decision. But I think this was of some concern to the faculty and the administration as well. . . . The rolling contract system appeared to be proving weak in the review process, and I think it was proving to be administratively cumbersome.

Schaefer departed in 1985 before the new faculty employment policy was finalized; his successor, Michael Bonner, inherited negotiations with the faculty committee. From those ongoing discussions, the faculty committee developed a long-term contract system proposal with an evaluation component and an early retirement plan. The board formally accepted the new system in May, 1986.

The contract system called for a series of one-, two-, or three-year contracts for the first six years of employment at the college. After this six-year probationary period, faculty entered a sequence of contracts as follows:

a. In the seventh year, the faculty member receives a four-year contract.
b. In the 11th year, the faculty member receives a five-year contract.
c. In the 16th year, the faculty member receives the first of continuing six-year contracts.

Under the provisions of the policy, all new faculty members were placed in the long-term contract sequence (there was no tenure-track). The policy stated that the Faculty Development Committee and the academic vice president would conduct a review at the end of the six-year probationary period to "determine whether or not the faculty member is to achieve *virtual tenure* as a senior colleague" (Emphasis added. Academic Manual, p. 30). This review resulted in either a one-year terminal contract or a long-term contract. So, while faculty were not tenured in the traditional sense after six years, those that passed the probationary period considered themselves to have a long-term employment relationship with the college.

The long-term contract policy included an "alternative" version of tenure. President Bonner explained, "Now, [tenure] was available in a totally different concept." As conceived, "tenure" in the new policy was not the primary means of faculty appointment. It was a secondary, honorific designation, infrequently awarded, to acknowledge sustained teaching excellence and service to the college. Post-probationary faculty members could apply or be nominated by a peer for this type of "tenure." According to the Academic Manual,

> The award of tenure at the College is a privilege and an honor recognizing the highest degree of commitment of faculty and college[,] each to the other. Given that a long-term contract system . . . exists at Rowlette College, tenure will be awarded only in rare circumstances when the criteria outlined [in the policy] are clearly met. (p. 37)

This new type of tenure did provide a lifetime appointment (with the customary dismissal-for-cause provisions), but it did not differ from the long-term contract policy. Once they had ten-years teaching experience, long-term contract faculty, like tenured faculty, were not subject to a regular contract-renewal review—their renewal was considered presumptive. Therefore, faculty and administrators did not view this version of tenure as offering more substantive job security than the multi-year contract system.[4]

The college set a restrictive threshold for awarding honorary tenure in the new long-term contract policy. A former administrator explained, "I thought the rule was that we would not offer tenure unless [candidates] walked on water." In 1989, the board awarded this new "tenure" to a faculty member, the first time it acted on a tenure decision in over ten years. Despite the availability of honorary tenure at Rowlette College, in the 1990s, only four other faculty earned this new type of tenure. Three of these four have since left the college—one professor contended that they use the designation as a stepping stone to move somewhere else.

If the Rowlette College version of tenure is only awarded in select cases, and if all long-term contract faculty have virtual tenure, why did the college enacted a new type of tenure? Trustee Dravis said:

---

4. According to the Academic Manual, "untenured faculty with more than six years of full-time service may be denied reappointment only for the following reasons: (1) enrollment decline, (2) program reduction, (3) financial exigencies, (4) unsatisfactory professional performance" (p. 39). These are the same conditions under which a tenured faculty member can be dismissed for cause.

> I didn't think we should get rid of tenure completely...
>
> *If the board stopped awarding traditional tenure and adopted a long-term contract system, why bother keeping tenure on the books?*
>
> I'm not quite sure. The tradition of tenure is so strong in higher education, I think we felt the college ought to be able to grant tenure, not take it away completely. But tenure at Rowlette College is honorary and is only awarded in exceptional cases.

The long-term contract policy also included two other provisions: a more sophisticated evaluation system and an early retirement policy. The board accepted the long-term contract proposal with the understanding that evaluation would be more stringent for both non-tenured and tenured faculty. The policy stipulated that all post-probationary faculty members (those on long-term contracts and tenure) "will be periodically reviewed" by the Faculty Development Committee and the academic vice president. Said a faculty member involved in the policy formation, "The board just wanted assurances that faculty evaluations would be rigorous. But they were more interested in personal assurances from members of the faculty rather than a formal policy that said so." The early retirement plan, a professor asserted, "was appealing to the board in addressing the issue of faculty quality." Several faculty members professed that the early retirement portion of the new policy was the most successful. One said:

> Virtually everyone eligible for early retirement took it. The top layers of salaries were then gone, which helped the college when financial difficulties came along again.... The early retirement buy-out worked; it achieved what it was supposed to. The policy change didn't work to release more faculty otherwise, through faculty evaluations [and non-renewal of contracts]. If anyone was hoping that the contract and evaluation system would spur more faculty to be dismissed, they would be disappointed. It hasn't happened.... People who've been here 12, 15, 18 years—the college won't let a single one of them go. And everyone knows they won't.

Summary of Change

Based on this case summary of faculty employment policies at Rowlette College, the academic vice president's 1996 letter that said "the Board of Trustees eliminated tenure ... in 1986" seems overly reductive. Rowlette did not go through a dramatic overhaul in policy like Scott College (tenure one day, no tenure the next). Instead, its change was slow, evolutionary, ambiguous, and uneven.

Did Rowlette College Really Change from Tenure to Contracts?

Both an affirmative and negative response are appropriate. On one hand, Rowlette College underwent a clear shift in appointment policy in the 60s, 70s, and 80s, evidenced both in policy manuals and in practice. In the 60s and early 70s, the official policy provided for tenure-track appointments, probationary periods, up-or-out decisions, and continuous tenure. In this period, faculty were awarded tenure, although perhaps not through the formal process stipulated in the policy. Today, faculty no longer are appointed to tenure tracks; rather, long-term contracts are the primary method of employment. The "tenure" that exists today is not a culmination of a probationary period, but an honor bestowed for sustained excellence.

On the other hand, the practice of how faculty operate, think of themselves, and relate to the institution has changed little in 30 years. Faculty consider themselves tenured, whether or not they have such a designation. "I have virtual tenure," maintained a long-time untenured professor. To the query of "Has anything changed in practice in the last 22 years?" a professor answered, "No, not really. We keep virtually everyone we hire. . . . There is the sense that tenure versus not being tenured means very little." President Bonner commented, "I don't think we ever acted as if we didn't have tenure."

The Meaning of Tenure at Rowlette College

The meaning of tenure at Rowlette College has changed—it is now more symbolic than substantive. The honorary tenure at Rowlette is "a symbolic asset, an aesthetic asset, rather than anything else," according to a former administrator. Because multi-year contracts were considered virtual tenure, interviewees attributed no extra protections in job security or academic freedom or no greater voice in shared governance to tenured professors. Trustee Dravis asserted that "some of the most influential faculty don't have tenure and don't give a damn." Faculty concur. "Not only does tenure make no difference in how you behave, it makes no difference in how the administration or trustees treat you." The benefit to this "honorary" tenure, according to one long-time untenured professor, lies in the meaning outsiders attribute to the title:

> *Is there any difference between tenured and non-tenured faculty members at Rowlette College?*
> [A tenured professor] can go out into the world and say he's tenured. I can't. But that doesn't matter to me.

A former administrator expressed the same sentiment:

> *What did those individuals awarded this "new" type of tenure gain?*
> I think they gained respectability in their peer groups outside the institution, when they went to their professional meetings. It was more convenient to say they were tenured.

No one interviewed—whether faculty, administrators, or trustees—thought that the college should have eliminated references to tenure (however defined) altogether. Even though tenure at Rowlette College did not include traditional AAUP-style provisions, and though most faculty members did not have tenure, interviewees expressed the belief that tenure was important to be "on the smorgasbord of things that are available to you."

REASONS FOR THE OVERHAUL IN POLICY

Interviewees identified several problems that sparked the revisions to the tenure policy:

Financial Considerations

The board of trustees became concerned with the tenure system during each fiscal crisis. President Bonner noted that since "the college has always been dependent on enrollment, . . .the leadership of the board did not feel that the college was in a position to make a commitment to a lot of people through tenure." For decades, the board's solution to this problem was to not award tenure, without making progress on an alternative system: "They had it on the books, they never took it off the books, yet they acted as though they didn't have tenure." Thus, the solution to the tenure "problem" for a long time was to ignore or neglect it. For over a decade, the board simply refused to award tenure. During that time, faculty acted as if tenure no longer existed. The eventual solution to the financial problem with tenure, as perceived by the board, was long-term contracts. Even though faculty report that the long-term contract system was like virtual tenure, it appeared to the board to be a "more reasonable" employment policy for the college, according to Trustee Dravis, because "it protects both the institution and the individual." The sentiment is the same at many contract colleges where the perceived benefit of contracts is "insurance against crisis" (Chait & Trower, 1997, p. 24).

Faculty Evaluation

An additional problem was that some faculty received tenure without going through any type of evaluation. At other times, the evaluation was perfunctory and superficial. Trustees were dissatisfied with this arrangement. Said one professor:

> [The board's] concern came from the evaluation process of faculty. If all faculty stayed here whether they had tenure or not—so, in effect, everyone did have tenure—there was concern that some faculty weren't being properly evaluated. The board wanted a new evaluation process. They indicated that long-term contracts would be okay . . . as long as the evaluation was more rigorous.

Trustee Dravis expressed the board's belief that, once tenured, "people can go to sleep on the job, not pulling their weight." The long-term contract system included ongoing review for all faculty, both tenured and nontenured, to ensure that "outstanding service will continue during the years of service to the College." Faculty members noted that the evaluation component in the long-term contract policy was an improvement "to the extent that we didn't have a good faculty evaluation system prior to long-term contracts [and] we now have a better system." But they also observed that the contract system did not promote more turnover than the tenure system or rolling contracts before it. It is a situation not dissimilar to Scott College. If long-term contracts were the intended solution for the problem of dealing with poor-quality teachers, it is not clear that the solution worked. Instead, an enticing early retirement program—like at Scott—produced more turnover in faculty ranks. Older faculty, said a professor, who "weren't all that good, who hadn't embraced the move to technology, who were 'old school,'" accepted early retirement, but "the policy change didn't work to release more faculty otherwise."

AN ANALYSIS OF THE PROCESS OF CHANGE

Rowlette College enacted several distinct faculty employment revisions over two decades, yet faculty claimed that "the change with tenure and contracts isn't significant." Instead, the overhaul from traditional tenure to long-term contracts at Rowlette College is dominated by inaction and distraction. How is this scenario possible? Unlike Scott College and contrary to my initial speculations about the process of change at institutions moving from tenure to contracts, Rowlette College's story is complex, lengthy, nonrational, and ambiguous. The loose coupling/organized anarchy model of organizational change (Cohen, March, & Olson, 1972; Cohen &

March, 1986; Weick, 1976) illuminates the circumstances and conditions through which the college underwent the various iterations in policy.

The three general properties of the organized anarchy model of choice and decision making—fluid participation, problematic preferences, and unclear technology (Cohen, March, & Olson, 1972; Cohen & March, 1986)—are applicable to Rowlette College.

Fluid Participation

First, participation in the change process at Rowlette College was sporadic, fluid, and changing. Cohen and March (1986) asserted that "participants in the organization vary among themselves in the amount of time and effort they devote to the organization; individual participants vary from one time to another. As a result, standard theories of power and choice seem to be inadequate" (p. 3). Similarly, Weick hypothesized that loose coupling exists when one organizational element affects another ". . . occasionally (rather than constantly) . . ." (Weick, 1984, p. 380). Rowlette College constituents affected faculty employment policy sporadically rather than constantly. The process of change from traditional tenure to long-term contracts occurred over 30 years, and the attention that each group—trustees, administration, and faculty—devoted to the issue waxed and waned over that period.

The Board of Trustees

Trustees were skeptical of the traditional tenure system and its viability in a tenuous financial environment. Despite their reservations and concerns, however, the board erratically focused on the faculty employment system. For example, between the ten-year period of 1974 and 1983, board minutes indicate that the trustees discussed their concerns with and took action regarding the tenure and rolling-contract provision only five times:

- In August 1975, the board approved the three-year rolling contract policy without addressing the ambiguity of whether tenure was still "officially" offered.
- No action occurred until two years later. In April 1977, the board appointed the tenure Task Force because trustees were still unhappy with the tenure situation.
- Eighteen months later, in October 1978, trustees put an official two-year moratorium on tenure, codifying a practice that started five years earlier.
- In May 1980, the board indefinitely extended the moratorium.
- In October 1981, trustees mandated that the administration and faculty work toward implementing a long-term contract policy.

Rowlette College 87

At other times during this ten-year stretch, trustees were preoccupied with different matters, most notably the financial condition of the college. When Stephen Dravis became a trustee in 1976, he directed some of the board's attention toward faculty employment policies, but the board did not consistently engage the issue. For a long period in the 1970s, the unofficial "non-tenure" employment policy was set by trustees through inaction rather than action, through neglect rather than attention.

The Administration

In stark contrast to Scott College, Rowlette did not have a dynamic, powerful leader who directed the change process in employment policies. While Rowlette does have a history of a totalitarian, autocratic president—Paul Potrowski, who presided during the great financial crisis of 1973 and the subsequent decade—interviewees at the college did not identify him as a significant player in setting or changing faculty employment policy. Instead, 16 presidents and academic vice presidents came and went during the 30-year period of change in employment policy at Rowlette College, and each individual devoted limited energy to the process. For example, when the board directed the faculty and administration to develop a long-term contract policy in 1981, Kenneth Schaefer was president. Before the policy was implemented in 1986, Schaefer departed and Michael Bonner arrived, so that the participation of leaders was not consistent. As a result, interviewees did not name any administrator as being particularly influential; instead, they identified a faculty member—the chair of the Faculty Development Committee—and Trustee Dravis as having the most influence in the change process.

Faculty

Members of the Rowlette College community universally agreed that the various changes in faculty employment policy over the years—the informal and formal moratoria on tenure, the institution of three-year rolling contracts, and the long-term contract policy—rarely captured the faculty's attention. They were not continually occupied with the issue; in fact, one professor maintained that his colleagues only dealt with employment policy when "these issues were pushed on the faculty to resolve." Informants offered two reasons for this lack of participation:

   1. Some faculty were uninterested in the concept of tenure.

Several interviewees maintained that numerous faculty weren't alarmed by the changes in faculty employment policy because, according to an administrator, "they were indifferent to tenure, from a personal belief in what it was." A professor affirmed:

> Instituting a tenure system has never been a high priority for us.... During my 30 years at the college I have not given much thought to it. It just hasn't mattered to me one way or the other. While a few individuals have been tenured ... in all my time at the college I've met only one colleague who wanted to make tenure a serious institutional issue.... On the whole, while it is true that our board has not promoted the development of a tenure system, I have to say that the faculty as a whole has remained rather consistently indifferent to the matter.

Some faculty members argued that they were uninterested in tenure because academic freedom and job security were not threatened under any of the various iterations of faculty employment policy. According to one professor, "No one felt that their job security was at stake. As far as I know, there has never been a loss of academic freedom." A colleague concluded that, as a result, "faculty felt they had virtual tenure ... Tenure didn't seem to be an important issue one way or the other." At first glance, it may seem curious that faculty would assert that job security was not a concern, given the retrenchments that Rowlette has endured. However, faculty explained that tenure status was not the determining factor in job loss during these difficult periods. Rather, as a professor said, "Tenure didn't protect anyone, as it shouldn't." As noted earlier, the movement for a faculty union arose from discontent with power and influence in decision making, not job security.

2. Faculty were preoccupied with other issues.

Issues like salaries and faculty-administration relations overshadowed academic tenure. Said a professor, "Tenure was always a back-burner issue ... The most important employment issue for faculty, apart from salaries, is workload. That is much more important than tenure. We've got more important fish to fry."

Problematic Preferences

The second loosely coupled characteristic at Rowlette College is problematic preferences. Cohen, March and Olson (1972) stated that an organization "operates on the basis of a variety of inconsistent and ill-defined preferences; ... it discovers preferences through action more than it acts on the basis of preferences" (p. 1). Similarly, Weick (1976) posited that in loosely coupled systems, "intentions are a poor guide for action, intentions often follow rather than precede action, and intentions and action are loosely coupled" (p. 4). Rowlette's preference to move away from traditional tenure was not established after an exploratory task force, a public debate of the issue, or some other rational-choice process. Instead, it happened in unplanned steps; it was incremental and evolutionary. Faculty learned that tenure didn't exist after trustees stopped awarding it. The *action* of refusing to tenure candidates in 1973 set a precedent for a preference that lasted over 15 years. In fact, the board did not impose the official moratorium until 1978, five years after the first *action* against tenure had occurred.

Furthermore, actions did not upset expectations or behaviors. While some faculty were no doubt alarmed that their tenure bids were put on hold, current faculty members reported that little change occurred in how faculty viewed their employment situation. Informants reported that the board and administration did not use the lack of tenure as an opportunity to arbitrarily dismiss faculty. Therefore, professors claimed that their belief in or expectation of job security was not altered by the trustees' actions.

Finally, the board did not seem to have clear sense of what it wanted to achieve by instituting three-year rolling and long-term contracts. One of the primary reasons offered for the board's "nervousness" with tenure was that trustees did not want to be obligated to maintain a large number of tenured (and higher-paid) faculty in times of financial crises. This desire for "flexibility" is problematic for two reasons. First, Rowlette's tenure policy had a provision for the elimination of tenured faculty during a financial exigency. There is evidence that the provision worked: during retrenchments in 1984 and 1994, tenured faculty were released. Second, there is no evidence that either alternative contract system provided trustees greater leeway in dismissing faculty. In fact, based on the opinions of multiple sources, the opposite is true: contracts were just like tenure. Long-time contract faculty had de facto tenure. Said President Bonner, "I don't think [the board] thought about the implications of a long-term contract system—that it was, in some ways, a tenure system."

Unclear Technology

Episodes in the story of Rowlette College's change from tenure to contracts are based on unclear technology. The technology of an organization is the process through which inputs are converted to outputs. In organized anarchies, it is not clear why some processes work. Organizations "operate on the basis of simple trial-and-error procedures, the residue of learning from the accidents of past experience, and pragmatic inventions of necessity" (Cohen, March, and Olsen, 1972, p.1). As a result, change in loosely coupled systems occurs "negligibly (rather than significantly)" and "indirectly (rather than directly)" (Weick, 1984, p. 380).

Rowlette's policy decision of instituting three-year rolling contracts in 1973 can be explained, in part, by trial-and-error procedures and pragmatic inventions of necessity. When the board implemented its unofficial, informal suspension of tenure, all post-probationary nontenured faculty remained on one-year contracts, a situation that was unsatisfactory to them and to the college administration. Therefore, it was necessary to provide some type of longer-term employment policy for faculty. Rather than resolve the ambiguities of the unofficial tenure moratorium, faculty and administrators instituted (or, to paraphrase Cohen, March, and Olson, "invented") a stop-gap measure of rolling contracts. Eventually, Rowlette College's trial-and-error tendencies led it to a long-term contract system with a more rigorous evaluation process.

It is unclear that the type of faculty employment policy (i.e. the "technology" of faculty quality or evaluation) produced any differences in turnover or faculty evaluation. The effect of the change in faculty employment policy was negligible rather than significant, indirect rather than direct. Multiple interviewees reported that instituting long-term contracts and "honorary" tenure did not produce an increase in faculty turnover. Instead, the early retirement plan, adopted as part of the long-term contract policy in 1986, had far greater impact than the employment policy. If the goal of the change in faculty employment policy was to produce higher quality faculty, then the college succeeded only indirectly through early retirements, by inducing "old school" faculty to leave the college and replacing them with newer faculty with fresh teaching perspectives.

The Garbage Can Model of Change

With these three characteristics of organized anarchies, Rowlette College's process of organizational change falls into the "garbage can model" of decision making (Cohen, March, & Olsen, 1972), where various organizational elements (or "streams") coalesce at a particular point to produce a decision. In a garbage-can model, problems require attention, solutions look for issues to which they might be the answer, and participants look for work. These three streams come together during a fourth element, the choice situation, the point at which a decision is expected. Each of these four elements were present in the "garbage can" of change at Rowlette:

Problems

As noted above, constituents at Rowlette College identified several "problems" that the elimination of a traditional tenure system was intended to solve. Some trustees put tenure in the garbage can of fiscal problems because tenure seemed to imply unrealistic long-term financial commitments. At least one faculty member noticed the nonrational basis for this reaction: "the board's decision [to stop awarding tenure] was supposed to be related to fiscal issues, but I didn't see the point of that, since the college has always been able to let go tenured faculty members in times of crisis." Tenure was also tossed in the garbage can of problems with faculty quality because it was linked to poor evaluation. Several interviewees told stories of being awarded tenure automatically, with no application, process, or review. Finally, tenure was put in the we-need-to-run-the-college-more-like-a-business garbage can, where it was targeted by trustees as an unfamiliar and archaic practice.

Solutions

The stream of solutions placed into Cohen and March's metaphorical garbage can attach themselves to various problems. At Rowlette, the problem of faculty quality was attached to tenure, even though it was not solved solely by a change in faculty employment policy. (In fact, many argued that the long-term contracts policy did not address the problem at all.) Solutions such as more stringent evaluations, early retirement, phased-length contracts, and post-tenure review also were added to the 1986 policy revision with the intent to increase faculty quality.

Participants

As discussed earlier, "participants come and go" (Cohen, March, & Olsen, 1972, p. 3) in organized anarchies. Such fluid participation had two important dimensions at Rowlette College. First, some participants entered and exited the college community entirely. Second, even long-time faculty and trustees who were part of the college for the whole history of change from tenure to contracts did not pay attention to the problems of faculty employment policies at all times. As a result of ever-changing leaders and uninterested participants, it became difficult to move faculty employment policies onto the Rowlette College radar screen. "Most issues most of the time have low salience for most people" (Cohen & March, 1986, p. 206). With a general apathy for the topic, participants most of the time were unmotivated to create a change. "The total system" in an organized anarchy, wrote Cohen and March (1986), "has high inertia. Anything that requires a coordinated effort of the organization in order to start is unlikely to be started" (p. 206).

Choice opportunities

At certain times over the history of Rowlette, the streams of problems, solutions, and participants converged. "These are occasions when an organization is expected to produce behavior than can be called a decision" (Cohen, March, & Olsen, 1972, p. 3). But in the Rowlette College case, choice opportunities were often delayed or ignored so that decisions were not made. For example, a 1973 report to the board of trustees recommended a series of changes to the Faculty Personnel Policy, including a study of the then-current tenure policy and the potential use of tenure quotas. However, the recommendations were tentative because of the expected "appointment of a new President next year. Important policies on faculty contracts should be provisional" (Board minutes, July 20, 1973). Because the participant stream in the decision-making process was fluid (the board did not want to take action without guidance from a new president), the choice opportunity was postponed. Decisions were routinely ignored or delayed in the 1970s and 1980s because of turnover of administrators, trustees, and faculty, and distraction from more pressing concerns.

Decision-making Styles

When organized anarchies make decisions, they can be grounded in clear cause-and-effect, cost-benefit, or other rational basis. Cohen and March called this decision-making style "resolution," in which "problems are actually worked through rationally until they are resolved" (Birnbaum, 1988, p. 164). However, organized anarchies rarely operate in this fashion; instead, Cohen and March (1986) hypothesized that decisions are more likely made by flight or by oversight.

Decision making by flight occurs when problems are associated with a choice until a better choice comes along. "The problem leaves the choice, and thereby make it possible to make the decision" (Cohen & March, 1986, p. 83). At Rowlette, trustees were wary of the long-term commitment tenure implied for the college to each faculty member. As the financial condition of the college slowly improved in the late 1970s and 1980s, fiscal issues took flight from faculty employment and moved to other arenas (e.g., increasing the endowment, improving the physical plant, raising faculty salaries). When the faculty employment policies was rewritten in 1986 so that tenure was not the primary method of faculty employment, the problem of financial implications left (took flight from) the tenure arena because the vast majority of faculty were not tenured. But, as Cohen and March noted, "the decision resolves no problems" (1986, p. 83). Rowlette still had the "problem" of whether it could afford to keep faculty long-term because, according to interviewees, involuntary faculty turnover was as negligible under long-term contracts as under tenure.

Decisions made through oversight are enacted so quickly in such an overloaded, problematic environment that no one has time to get involved in the decision (Cohen & March, 1986). When the board was faced with stiff financial pressure in 1973, they made the decision to suspend tenure by oversight. Faculty and administrators were not involved in the decision-making process because they were distracted by the more pressing matter of the financial viability of the institution.

A Symbolic System

As a result of the ever-changing players, ill-defined problems, loosely coupled solutions, and decisions made through distraction and inaction, Rowlette College developed a weak information base, in which "information about past events or past decisions is often not retained" (Cohen & March, 1986, p. 207). All of these characteristics confounded decision making and organizational understanding. For example, loose coupling illustrates how the mysterious 1977 Task Force on Tenure had such little effect on policies or people at Rowlette. Task forces, planning committees, and other such groups are classic garbage cans in an organized anarchy because they "absorb problems, solutions, and participants like a sponge and prevent them from sloshing around and disturbing arenas in which people wish to act" (Birnbaum, 1988, p. 165). So, in effect, it does not matter if (a) the task force was ever formed—the very act of mandating its formation was an important symbolic step for the board—or (b) if the task force produced any report or recommendations—it may have only acted as a holding tank in which trustees could place their concerns about employment policy for a period of time. In the long run, as a faculty member said, "I can't imagine what difference such a task force or its report would have made."

This quotation speaks to the symbolic nature of "tenure" as employment policy. Most faculty felt like they had tenure (i.e., academic freedom and economic security) regardless of the official policy. Therefore, action by the board as a result of this task force wouldn't have made any "difference" because the board was attending to the rationalized myth (Meyer and Rowan, 1983) of the written, codified faculty employment policy. Organized anarchies and loosely coupled systems are symbolic entities that focus on rationalized myths and beliefs (Birnbaum, 1988). Meyer and Rowan (1983) defined a rationalized myth as an organizational structure, rule, or goal that is influenced by societal expectations—they are myths because they do not actually determine how the organization operates. Under this theory, Rowlette's tenure policy was an rationalized myth. It may have been adopted initially because it is considered by the external higher education community to be the mainstream model of faculty appointment. It may have been attacked by the board of trustees because of the rationalized myth in the business world that asserts tenure is a means of guaranteed, ironclad lifetime employment. But, in practical terms, tenure did not actually determine if faculty remained at the college a long time (both tenured and nontenured faculty did), nor did tenure determine if faculty had freedom in the classroom and in scholarly pursuits (most interviewees asserted all faculty, regardless of tenured status, enjoyed those freedoms). Trustees also subscribed to the rationalized myth that contracts could be temporary. Trustees relied on a perceived difference between tenure and contracts rather than an actual difference. They believed "that a contract is a contract—that you could end it or break it." So while evidence may not have existed that contracts were substantively better (or even different) than tenure, decision-makers relied on the rationalized myth that a multi-year contract system was short-term and flexible and tenure was lifetime and rigid.

In practice, tenure did not provide greater job security or academic freedom, nor did contracts beset turnover. So, the consummate rationalized myth at Rowlette College was that a change in policy would somehow change practice. Rowlette's process of moving from traditional tenure to rolling contracts to multi-year contracts is essentially a symbolic story in which organizational actors created a façade of change while not really affecting the way by which faculty are employed at the college. When trustees mandated that the administration and faculty give attention to updating and improving the faculty employment system, leaders appointed committees, which wrote reports and recommendations on policy changes, which eventually appeared as new policies in the faculty handbook. But these events were symbolic, rationalized processes devoted to the appearance of change. One professor acknowledged that, when the board requested a multi-year contract policy from the faculty and administration in the early 1980s, the academic vice president "tried to make it look like something changed without actually changing much at all." Thus, faculty and administrators alike reported that, in practice, the manner by which faculty think of their employment situation has not changed: they consider themselves tenured, whether or not they have the designation.

Exhibit 4.1

Rowlette College Board of Trustees
October 1978
Resolution on Tenure

WHEREAS, it is the sense of the Board of Trustees that the Tenure system is not supportive of the best needs of the College and is not a satisfactory basis for recognizing the service of faculty in a manner that serves the interests of the total College community, therefore be it

RESOLVED, that the Board of Trustees believes it is in the best interest of Rowlette College to declare a two-year moratorium on the awarding of Tenure, during which time the College shall seek a means for development of a more satisfactory system of recognizing faculty service to the College which provides adequate security to the faculty member in a fashion other than Tenure.

Further, such an alternative system developed with the fullest faculty participation and the most careful academic administrative consideration shall be reviewed by the President and presented to the Board of Trustees for its consideration. The Board directs the President to report to the Executive Committee which is designated as the Board liaison committee on this matter at the Fall and Spring meetings of the Board on the progress in this effort.

The Education Committee shall be kept fully informed and its advice and counsel sought by the Executive Committee.

Action by the Board of Trustees on such an alternative system to Tenure should take place by the Spring 1980 meeting of the Board.

CHAPTER 5
Lakeview College

Lakeview College is a mid-sized, open-admissions, urban institution that specializes in the fine and performing arts and communications. Lakeview historically did not offer tenure—all full-time faculty were on one-year contracts—until 1997, when the college instituted a tenure system.

A SHORT HISTORY

Lakeview College was founded in 1890 as the City School of Oratory. Two women from what is now Emerson College in Boston started the college to train students in speech and declamation, popular academic and social pastimes of the day. The college remained "tiny" for many decades, typically enrolling around 100 students. According to college documents, "in 1928, the college was incorporated into [a teachers college.] A renewed, coeducational version of the college emerged in 1936, emphasizing the growing field of radio broadcasting. In 1944, the name was changed to [Lakeview College.]"

After World War II, Warren Lynch opened a radio station in Lakeview City. The college's leaders asked Lynch to become president, to which he agreed. During the 1950s, the college broadened its academic programs to include television and other mass communications. Lynch served as president until 1963, when his son, Kevin, took over. At that time, Kevin and his wife were the only full-time employees of the college. "Lakeview was a dying institution by 1962. The college had fewer than 200 students, a part-time faculty of 25, and no endowments, subsidies, or visibility" (College history). The younger Lynch instituted many of the programs and policies that define the college today, including:

1. An open admissions policy.

Lakeview accepts nearly all applicants for admission (its acceptance rate in 1998 was 90 percent). The college serves a diverse constituency of approximately 8,000 undergraduate students—28 percent of whom are 25 years of age or older, 27 percent part-time—and 600 graduate students.

2. A curriculum focused primarily on the fine and performing arts and communications.

Lakeview's program of study includes majors in areas such as advertising, computer graphics, fashion merchandising, film production, interior design, and music, but does not offer majors in traditional liberal arts areas like English, history, biology, and political science.

3. Part-time faculty who were practitioners rather than full-time traditional academics.

Lynch initially hired only part-time instructors who were practitioners in the field: working journalists, television and film producers, actors, theater directors, dance choreographers. The full-time faculty that the college hired did not come from traditional academic paths either; many of them did not have graduate degrees.

Because these characteristics are still integral to the college's identity, many people at the institution refer to Kevin Lynch as the "founding president" and "founding figure" and the last 35 years as the "modern incarnation" of the college. During his presidency, Lynch governed the college by "the proprietary model," said a trustee. "By that, I don't mean anything pejorative. But the president who created this school just ran it. He ran everything. It was a big step when a College Council [a faculty-administrator advisory board] was created, but the Council didn't have any power. They didn't do anything. He ran it all." According to faculty, Lynch insisted on an informal operating model. He "didn't think the college should have any kind of formal structure" and "he hated committees." As a result, the college was "light" on administration, and shared governance did not exist. "Kevin believed in shared governance on an intellectual level," said one professor. "On a practical level, it just never took hold." He also was opposed to rank and tenure.

As the college grew, however, Lynch's "proprietary" method of managing the college became dated. Lynch retired in 1992, succeeded by Craig Murin, who had been president at a state-supported university and provost at a private university.

IMPORTANT CONSTITUENCIES

Like the other colleges in this study, Lakeview's administrators, faculty, and trustees were involved in the process of change in faculty employment policies. As this section explains, however, a fourth constituency—the department chairs—were integral to the culture and structure of the college and to the change process.

Administration

President Murin was in office when the college shifted faculty employment policies in 1997. He was quite different than Lynch. Said a colleague, "Craig came out of a traditional route to the presidency. He had been a [college president elsewhere] and had been at a variety of institutions. He was more rooted in traditional higher education culture than his predecessor." Faculty reported that Murin was a "believer in the sharing of power" and "felt very strongly that faculty should have a voice in decisions made in the college."

Another important administrator in the history of Lakeview was the executive vice president and provost, Mark Cooper, who had been a student at Lakeview in the tumultuous 1960s. He gave the valedictory speech wrapped in the Vietnam flag. Then-president Lynch hired him in the business office and he worked his way up to executive vice president. Immediately before he retired, Lynch appointed Cooper as provost. Unlike most provosts, however, Cooper had neither teaching experience nor a doctoral degree. President Murin recalled that Lynch suggested to him that he "do all the fundraising and let Cooper run the college. Cooper could run the Pentagon." Murin continued:

> Mark [was responsible for] everything. He's the provost but he was also in charge of all financial matters, all the security arrangements, all maintenance, buildings and grounds, and the bookstore. The chairman of the board told me "You have to do something about that. If he ever gets hit by a car, we're in real trouble." Mark doesn't tend to put things in writing, so a lot of these things are in his head.

Murin expressed concern about this unusual administrative style. One of his first initiatives was to transfer the authority for budgeting and personnel to the vice president for finance.

Faculty

Experienced faculty and administrators describe the institution as a place that, for a long time, attracted an "anti-establishment" faculty. Provost Cooper recalled, "This was a faculty back in the 60s that didn't wanted to be accredited because it was viewed as a sell-out. That was a compromise, that was the establishment. We didn't want to be part of that establishment. We didn't want the trappings of a traditional institution. We were an alternative band of, not reformers in higher education, but revolutionaries." As noted above, these were also faculty who did not come from traditional academic backgrounds. Interviewees asserted that many faculty lacked interest in shared governance because they did not have experience in higher education and "all the crazy vagaries of academia," according to a professor. "It [was] rather difficult to get faculty engaged in issues here." As the college hired an increasing number of faculty with typical academic career paths, however, faculty began to expect "traditional faculty roles as to power, as to prerogative, as to status," according to a trustee. "Tenure was a glaring omission in the faculty's status among their peers. . . . It was something of an evolutionary process that made it time for there to be institutional recognition of the stature and status of our faculty."

The faculty organization, Lakeview College Faculty Association (LACFAC), was founded in the early 1980s. "It had to meet off-campus in secret," said a professor. "Once it came out of the closet, the administration sat up and took notice and said, 'Of course the faculty needs an organization.'" LACFAC had difficulty earning the respect of the Lynch administration, according to a former association president. Originally, only faculty who paid dues were considered members of the faculty association; "whenever we would bring something up in a meeting about the position of LACFAC, [administrators] would say, 'Oh, that's only 60 percent of the faculty; we can disregard that.' [So] we changed the bylaws to say that anyone who was a full-time faculty member was, by designation, a member of LACFAC. . . . That allowed us to speak for the whole faculty." Nevertheless, faculty reported that decisions were typically made "at a private level," without faculty input. "Often, decisions were made over dinner."

Trustees

At the time of the research for this book, the board of trustees consisted of 37 members. While most trustees were from the business or corporate world, seven were educators and 11 had backgrounds in the arts or communications.[1] Trustees had a "traditional aversion" to tenure at the beginning of the change process but, by the end, voted unanimously to adopt the new tenure system. Interviewees attributed the turnaround in trustees' view to the involvement of the chairman of the board, Michael Cerra, an attorney. Murin noted with amazement, "He got very interested in this subject. When he gets interested in a particular subject, he goes all out . . . In my

---

1. The board of trustees consisted of 10 corporate executives, 8 attorneys, 7 business owners or entrepreneurs, 7 educators, 4 arts patrons, 2 medical specialists, 2 journalists, 2 artists, 2 television or radio producers, 1 television or radio personality, 1 government official, and 1 non-profit executive.

presidencies, I've had seven board chairs, and I've never had anybody who's . . .put that much time in an endeavor." Murin maintained that "if [Cerra] had been billing us [for all his work on the tenure policy] like he would have at his law office, it probably would have cost $100,000 to do this job." The president recalled an example of Cerra's devotion to the tenure issue at Lakeview:

> I was reading the New York Times one Sunday morning and there was an account of a debate between [two national experts on tenure] at Brooklyn College. It was very interesting, so I called up Mike and said, "I saw this article in the Times. I'll send it to you. There was this debate at Brooklyn College [on tenure.]" He said, "Yeah, I know, I was there." Can you imagine that? He had taken a plane and gone to New York to sit in on the debate to hear what they were saying.

Chairs

In addition to faculty, administrators, and trustees, Lakeview College had a fourth group of actors: department chairs. In the nascent stages of the college's modern era, President Lynch hired individuals to develop the academic curriculum of each program of study. These chairs were "entrepreneurs," "authors of their enterprise," and "visionaries." At first, they were the only full-time faculty members in their departments. Provost Cooper noted that "those pioneer chairs, almost without exception, came directly from the arts or media, not out of the academy. They didn't bring the traditions [of higher education]. Their expectations were not the same." According to a faculty member, "the departments grew out of visionary chairs, who had enormous and virtually unhampered discretionary powers. It used to be that faculty [were retained] just by the rule of the chair, period." Sometimes, the result was, in the view of faculty, an abuse of power:

> The chairs simply did what they wanted to. For example, the faculty handbook states that if there is a resignation or space for a new faculty member, there is a search committee. Chairs would blatantly ignore that. They would take an artist-in-residence and promote him or her, as if this were an industrial model of promoting from within the ranks. . . . There were some really ugly instances of chairs simply ignoring the wishes of faculty. Faculty might have interviewed 15, 20 candidates and the chair would say, "I'm going to hire John Doe because he is my favorite."

Full-time faculty considered themselves a separate group from the chairs. For example, if a faculty member became a chair, he or she automatically would be expelled from LACFAC. The chairs developed their own group, the Chairs' Council, which one faculty member described as "the cabinet of the provost."

Several faculty described the internal structure of the college as a tripartite system, with three unique "nodes" or constituencies: central administration, the chairs, and faculty. One faculty member asserted that "the model was . . . administrators on top, the faculty hoi polloi on the bottom, and the chairs in between. It was a straight hierarchy." When President Murin arrived, he found "a federation system, with very powerful chairs operating at the dean's level."

PROMINENT CHARACTERISTICS

Several important characteristics of Lakeview arose during my site visit and in interviews with faculty and administrators: (1) Lakeview has undergone staggering growth in the last two decades, impacting its culture and identity, and (2) the college has evolved in its traditions of governance.

Expansion and Growth

Lakeview College is nestled amid towering skyscrapers, hotels, museums and cultural venues, and a lakeside park in an historic downtown area. Unlike the other three sites in this study, Lakeview does not have a traditional campus *per se*—its 11 office-like buildings are scattered throughout several city blocks, and its students and faculty mingle among the city's workers and tourists and dart around its delivery trucks and taxi cabs. Faculty and administrative offices, classrooms, and academic facilities are often squeezed into small spaces. For example, in an area more suitable for one secretary, the anteroom in the president's office holds two assistants and a student worker; one of their desks extends from a closet. Visitors wait in one of two plain chairs surrounded by storage boxes and a copying machine.

Lakeview's cramped physical plant is indicative of the college's staggering growth in the last two decades. As an observer noted, Kevin Lynch "hit on the right formula" by developing an open-admissions policy, a practitioner focus, and arts and communications curricula. The college's enrollment grew from several hundred in the early 1960s to 2,000 by 1976, over 4,500 by the mid-1980s, to more than 8,500 in 1999. An administrator proudly commented that "even in the 1980s, when [other] campuses were going through downsizing and whole departments were wiped out, we were growing and hiring and desperately trying to find more [faculty]." As a result of this growth of enrollment, "in recent years the college had had its hands full just finding additional space in the [neighborhood] for its burgeoning enrollment" (Presidential speech, 1999). Since Craig Murin became president in 1992, the college has acquired seven new buildings, for a total of eleven.

The size of faculty has increased to meet enrollment demands. Full-time faculty numbered 227 in 1998–99, a 100 percent increase since the early 1990s. They are dwarfed, however, by the number of part-timers and adjunct professors—over 1,000 in the 1998–99 academic year, responsible for 70 percent of the courses offered.

Traditions of Governance

As several aspects of this case description suggest, Lakeview College developed a unique system of governance. An entrepreneurial president allowed decentralized "fiefdoms" to develop with strong, powerful departmental chairs. Because so many chairs and faculty came from outside academe, there was not a faculty culture to resist administrative decision making. Even though faculty began an organization (LACFAC) to represent their interests, "the faculty organization was never recognized as a bargaining unit." Instead, as one professor reported, faculty asserted their desires to the administration individually: "You could have ready access to the administration. [For example,] you could further yourself from a salary standpoint by doing 'the right things' . . . through individual negotiation. So, there was always this suspicion of great salary inequities in the institution."

As the college grew and matured over 30 years, newer faculty members exerted pressure for more traditional models of collegiate governance. Ironically, the system of decentralized authority, in which chairs were given wide range of authority, contributed to its own demise. Under the strong-chair model, successful chairs whose programs increased in popularity and quality were rewarded with larger enrollments and more faculty. These new full-time faculty came largely from traditional academics backgrounds. It was these very people who, after becoming a critical mass across campus, began to demand a greater voice in decision making.

When President Murin arrived in 1992, he sought to reform Lakeview's governance system in two ways. First, Murin increased the number of chairs from 13 to 17, and replaced the "chair-for-life" arrangement with a three-year rotational appointment. By 1999, only three of the "old-style" chairs remained at the college; the others had retired. Second, he overhauled the College Council, an advisory group. As Murin explained:

> The college was a federation [of] various departments. There was no faculty governance. . . . It [was] hard to get them interested. If you have a college with no historians or political scientists or sociologists—people dealing with people—you don't get them involved.

Where did the push for faculty governance come from?
It came from me. There were faculty who were eventually supportive of it, but it was hard going.

Murin appointed a committee of administrators, faculty, and chairs—chaired by a professor—to develop a new College Council. Previously, every department chair was on the council. The new council consists of 46 members and has a faculty majority: 25 elected faculty members, 6 administrators, 7 chairs, 3 students, and 5 staff members. According to the faculty handbook, the College Council "is the principal advisory group from the College community that recommends to the president on a broad range of policy issues concerning College matters with the expectation of a timely response." (See Exhibit 5.1 for a complete description.)

THE PROCESS OF CHANGE IN FACULTY EMPLOYMENT POLICIES
The System of Faculty Employment

Lakeview had no academic tenure or rank system. The college employed all faculty on one-year contracts. "Not having the traditional titling and trappings [of rank and tenure] was quite hip" at one time, reported Provost Cooper. "Certain faculty in the late 60s and 70s saw it as a badge of singularity and celebration." The college hired new faculty on a "probationary" status instead of on a tenure-track. After three years, faculty advanced to "non-probationary" status, pending approval of the chair, who would write a recommendation to the academic dean. In 1986, the probationary period was extended to five years, and according to a professor, "participation of faculty in the department, albeit advisory and unevenly applied, was supposed to guide the chair's recommendation to the dean." A colleague noted that the process was "unsystematic and very loose." There was not a college-wide interdisciplinary committee to review non-probationary decisions. Several professors reported this system had adverse effects on junior faculty members. One said, "It led to a lot of sycophancy, a lot of brown-nosing, a lot of behavior that was, quite honestly, unprofessional on the part of faculty." Another reported that, because of the explosive growth in the 1980s,

> There were always more probationary faculty than non-probationary. The probationary faculty did not dare to do anything risky. They wanted to quietly serve out their probationary years under this regime. There was a real fear of "don't rock the boat." So, even if the non-probationary faculty came up with a proposal that made all kinds of sense, you had a hard time selling it to the probationary people.

Although non-probationary faculty were still awarded one-year contracts, they considered themselves to have long-term status. One professor recollected, "when I got my letter saying that I was a post-probationary faculty member, there was a sense of, 'oh, okay, I'm here, it's going to be a long-term relationship.' Even though we were only on one-year contracts, there was that sense, confirmed by a letter, that you had achieved another level at the institution." Many faculty felt that the probationary/non-probationary system, in practice, was very similar to tenure: "We had a tenure system but not in name." Trustee Cerra came to a similar conclusion: "If you were non-probationary, you could grieve a dismissal [as stipulated in the faculty handbook] and go through a whole complicated process that, in effect, forced the college to justify removal, in the same way as traditional tenure."

Many faculty reported that, in addition to the near-unilateral role that the chairs played in the faculty evaluation process, the probationary/non-probationary system was problematic for symbolic reasons. Said one, "A number of people disliked the language. It made them sound like they were at a penal institution." Another asked rhetorically, "If you were a probationary faculty member, did you see your probationary officer often? Did you wear a collar? Just the very terminology carried overtones of a very paternalistic type of governance."

The Movement for Faculty Rank

Faculty discontent with Lakeview's employment policy became evident in the late 1980s over rank, not tenure. In 1988, a Faculty Rank Committee ("an infelicitous name if I've ever heard one," commented a professor) began work on a proposal to place faculty in traditional categories of assistant, associate, and full professor. Under the plan, all faculty would have had to apply for rank: no one was to be grandfathered. Interestingly, tenure was not part of the plan—at that point, faculty were primarily interested in title. One professor explained that "the faculty felt that they needed the customary benefit of professional title to help them with external organizations and individuals to recognize who we were. We needed the traditional, standard titles that others were afforded." President Lynch insisted that, for the Faculty Rank Committee's proposal to be accepted, a 66–percent super-majority of faculty had to support it. Faculty who did not cast ballots were considered to vote "no." The proposal received a majority of votes, but not enough to pass. Observers attributed the defeat, in part, to a schism in the faculty: "Working professionals who had entered teaching largely opposed it, while the growing numbers of academically trained faculty supported it" (Presidential speech, 1999). After the rank proposal fell through, faculty leaders brought up the issue with President Lynch again, "but it just didn't go anywhere."

Tenure Proposal of the Committee on Faculty Status

After Murin became president in 1992, he signaled to LACFAC officers that he would be willing to consider a proposal on rank and tenure. The board chairman recalled that, after the defeated proposal on rank, the issue "just sort of dropped off my radar screen entirely. It was the changing of the presidency and Craig Murin's general sympathy for the concept that played a significant role in its revival." Murin was interested in a tenure system because the probationary/non-probationary process "wasn't a formal system. It was based too much on departmental recommendations to the dean and provost."

Four LACFAC officers spent the 1993–94 year researching rank and tenure at other universities. They presented their findings at two general faculty meetings in spring 1994, and, that fall, the entire faculty voted to develop a proposal on rank, tenure, and salary equalization. Salary equity issues were added to the slate because President Murin demonstrated that "the three were integrally related." Salary disparities existed among faculty with similar lengths of service because of the college's history of making "private deals" with individual faculty members. Murin said:

> I pointed out to them that the problem with rank was that it would cost a great deal of money [to equalize salaries among faculty at the same rank]....
> If we do rank, we're going to have to have money. If it turns out that we have a professor who's making $55,000 and another professor, for whatever reason, happens to be making $40,000, who happens to be female, then we've got a real problem.

In spring 1995, LACFAC appointed a Committee on Faculty Status, including 10 faculty, 2 chairs, the academic dean, and a consultant. A LACFAC officer indicated that the committee's name and structure were important symbolically: "It took quite a while to get to that name. It wasn't going to be the Rank Committee because it wasn't only about rank. By calling it the Committee on Faculty Status, that gave us status to begin with. But, it was a different type of committee. It was a committee of LACFAC, not a committee appointed by the president. This was to be a faculty-led effort."

By spring 1996, the issues of rank and salary equalization were put on the back burner and the committee focused exclusively on tenure. Interviewees offered several reasons for this development. First, President Murin indicated the college would endure a financial burden in offering salary equity among faculty at similar ranks: "The faculty would have to stipulate that they were willing to use the money set aside for faculty raises—or at least part of it—to set up a rank system." Second, the Committee on Faculty Status found that tenure "had the most widespread support" among its members. Finally, several interviewees commented that the committee pursued tenure first because "the system we [had] in place [was] in many ways equivalent to a traditional tenure system."

The committee met biweekly between spring 1995 and summer 1996 to write a tenure document. The chair of the committee described the process as "very collegial," but noted some faculty mistrust of the two chairs and the president's consultant at the beginning of their work. "It turned out that the chairs and [the consultant] were really above-board and brought to the table significant issues that the faculty should consider." In fall 1996, the Committee presented its work to the entire faculty, 86 percent of whom voted to adopt a tenure system.

The Board's Reaction

The president introduced the faculty proposal to the board of trustees in September 1996. The board's reaction was "openly hostile," according to Trustee Cerra. President Murin remarked, "You'd think I tried to introduce cholera rather than tenure into the college." The board's response was "fueled by the negative publicity which tenure was receiving nationally, as well as by the traditional notion that tenure meant an ironclad guarantee to lifetime employment" (Presidential speech, 1999). Despite the board's reaction, Cerra was not inclined to scuttle the proposal: "One, we didn't know enough about [tenure] and its implications and, second, . . . it was clear that Craig thought this was a good idea." However, the chairman was unhappy with the faculty's work. "The policy statement that the faculty prepared was woefully inadequate. It was naïve, poorly conceived and, well, terrible." Cerra did not like the faculty's reliance on "ambiguous language" of the AAUP's policy statements.[2]

At its October 1996 board meeting, Cerra appointed a five-member Board Committee on Tenure, whose purpose was to rewrite the faculty proposal in a form that the board could accept. The board tenure committee, which Cerra chaired, met biweekly from November to May 1997. During its seven-month existence, the board committee interacted with the Committee on Faculty Status several times. At first, the two groups were "talking past each other." The board committee, said Chairman Cerra, thought that faculty "didn't really know what they wanted." One faculty

---

2. In a 1998 speech, President Murin further explained the rationale behind Cerra's complaint: "Those of you who have had to administer an institution governed by AAUP-sanctioned policies and practices know that the most central procedures, particularly those involving termination and financial exigency, are often rife with confusing or ambivalent wording. Administrators who must carry out such policies are often accused of procedural violations."

member charged that "the board chair got a hold of the document and . . . made it more legalistic. . . . The faculty made some concessions with the board committee." But, overall, both faculty and trustees described their interactions as collegial and cooperative. Cerra said, "when faculty saw the kinds of things that we needed, they were able to understand the board's concerns, and I think the [board] was able to understand the faculty's issues. . . . This was a win-win negotiation."

One of the key differences between the faculty and board proposals was post-tenure review (PTR). When the board raised the issue, the faculty status committee said "that was a separate issue and we would be glad to visit it later, but let's just strictly deal with tenure." The faculty committee chairman reported, therefore, "it was a bit of a surprise" that the board's document included a post-tenure review. But, faculty concluded that PTR was crucial to obtain board approval of the tenure proposal. An administrator called post-tenure review "the force that allowed the document to be passed. . . . This quieted the argument that always gets dredged up about deadwood on the faculty."

The two groups also extensively debated the definition and procedures of financial exigency and due process. In the area of financial exigency, faculty and board members agreed to allow the board to dismiss tenured faculty because of "imminent, serious fiscal difficulty," rather than permit action only after a crisis had materialized, an AAUP provision. In the area of dismissal for cause, the new tenure document allowed for fewer levels of appeal than usual. President Murin outlined why this policy was acceptable to both trustees and faculty:

> In this instance the Board convinced the faculty that excessive appeals were not in anyone's best interest. Besides, aggrieved parties usually took their cases to court regardless of the number of appeals available internally. The document spells out the dismissal "for cause" reasons with more specificity than is usually found. The reasons cited are clearly egregious, thus making it difficult to initiate proceedings on flimsy grounds. (Presidential speech, 1998)

Once the board and faculty committees reviewed and approved the new tenure policy, the Academic and Student Affairs Committee of the board unanimously approved the document. On May 31, 1997, the full board also unanimously approved the tenure policy. These votes represented a complete turn-around for most board members, who nine months earlier vigorously opposed the move to tenure. Chairman Cerra attributed the change to the make-up of the board's ad-hoc tenure committee as well as the amount of substantive work the board completed. Cerra intentionally put several skeptics of tenure on the committee: "I wanted to select people

Lakeview College

that, if they were convinced, would then convince others." He elaborated on that strategy:

> The members on the tenure committee were very well respected members of the board. The board was kept apprised of how often the committee was meeting, how much work it was doing. They recognized that some of those members were very skeptical of tenure at the beginning. I think that, when members of that committee—after long, intensive examination of tenure and its implications—had all reached the conclusion unanimously that this was a good thing for Lakeview, it was very difficult for other board members to say, "well, I still don't like it." Overwhelming information and study sometimes can have an intimidating effect on those who don't agree with the point of view but don't have the resources or the information to argue with it.

Under the new policy provisions, all 150 non-probationary faculty, approximately 83 percent of the full-time faculty, were grandfathered into tenure beginning in the 1997–98 academic year.

SHORT TERM OUTCOMES

At the time of the research for this book, Lakeview College was completing its second year under the new tenure policy. While interviewees claimed the "jury is still out" on the long-term effects of the new policy, faculty and administrators alike observed a shift in power and decision making at Lakeview. Prior to tenure, the department chair had virtual sole authority to determine if a faculty member should receive non-probationary status. While the old policy stipulated that "full-time non-probationary faculty members within the department are to be consulted by the chairperson and those faculty opinions are to be reflected in the chairperson's recommendation," faculty members noted that such involvement was erratic and inconsistent. The new tenure provision codified faculty engagement in the tenure-review process in two ways. First, the policy emphasized that the recommendation on the tenure candidate was the recommendation of the *department,* not the department chair. Furthermore, "The Chair or any faculty member in that Department with a Tenured appointment may append a written dissent or supplemental statement to this report." This provision guaranteed that tenured faculty members had a voice in the process, whether or not they agreed with the majority opinion. Second, the new tenure policy instituted an interdisciplinary, faculty-led All-College Tenure (ACT) Committee, which also reviewed each tenure candidate and made recommendations to the academic dean and provost. The formation of the ACT committee was "a real culture shift" for Lakeview. The chairs "had to share power with faculty," beamed a professor. Another said, "[the chairs'] discretionary powers have been hampered by the fact that there is a committee above them. . . . A committee working beyond departments and across departmental lines unbalanced that earlier hierarchical process." An administrator emphasized that the policy changed from one "that is very chair-driven to a process where the chair is one of four other voices. . . . Although we value the chair's input, there is other input as you move through the tenure-track. That's been a hard transition for chairs who've been here a long time."

It is important to note that, although a professor proclaimed, "tenure, to a certain extent, has helped lessen that autocratic management style" of the chairs, the shift to tenure is not the sole cause of the change in power relations between faculty and department chairs. An administrator emphasized, "the reduction in authority of the chairs . . . had already begun" prior to the shift toward a tenure policy. As noted earlier, several years before the introduction of tenure at Lakeview, President Murin overhauled the governance system, making the chairs' authority more diffuse and eliminating their "chair-for-life" status. Nevertheless, the implementation of a tenure system has especially affected faculty's involvement in campus governance. Provost Cooper noted that "faculty are much more intent, or more willing, or feel more enfranchised to take a strong role, an outspoken role" now that they have tenure. A professor concurred, declaring "people are speaking out more strongly, more directly, about issues on campus." Another noted that "faculty are only gradually becoming aware about the extent to which they have been empowered by this. I don't think it was the board's goal to empower the faculty."

REASONS FOR THE OVERHAUL IN POLICY

Interviewees offered several reasons why the probationary/non-probationary system of employment was a problem and why tenure was the solution:

Power

Faculty generally offered two reasons for tenure. First, as noted above, faculty almost universally described tenure as prohibiting "arbitrary" decisions by the administration and "the abuse of discretionary powers, largely by the chairs." While some of the chairs' power had been eroded because of President Murin's changes to the structure of governance at Lakeview, faculty saw tenure as an added step in affording them participation in decision making, particularly in departmental issues of hiring and tenure review. Tenure solved "the inconsistency of how faculty were treated among departments," expressed a former LACFAC officer, because department chairpersons were no longer making those decisions unilaterally.

Tenure solved this problem of power and administrative inconsistency because nearly all faculty received tenure automatically. Lakeview does not yet have a history of the administration denying tenure to a junior faculty member.[3] If and when the administration denies tenure to a candidate, the faculty's perspective on power and consistency in personnel decisions may change.

Faculty Status

The second problem that tenure "solved," according to most faculty, was that of professional recognition. A professor stated that "[tenure] would give us recognition outside the institution. It was a clear and consistent system that provided credibility to the outside." Faculty saw tenure as a signal of respect, to offset the "sense of not being part of the academy at large." Many participants linked faculty's demand for "status" to the growing maturity of the college. Trustee Cerra commented that "Lakeview has moved from a somewhat iconoclastic, unique, we're-not-like-all-of-those-other-institutions, into a large, private college that increasingly craves to be welcomed into the educational mainstream; that, while keeping its differences, needs to be acknowledged by its peers as 'one of them.'"

Another component of this status issue existed internally. With a mix of traditional course offerings and unconventional programs (e.g. English and Interactive Multimedia), faculty "were suspicious of each other in terms of academic qualifications." With a formalized tenure process capped with a review from an all-college committee, "tenure has proven that folks in art go through just as rigorous process as English . . . It diminished the feeling of superiority."

Not all faculty, however, believed that the prestige and status that faculty associated with tenure was a benefit. One faculty opponent decried the move:

> The desire to make this place like other, more prestigious institutions was a bad mistake.
>
> *Why was that a mistake?*
>
> One of the reasons I'm here is because of the kinds of flexibility this place represents, the desire to support the arts in ways that you wouldn't get in other institutions; the absence of what some people call safeguards or what I consider obstacles to achievement. . . . This place is also unique [because of] the commitment to open enrollment. Why in the world, with [other well-known, highly competitive universities in the area], why in the world would you want to be like them? Students who want that can go to those places. This is a place that people can find themselves; where late-bloomers can bloom. When you start doing this other stuff, you lose that identity.

---

3. In 1998-99, the first year of the new tenure policy, all nine candidates successfully earned tenure.

An Employment Policy Just Like Tenure

The old employment policy was, according to many, very much like tenure. As expressed by the chairman of the board:

> We had a system in place in which removing faculty was extraordinary difficult. The notion that the alternative to tenure is employees-at-will I find simply ludicrous. Even schools that have rolling contracts have all sorts of problems with nonrenewal of contracts. . . . I came to see [the non-probationary status system] in much the same way as traditional tenure. In my point of view, I grew more and more convinced that we had a terrible system. The movement to tenure—if we could craft it our way as opposed to simply adopting the AAUP model—gave us the opportunity to substantially improve our faculty employment processes.

Others described the previous system as "equivalent to tenure" and "a de facto tenure system." "If the system resembled tenure," asked on faculty leader, "why not develop it into something that was academically recognized?"

Ironically, now that Lakeview faculty have tenure, several commentators believe that faculty have less security and protection than they did under a non-tenure system. Trustee Cerra maintained that "faculty have less protection now than they had before. . . . It is far clearer now what we can do and how we can do it. It was far more uncertain [under the probationary/non-probationary system] what rights we [the trustees] had [to dismiss faculty.] We were extraordinarily vulnerable to try to do something and then be tied up in litigation." While the vast majority of faculty supported the move to tenure, one faculty dissenter concurred with the board chair, saying, "After you were here and moved to non-probationary status, you had it made. The standards were not nearly as high as they are now. . . . [Faculty] traded in a golden goose for a crow."

Faculty Evaluation

Tenure was intended, according to the board chair, "to increase the rigor of the process by which people move into a protected employment category. We had a process in the past in which that movement to non-probationary status was essentially a departmental issue. Now, we've created an All-College Tenure Committee that [is] . . . a way to deal with lax departmental standards." An administrator agreed, saying that the college administration embraced the tenure proposal because "the rigor of the evaluative process is probably greater" under tenure. In addition, Chairman Cerra said post-tenure review was a "mechanism to put pressure on the lazy or incompetent," not as a way to fire them, but "to make them go through a difficult process of explaining themselves."

Faculty Recruitment

Many interviewees mentioned issues of faculty recruitment as a "problem" to be solved by tenure; now that faculty have "stature," it increases the potential for recruiting strong faculty. The academic dean reported, "Tenure has allowed us to attract people who otherwise might not have come to Lakeview." But, this benefit is a double-edged sword. The provost expressed concern that the non-traditional faculty who come out of industry and the arts rather than academe may suffer because of the tenure system. "I didn't want to lose those people who often are entirely successful teachers and role-models . . . I have no evidence so far that it's making it more difficult to recruit non-traditional faculty. Conversely, I don't have a lot of evidence that it's making it easier to get traditional faculty. The jury's out on that one."

AN ANALYSIS OF THE PROCESS OF CHANGE

Lakeview College's movement from a system of one-year contracts to a tenure policy, in some ways, is the mirror image of Scott College. Participants in both cases reported that the underlying struggle was about power. Scott's story of change involved a strong leader taking power and authority away from the faculty; the abolition of tenure was part of a larger effort to curtail shared governance and increase faculty "accountability." Lakeview's story is the opposite. Here, a president sympathetic to norms of shared governance and tenure allied with faculty who wanted to increase their status in addition to their voice in governance and in recruitment and retention of their peers. This new dominant coalition changed the distribution of authority in the college. Tenure was a means to share power more broadly among faculty, department chairs, and the administration.

Tenure was also a signal and a symbol. While a power framework might explain part of the Lakeview case, power theories rely on intentionality and strategic purposefulness of organizational participants (Pfeffer, 1981). But Lakeview's movement to tenure was as much symbolic as substantive, driven by intentionality but also by ambiguity of purpose. The change to tenure was important for what it expressed as well as for what it produced (Bolman & Deal, 1991). This analysis, therefore, draws on both power theory (Pfeffer, 1981) but also on the symbolic frame of organizational understanding (Bolman & Deal, 1991; Cohen & March, 1986) to illuminate the circumstances and conditions by which the change to tenure unfolded.

Power as a Framework for Change

Issues of power and control are evident at Lakeview. For much of its modern history, prior to the arrival of President Murin, decision-making power and authority rested with the department chairs and the administration, not with the faculty. A number of power-related characteristics describe the organizational milieu at Lakeview *prior to the change* in faculty employment policy:

Dependence

Emerson (1962) and Pfeffer (1981) stated that power results from one party having control over what another party wants or needs. At Lakeview, for many years, chairs had near-total authority in determining faculty members' promotion to non-probationary status. While the evaluation policy articulated a role for faculty members in the department, interviewees reported that, in practice, such a role was often negligible. Because faculty were so dependent on the chair for a favorable recommendation, several participants described faculty behavior as sycophantic and cowardly.

Informal Decision Making and Centralized Authority

In the early stages of Lakeview's modern incarnation as an arts and communications college, the administration maintained informal policies and a small staff. Because policies were informal and oral, faculty members regularly made individual deals (e.g. salary review). This practice kept power in the hands of those who controlled individual negotiations—the president and provost. In addition, individual administrators had decision-making authority over a significant number of areas. Both outcomes greatly enhanced administrative power in the organization. While President Lynch obviously exemplified this phenomenon, so too did Provost Cooper, who had wide discretionary authority over finances, security, maintenance, and building and grounds. Furthermore, as President Murin discovered upon his arrival, "Mark didn't tend to put things in writing, so a lot of these things were in his head." Murin's mandate from the board was to provide more administrative structure to the institution to reduce the power and authority of any one person.

Control over the Decision Process

"It is possible for a social actor within the organization to have power because of his or her ability to affect some part of the decision process" (Pfeffer, 1981, p. 115). Pfeffer further noted that one of the ways to affect the decision process is by "having laws, regulations, or pressure from some powerful actor imposed to impact the constraints and values used in the choice process" (p. 117). Kevin Lynch had this power to affect decision processes. The faculty vote on academic rank is an example of how Lynch used "laws, regulation, or pressure" to influence a seemingly democratic process. In 1990, when faculty voted on the Faculty Rank Committee's proposal, President Lynch, who was not an advocate of rank and tenure, set a high threshold for passage of the proposal. Not only did two-thirds of faculty need to approve the measure, but absentees and abstentions were counted as "nays." A majority of the faculty, in fact, voted to adopt rank, but the proposal did not reach the super-majority that Lynch required.

For many years, academic administrators had the balance of power at Lakeview—they garnered the dependence of faculty, made decisions informally, and had the ability to control the decision process. By the late 1990s, however, power had dissipated—faculty shared leadership positions in the campus governance system with administrators and chairs. The implementation of tenure contributed to this shift. But how was power transferred from the administration and chairs to the faculty, especially without outward signs of political unrest? Several conditions enabled the power dynamics to change in the organization.

A Shift in Presidential Leadership

The most significant circumstance that contributed to the college's cultural shift generally and the move to tenure specifically was the appointment of a new president in 1992. For 25 years, Kevin Lynch, Lakeview's "founding father," was at the helm. When he took control over the college in 1965, it was very much like a family business; he "inherited" the presidency from his father. In this small organization, Lynch preferred an informal structure that he could control. Observers said the college was "very unsystematic" and "loose in the way things were administered." Lynch "ran everything" and did not support academic rank or tenure.

Lynch retired because the college became too big to control. Lynch's entrepreneurial formula for Lakeview worked so well that it grew beyond his management capabilities. As one faculty member who was close to the former president conveyed, President Lynch recognized that the model of strong, centralized, autocratic management was no longer viable:

> When the former president was getting ready to retire, he said to me, "This place is getting too big. I used to run this institution out of my back pocket. I can no longer do that. There are a lot of different people around, different ideas. It's time for me to go." I think that was an indication of a huge change in the institution. He knew that more administrators were going to be needed. He hated committees. He realized that, with this kind of growth, [greater participation in governance and decision making] was going to happen. . . .

Perhaps with the growth, internal changes need to happen. But [the president's] desire was not to participate in those changes.

President Lynch decided to step down rather change his decision-making style. The board of trustees searched for a new president who could "guide the College into a more structured and contemporary institution" (Presidential speech, 1998).

Craig Murin was that different type of leader. He spent much of his career in academe as a college president, chancellor, provost, and faculty member. He was socialized in traditional academic settings that emphasized shared governance and participatory decision making. Because he was "a believer in the sharing of power," he pushed the faculty to claim a more traditional role in campus decision making. He overhauled the College Council, "providing much greater faculty participation in governance" (Presidential speech, 1998). Likewise, he had "sympathy" for academic tenure. "Philosophically, I have always favored tenure in higher education" (Presidential speech, 1998). When faculty leaders approached him about supporting a proposal for academic tenure and rank, therefore, he was amenable to it—unlike his predecessor.

One might wonder why a president would want to introduce shared governance and academic tenure to a college, thereby limiting the power of the administration. There are several explanations. First, Murin was a president and provost at institutions with tenure. Like Kelly at Scott College, Murin "learned" from his previous and successful experience as a leader on a campus with tenure, even though there could have been ambiguity in the inferences he drew from those experiences (Cohen & March, 1986). Based on his prior experience, he believed that autocratic, centralized power, as practiced by his predecessor, was not respected in higher education and would not lead to a respected president. Instead, he embraced a view of consultative leadership and participatory governance. Second, his experiences led him to believe that "good" institutions offer tenure. For Murin, the lack of tenure at Lakeview was too informal, did not convey adequate prestige, and signaled an institution outside the mainstream. Third, no doubt he was aware that the most respected institutions in American higher education offer tenure. By introducing tenure to Lakeview, not only did he raise the stature of the college but he elevated his own professional stature as well. He would be a leader of a tenure-granting institution rather than a "backwards" college with contracts.

An Increasing Schism of Faculty

Another condition that enabled power to shift from chairs to faculty was the increasing demand of a group of professors for a more traditional voice in decision making. Power theory posits that conflict is reduced when par-

Lakeview College 117

ticipants' backgrounds and values are similar to each other (Pfeffer, 1981). In the Scott case, many faculty respected, or at least tolerated, the strong administrative management because prospective faculty who would be uncomfortable with the college's cultural and religious environment were screened out during the recruitment process, and new faculty were socialized to expect little voice in governance. In contrast, the Lakeview case involved a growing number of traditional faculty who were interested in shared governance and tenure, while administrators, chairs, and practitioner faculty remained content with the status quo. As this dichotomy widened, so too did the struggles for power within the faculty.

In its early years, Lakeview College recruited part-time practitioners. These faculty, like the chairs, came out of industry and the arts, where there was no norm of shared governance and no expectation of tenure. In fact, interviewees attribute the early success of the college, in part, to the chairs' entrepreneurial ability to quickly add a new course or revise curriculum without faculty involvement. As the college's enrollment burgeoned, Lakeview recruited full-time faculty, including those who came from traditional academic career paths. Over time, these faculty members gained a critical mass and began to question the college's governance and employment norms.

Changes in socialization also account for the differences among faculty in campus culture. Many of the early brand of faculty and administrators were anti-establishment, uninterested in traditional higher education "trappings" of tenure and rank—so much so that they prided themselves on the college's lack of accreditation. By the 1980s and 1990s, the views of these "revolutionaries" were not as dominant, Provost Cooper reported, because of "the change in popular culture and public culture." So, while the college's administration and faculty in the 1960s and 70s shared a similar anti-establishment world view, by the late 1980s, two different outlooks prevailed: one group of faculty represented the iconoclastic status quo, and the other expected the traditional practices of rank, tenure, and shared governance. The provost commented that "the newer side of faculty [who support academe's traditional expectations and beliefs] kept getting larger and larger, and the other side [the anti-establishment, radical faculty] kept shrinking and shrinking." Conflict between the two factions grew—witness the polarized vote over academic rank in the late 1980s.

Realignment of the Dominant Coalition

These first two factors—a change in presidential leadership and an increasingly traditional faculty—coalesced at a particular point in time. The faculty's work on rank and tenure, previously derailed by President Lynch, was now supported by Murin. The college, in effect, went through a change of political parties. The dominant coalition of the faculty and President Murin replaced the former alliance among President Lynch, Provost Cooper, and the department chairs. Murin delegated many of Cooper's responsibilities to other staff members, reduced the number of chairs, and eliminated their permanent status. Now enfranchised, faculty worked to implement a tenure system, which codified their role, strengthened their power in governance, and brought Murin a degree of professional stature that he lacked before Lakeview had tenure.

Power theory not only accounts for the historical changes that laid the groundwork for the change to tenure; it also explains, in part, how the college adopted tenure. For example, the ad-hoc board committee on tenure played a crucial role in the process of moving from one-year contracts to tenure. Chairman Cerra used "an old and time-honored [political] strategy" (Pfeffer, 1981, p. 166) of co-optation in appointing individuals to that committee.[4] "Co-optation involves giving a representative of the organization or subunit whose support is sought a position on a board, committee, or other body of the unit seeking the support" (Pfeffer, 1981, p. 166). Cerra specifically co-opted two groups of board members. First, he appointed trustees who were widely respected by the board as a whole. Their informal influence and authority gave legitimacy to the committee's work and made it difficult for less-admired members of the board to disagree with the committee's conclusions. Second, Cerra tapped several members who were skeptics of tenure. If they changed their opinion of tenure (which, in fact, they did), Cerra believed that they would be persuasive in convincing other skeptics. This political strategy worked.

The board committee invoked another political device by developing expertise in tenure policies. Pfeffer (1981) explained that "at each stage in the decision making process, the definition of constraints and preferences, development of alternatives, and gathering of information about those alternatives, there is a presumed legitimacy in place" (p. 121). The board committee acquired legitimacy with other trustees because it carefully researched and studied the issue of tenure. Cerra explained, "when people [on the full board] asked questions [to the committee], it helped that the questions all had answers." So, even if board members disagreed with the move to tenure, they would have found it difficult to contest the committee's findings. "To challenge the process . . . is to openly express distrust of the process and those actors involved in the process. . . . This fact leaves those in the position to define and develop information about alternatives with enormous power" (Pfeffer, 1981, p. 121). Because the ad-hoc board committee had such power, it is not surprising that the board as a whole unanimously endorsed the committee's tenure proposal. Cerra observed,

---

4. Cohen and March (1986) referred to this strategy as opposition participation (p. 209).

"Overwhelming information and study sometimes can have an intimidating effect on those who don't agree with the point of view but don't have the resources or the information to argue with it."

The Symbolic Nature of Change

To understand how the process of change from contracts to tenure unfolded at Lakeview College, one must recognize the shifts of power in the organization: from an autocratic, centralized system of authority and governance to a norm of inclusiveness and participation. This shift happened because the college hired a new president who felt at home with shared governance and because an increasingly large contingent of the faculty desired a traditional role in decision making.

Another component to Lakeview's shift in faculty employment policy involves a symbolic framework, which focuses on "images, drama, magic, and sometimes even luck or the supernatural" to explain organizations and organizational change (Bolman & Deal, 1991, p. 10). Complex organizations "are full of questions that cannot be answered, problems that cannot be solved, and events that cannot be understood or managed. Whenever that is the case, humans will create and use symbols to bring meaning out of chaos, clarity out of confusion, and predictability out of mystery" (Bolman & Deal, 1991, p. 253). This framework explains the move to tenure in terms of metaphor, symbol, and ceremony. The change process at Lakeview is, in part, a tale of a college "growing up," or, as one faculty member described, of transitioning from the first generation of visionary founders, to the second generation of disciples, to the third generation of traditional academics. In its recent history, then, Lakeview experienced three stages of development. Each period has a different dominant organizational metaphor.

The Lynch Presidency: The Founding Father and the Ma-and-Pa Store

During the Lynch presidency, the college developed many characteristics that defined the institution for nearly 30 years. Among the dominant organizational "myths" was an emphasis on loose structure, strong administrative decision making, entrepreneurial chair leadership, and practitioner faculty who had no role in governance. At that point, Kevin Lynch and his wife were the only full-time employees. A faculty member described "an evolution of this college from a Ma-and-Pa store to an academic institution.... Ma and Pa were running the store and the kids were told what to do. The kids were the faculty." Therefore, an appropriate metaphor of organizational life for this period is the "Ma-and-Pa store." President Lynch himself was a symbol of the institution, a visionary leader who grew the college on his own terms, without much need for bureaucratic structure, traditional academic practices, or conformity with the greater higher education community. Another symbol of the organization during this stage is the future provost wrapped in a Vietnam flag delivering the valedictory speech. The chief academic officer—like most of the faculty for many years—was a revolutionary, not a traditionalist. Signs of normalcy for most higher education institutions—accreditation, rank, tenure, shared governance—were, at Lakeview, symbols of the stagnant status quo. The college rejected those symbols.

The Transitional Period: Adolescence

As the institution grew and matured, it encountered what researchers have called an "inexorable push toward homogenization," or isomorphism (DiMaggio & Powell, 1991, p. 64). Peer pressure would also be an apt description. According to isomorphism theory, institutions change to resemble other organizations for several reasons. First, organizational actors are subject to the *norms of professionalization.* For example, many faculty and administrators in higher education are socialized during their graduate training to accept that characteristics such as shared governance and tenure are normative. As more traditional faculty members came to Lakeview—less interested in being iconoclastic, more aware of the higher education world beyond the college—they were concerned about their status with their peers at other institutions, where rank and tenure are symbols of professional legitimacy. A professor noted that faculty viewed themselves as "second-class academic citizens because they didn't have these things." This group of professors reached a critical mass by the late 1980s and began to advocate for a more typical faculty employment policy. Even the name of their committee signaled their desire for recognition. As a former LACFAC president said, "By calling it the Committee on Faculty Status, that gave us status to begin with."

Second, colleges *mimic* well-known, established higher education institutions. Faculty, trustees and the new president wanted to, as a professor described, "make the college come of age, to take the college into a mature stage of academic life." Faculty felt that tenure would signal to peers the college's maturation. President Murin agreed: "I thought [that] creating a tenure system would be a good sign of the maturity of the college." The college would shed its anti-establishment past and emulate other successful higher education institutions.

Tenure: A New Symbol for Lakeview

Much like a teenage debutante, the "mature" Lakeview College had its debut with the adoption of tenure in 1997. The move to tenure was a signal to internal and external constituencies of the college's rite-of-passage.

Lakeview reinvented its predominant organizational myth; the dominant metaphor shifted from rebel to conformist. Tenure signaled that the college was different than before, even if, substantively, not much had changed in how faculty were appointed and retained.

While participants may agree that tenure was a symbol of a new era, they do not agree on the interpretation of that symbol. This ambiguity (Cohen and March, 1986) was exemplified by the disparate comments of administrators, faculty, and board members. President Murin advocated the shift to tenure as a sign of institutional maturity—a baptism into the community of the faithful. Faculty viewed tenure as a means of increasing their status in the profession—an initiation into the priesthood of professional legitimacy. But they also envisioned tenure as a means of enhancing their influence in the institution. Tenure was a proxy for power. Trustee Cerra, however, did not frame the change to tenure in terms of power. Instead, he believed that tenure was a symbol of improved faculty quality, not through a substantive outcome of higher turnover rates, but through the "ceremony" of post-tenure review, which demonstrated that the trustees were seriously attending to potentially unproductive faculty members.

In a symbolic system, these participants attributed diverse meanings to tenure, which allowed them to agree on tenure as a solution to their own particular problem. Tenure was itself a metaphor. For President Murin, tenure was prestige and normalcy. For faculty members, tenure was power and status. For trustees, tenure was quality control. The ambiguity of purpose in the change process allowed these various players to adopt a new organizational metaphor without having to agree on its meaning.

Summary: Integrating the Two Frameworks of Change

Lakeview's alteration in faculty employment policy is part of a broader story about a shift in power relations from a centralized autocracy to a participatory collegium. The Lakeview case is also about the symbolic meaning of tenure in an institution undergoing transition. These two frameworks can be integrated when viewed along a continuum of time. (See figure 5.1.) Power theory resonates well when Lakeview is examined at two different moments in time. During the "Autocracy Period" of President Lynch, decision-making influence was limited to only several people. Nontraditional faculty had little interest in governance. Department chairs—strong "third nodes" in the organization—were entrepreneurs subject to few rules or constraints. During the "Normative Period" of President Murin, chairs lost power, faculty's representation in the College Council grew, and the norm of governance became open, shared, and inclusive. Lakeview embraced the normative governance model of higher education. Part of this new model involved academic tenure.

The symbolic frame supports this view of organizational change when each period is examined through its dominant organizational myth or metaphor. During Lynch's presidency, the dominant metaphors were the Ma-and-Pa store, faculty-as-kids, and nonconformity. New presidential leadership, an increasing cadre of traditional faculty, and a realigned dominant coalition contributed to a transitional period when the goals of the college (or the operational metaphor) changed. In this new period, tenure was a symbol of institutional maturity, coming-of-age, faculty quality, status, professionalism, and power.

FIGURE 5.1

Time

Autocracy
President: Lynch, the founding father
Faculty: Kids, no participation in governance
Strong "third node" department chairs
Metaphors: Ma-and-Pa Store, revolutionaries, iconoclasts
Symbol: Future provost wrapped in Vietnam flag

Transition
Shift in presidential leadership
Bifurcation of faculty
Realignment of dominant coalition
Isomorphic pressure for status and conformity

Normative Governance
President: Murin, career academic, believer in shared governance
Faculty: Professionals, participation in governance
Metaphor: academic tenure, conformist
Symbols: All-College Tenure Committee

EXHIBIT 5.1

225.4 Lakeview College Council (LCC)

The Lakeview College Council is the principal advisory group drawn from the College community that recommends to the president on a broad range of policy issues concerning College matters with the expectation of a timely response. The membership of the Council is composed as follows:

Faculty: one faculty member from each department, totaling sixteen (16) members; four (4) faculty members elected at large; the elected president of the CCFO during her/his term of office; one (1) faculty (full or part-time) elected from graduate-only departments; one (1) faculty (full or part-time) elected from course offering, non-departmental programs within the college; two (2) part-time faculty;

Six (6) administrators comprised of the Provost, the Academic Dean, the Dean of the Graduate School, the Vice-President/Finance, the Dean of Students, and the Director of the Library;

Six (6) Chairs plus the Chair of the Chairpersons' Council;

Students, including two (2) undergraduate students and one (1) graduate student;

Three (3) members selected from full-time employees of the College, appointed by the President; and two (2) staff elected by the Staff.

The total number of members of the Council at no time includes more than 46 members.
All full-time faculty members are elected for three-year terms and may be re-elected to a second term. Chairs are elected for three-year terms with the same proviso expect for the Chair of the Chairperson's Council, whose term is one year unless re-elected for a second term. All members may serve additional terms after a hiatus of one year following six years on the Council. Departmental faculty representatives are supposed to report decisions of the Council regularly to their departments.

Any member of the College community may submit agenda items in writing to the Executive Committee of the Council for its consideration.

The Council meets monthly from October until June except for February.

CHAPTER 6
Accomac College

ACCOMAC COLLEGE, A PUBLIC LIBERAL ARTS INSTITUTION OF 1,600 students, abolished tenure in 1971, four years after becoming a full-fledged baccalaureate college. Tenured faculty had the option of retaining that status, while new faculty were placed on a multi-year contract system. In 1993, Accomac reinstated tenure.

A SHORT HISTORY

Accomac College has the longest history of the institutions in this study. Nevertheless, it too is a newcomer to higher education as a four-year college. Accomac was founded in 1840 as a state-sponsored, publicly supported, nonsectarian "female seminary" (girls' boarding high school) with an independent board of trustees. It became the state's first junior college in 1927, "affording students the unique opportunity to complete four years of high school and two years of college at the same institution" (College Catalog, p. 10). The State Commission on Higher Education recommended the institution for dissolution in 1947, but "a large public outcry ... not only saved the school but created the momentum for renaming it Accomac Seminary Junior College (1949) and its eventual evolution into a four-year baccalaureate college (1967)" (College catalog, p. 10). The institution began admitting male students in the 1940s.

The school-then-college has had stable leadership throughout the 20th century. From 1900 to 1996, Accomac had only five presidents. Current long-time faculty recalled the infamy of Roderick Hopper, the first male president, who served from 1969 to 1981. Under Hopper's leadership, the institution embraced what he labeled the "new higher education of the 70s," which included experimental educational initiatives such as eliminating grades and abolishing academic tenure. A professor hired in 1969 explained, "In the early 1970s, the college perceived itself as experimental and moving in new directions. I guess getting rid of the old traditional tenure system was part of where they were going." A colleague said, "[President Hopper] was a '60's person.' He brought in a large group of young faculty who wanted to change everything.... In spring 1971, there was a faculty vote against tenure. When we came back from summer vacation [in 1971], the board of trustees had abolished tenure."

According to multiple sources, Hopper was mercurial, authoritarian, arbitrary, and capricious. He was "fast and loose" with faculty employment policies, hiring several faculty with tenure after it was officially eliminated. Professors also recalled occasions when he would ignore faculty recommendations for contract renewal, dismissing faculty "because he didn't like them." Faculty voted no confidence in Hopper in 1974, an indictment which he survived. He was eventually forced to resign in 1981 after damaging publicity over a sexual affair. A faculty member summarized opinions on Hopper by saying, "Never in my life have I met a man who engendered such strong negative emotions."

The next president, Duane Robinson, who served from 1983 to 1996, was very interested in building the reputation of the college as a liberal arts institution and "regularizing" the college. After six years as president, Robinson indicated to faculty leaders that he was willing to support a move back to tenure. After a lengthy process, the board of trustees adopted the new faculty employment system in June 1993.

At the time tenure was reinstated, Accomac College served 1,519 undergraduate students and employed 104 full-time faculty. According to 1998 figures, the student-faculty ratio was 14:1, 95 percent of the faculty had earned doctoral or terminal degrees, and the college's endowment stood at $12.5 million.

PROMINENT CHARACTERISTICS

Within only several hours of my site visit to Accomac, two important characteristics emerged. First, the campus "looked" like a private college. Second, campus constituents were very proud of the college's recent and successful rise in national scope and reputation.

Private College Atmosphere

Along the wooded country highway to Accomac Village, the rural historic site of the college, the dense trees suddenly gave way to the grand view of the majestic Elizabeth River. Sailboats darted through the chop toward the campus's boathouse. Accomac's 275-acre campus lies along a horseshoe bend of the river, and the college takes full advantage of its recreational and academic resources:

> The College beach, boathouse, dock, and fleet of watercraft provide a resource for recreation and learning that is virtually unmatched nationwide. The campus is located on a broad, baylike bend of the Elizabeth River—an ideal spot for sailing, kayaking, and canoeing. The College fleet includes numerous small craft and canoes, in addition to several larger off-shore racing and cruising boats. The College counts four All-American sailors and one Olympic silver medallist among its alumni. The riverfront is a psychological as well as physical point of reference for the Accomac community: a favorite place for walks, picnics, conversations, relaxed studying, and sunset watching. (College Catalog, p. 6)

The college's Federal-style buildings of red brick and white columns and its verdant lawns blend neatly with the littoral surroundings. The pastoral of red brick, green grass, and blue sea and sky is idyllic, Romantic, classically *collegiate*. Accomac looked like what a small *private* college is supposed to look like.

That is the effect that the college hopes to achieve. Accomac prides itself on its private, "clubby" feel. Its catalog reads,

> The State ... has set [Accomac] apart; unlike the other state colleges and universities, Accomac offers an undergraduate liberal arts education and small-college experience of the kind more commonly found at fine private colleges. Accomac shares the hallmarks of private institutions: an outstanding faculty, talented students, high academic standards, a challenging curriculum, a sense of community, and a spirit of intellectual inquiry.

Accomac shares other attributes with small private liberal arts colleges. Its average class size is 19, and it is primarily residential—70 percent of full-time students live on campus, the highest percentage of all public higher education institutions in the state. When interviewees compared Accomac to other colleges, they routinely identified respected private institutions such as Swarthmore, Franklin & Marshall, Hamilton, and Davidson. This is not to say, however, that Accomac hides from its public status. In fact, the college "is committed to the ideal of public education—affordable, accessible, thriving on the diversity of the state's citizens" (College Catalog, p. 4). Rather, the traditional, selective, prestigious liberal arts colleges to which Accomac aspires are private.

Accomac achieves its "private" feel, in part, because of its semi-autonomy from the state. In 1992, the state legislature granted the college extensive freedom from state oversight. Unlike other public higher education institutions, Accomac's board of trustees was given control to manage the College's property and assets, including accepting and spending gifts and endowment money, establishing capital and operating budgets, borrowing money, and establishing procurement procedures. It also was given authority to establish a College personnel system separate from that governing all other state employees. The board of trustees continues to be under the oversight of the [state] higher education commission on such matters as the mission of the College, review and approval of academic programs, and fiscal accountability. (1994 Reaccreditation Self-Study, p. 6)

A media account of the change summarized the effect of the 1992 legislation: "Campus leaders say Accomac now operates more like a private college because officials can plan with greater predictability than in the past."

Rise in Prominence

Many faculty, administrators, and trustees spoke with pride about Accomac's increasing national recognition, student selectivity, and prominence. When President Robinson arrived in 1983, "the College embarked on an ambitious plan to increase state support for the institution, to raise the quality and improve the diversity of the student body, to recruit nationally a faculty committed to the teacher/scholar model of higher education, and to improve the physical plant" (College Reaccreditation Self-Study, 1994, p. 5). This endeavor resulted in the *Campaign for National Prominence*, launched in 1990, which was intended to increase the size of the faculty, lower the student-faculty ratio, and improve the college's academic facilities. By several measures, the campaign worked. The number of full-time faculty grew from 72 in 1983 to 103 in 1993. Eighteen percent of full-time faculty were members of racial minorities in 1993, compared to eight percent in 1983. The student-faculty ratio declined from 16:1 in the late 1980s to 14:1 in 1993. Accomac was cited regularly in *U.S. News and World Report* in the mid- to late-1990s as one of the top ten regional liberal arts colleges in the nation, and received recognition by *Money* magazine in the late 1990s as one of the top ten "best buys" in the country among both public and private institutions.

In 1992, in addition to granting the college fiscal independence, the state legislature designated Accomac a "public honors college" with the intention of signaling the college's quality and prestige. The two actions of the legislature—fiscal autonomy and the "honors college" appellation—were integrally linked. The state secretary of higher education said that the legislation was to place "the College in the first rank of public liberal arts colleges in the United States. Armed with new freedom of operation and new incentives, Accomac will be able to continue its march toward national prominence" (quoted in 1994 Reaccreditation Self-Study, p. 6).

IMPORTANT CONSTITUENCIES
Board of Trustees

Accomac is one of two public colleges in the state higher education system with an independent governing board. (A board of regents governs the other state-supported institutions.) The governor officially appoints 23 of the 25 members of the board, although they are cultivated and nominated by the college itself.[1] Trustees are appointed for no more than two six-year terms. One board member is a current Accomac student, who serves a one-year term. In contrast to the two colleges in this study that eliminated tenure, Accomac's board is not comprised of just "business people." Of the 21 board members listed in the 1998 college catalog, nine came from the corporate world. Others included two members of Congress, a retired college president, a retired governor, a retired commander of NATO, a president of a nonprofit organization, a government official, two attorneys, and three private citizens.

Interviewees did not characterize the Accomac board as "anti-tenure." One administrator noted, "It's not as though the board saw the wisdom in [moving back to tenure] as self-evident," but most commentators asserted that the board was open to the suggestion. Interviewees attributed this positive tenor to various factors. First, many people stated that the board was supportive of President Robinson's initiatives and, as will be discussed below, he advocated the reinstatement of tenure in the early 1990s. A professor said, "Robinson had the board in his pocket . . . The board was so grateful to Duane for turning this place around and putting it on the map that it would have done anything he said." A trustee concurred: "When you have a president who did as much as Duane Robinson, it is very hard to say no to him. Duane was on a roll. He was doing great things." Second, observers noted that the chairman of the board, Steven Connallon, a former president of a large research university, was "the most academically knowledgeable person [on the board] and supported the president's argument [for moving back to tenure.]"

The Administration

Two administrators played prominent roles in the change in faculty employment policies. As president, Duane Robinson was a well-respected leader. Many faculty and administrators identified Robinson as the force

---

1. The other two members of the board are the president of the alumni association and president of the Accomac Village association.

behind the college's improvement in the 1980s and 1990s. An administrator said, "His vision was shared to a certain extent, but he was the prime pusher. He felt that if you're going to become a first-rate liberal arts institution, along the lines of the privates, with the same student-faculty ratio and traditional attitude toward education, you probably ought to be like them in most respects."

The other important administrator in the change process was the provost, Paul Longo. Longo came to Accomac in January 1991 from a private college in New York, where he had been dean of faculty. Longo reported that Robinson hired him because "he was looking for someone with experience at a highly selective private liberal arts college to try to bring that aura as well as policies to bear on this institution." A faculty member noted that the college brought in Longo "to raise standards" and that he was "at least sympathetic to the idea" of instituting a tenure system. Longo became the point person in the administration for negotiating the tenure issue with faculty.

Faculty

During my interviews, professors universally described current faculty as having "incredible power" and "tremendous influence" in curriculum and policy issues at the college: "If we want something and pursue things in a skillful way, we can, by and large, get it." But long-time faculty also noted that, for an extended period, they were subject to the whims of President Hopper. As a result, faculty still are "very suspicious of administrators acting in an arbitrary way," said Provost Longo. "People who have been around for 25 or 30 years remember things." A professor hired in 1982 (after Hopper departed) observed that there was a lingering uneasiness with administrators because of "being run over rough-shod by President Hopper. That still is a dominant force in the psyche of the faculty here, which is interesting because we're talking about only one-fifth or one-fourth of the faculty who were here then."

Faculty governance reflects that concern. A professor explained that the faculty constitution was written the year after Hopper left: "We're all ready for him if he ever comes back." Faculty governance operates on two levels: the Faculty Senate and the faculty as a whole. The Faculty Senate, the "executive committee of the Faculty" (Faculty Handbook, 1994, p. 47), is composed of the chairpersons of the four academic divisions, four elected faculty members, and the provost, *ex officio*. The president of the senate is elected by the faculty at large. "In matters of minor importance, the Senate may act for the Faculty" (Faculty Handbook, 1994, p. 51). However, all matters of "major importance" must be brought to the facul-

Accomac College 131

ty as a whole. The Faculty bylaws recognize that the board of trustees has final decision-making authority, but stipulate that

> On matters that are the primary responsibility of the Faculty, the power of review or final decision lodged in the Board of Trustees or delegated by it to the President of the College shall be exercised adversely only in exceptional circumstances, and for reasons communicated to the Faculty. (Faculty Handbook 1994, p. 46)

The faculty handbook also includes a process for faculty to appeal decisions made by the president directly to the board of trustees:

> When the Faculty recommendation has been formulated, the Provost will either act upon the recommendation or recommend a course of action to the President. The President, in turn, may either act upon the Provost's recommendation or recommend a course of action to the Board of Trustees. Actions or recommendations of the Provost which are adverse to the Faculty's recommendation may be appealed by the Faculty Senate to the President; actions or recommendations of the President which are adverse to the Faculty's recommendation may be appealed to the Board of Trustees. (Faculty Handbook 1994, p. 12)

THE PROCESS OF CHANGE IN FACULTY EMPLOYMENT POLICIES
Multi-year contracts and "critical review"

Accomac originally implemented an academic tenure system in 1968, soon after the college achieved baccalaureate status. The Accomac board of trustees voted to stop offering tenure as the college's faculty appointment policy in July 1971. Tenured and tenure-track faculty members retained that status, although the new policy gave tenured faculty members the "option" of waiving their tenured status:

> Faculty members whose first full-time contractual services in the College commenced prior to July 1, 1971, shall be given the opportunity to select contractual arrangements . . . without tenure. To exercise this option, they should, in writing, inform the President of the College concerning their choice and should specifically waive all benefits under the terms of their earlier contracts, including the right to tenure. (1971 Regulations and Procedures Governing Academic Freedom and Responsibility, p. 4)

The college placed new faculty on a multi-year contract system. Faculty were hired on a two-year contract, then earned a three-year contract. After the fifth year, they moved to renewable five-year contracts. According to a faculty member, "There was simply a series of contracts—if you were doing well, you could presume that you could stay, but there was no protection in the bylaws."

At the beginning of the 1974–75 academic year, 13 of 62 faculty members (21 percent) had tenure. Those faculty who remained on the tenure-track in 1971 had worked through the system by 1974, so that no new recommendations for tenure were expected. In 1975, the college entertained the idea of bringing back a tenure system, a move supported by the president, who, according to a professor, "tried to redeem himself" after the 1974 faculty vote of no-confidence. At its spring 1975 meeting, the Academic Affairs Committee of the board of trustees "asked the administration to propose a plan for awarding tenure to additional faculty members in the future" (memo from provost, March 11, 1975). The administration (not the faculty) developed a proposal, including the following principles:

1. Tenure would be awarded selectively. "Tenure would not be automatic, as it is in some public school systems" (memo from provost, March 11, 1975).
2. A tenure quota: "an upper limit of approximately 50% of the total full-time faculty of the college may be tenured at one time. The same limit applies to the number of tenured faulty within divisions" (Regulations and Procedures document, 1975).
3. The proposal also stipulated a "periodic review" process: "The Coordinating and Review Committee must every five years review a tenured faculty member's performance in regard to the criteria for possible dismissal . . ." (Regulations and Procedures document, 1975). This provision resulted from "the widespread criticism of the tenure system as allowing a relaxation of professional effort after a faculty member is awarded tenure" (memo from provost, March, 11, 1975).

Faculty rejected the tenure proposal, according to a professor, because of the periodic review provision: "The faculty felt that was contrary to the principles of tenure."

Faculty employment policies remained unchanged until the early- to mid-1980s. As President Robinson articulated his desire to increase the quality of the college, faculty became worried that their past performance as teachers and scholars would not be adequate for continued renewal of their five-year contracts. Said a professor, "People became increasingly concerned that the evaluation process [under the contract system] would be used to 'up' the bar and that, if we had a series of contracts, the bar could be raised without protection." As a result, faculty pushed to amend the contract system in 1987 to include a "critical review." The policy instituted a contract sequence of two, two, three, and five years. Under the revised policy,

> The third evaluation for reappointment, which takes place in the faculty member's sixth year of service, constitutes a critical evaluation following which a faculty member appointed to a first five year contract may expect ... to continue in his or her academic position as long as a level of performance is maintained consistent with the then prevailing standards of the institution.

For critical-review cases, faculty were reviewed by a division committee, the division chair, and a college-wide evaluation committee composed of six faculty members, before being submitted to the provost and president for administrative review. Once the critical-review provision was adopted, the contract system, said a faculty member, "was called de facto tenure widely by both the faculty and the administration." A colleague commented, "Once you got your first five-year contract, the next contracts were a given."

Administrators were unhappy with the contract system because it did not promote either involuntary turnover or rigorous evaluations. Said a faculty member, "Once you passed critical review, I don't think anyone was ever asked to leave." A campus reaccreditation report indicated that, from 1983 to 1992, the college did not renew contracts for only five faculty members. Moreover, the president observed that "the contract system lacked rigorous examination." Provost Longo concurred:

> Everyone was just sailing through with no questions being raised. The first spring I was here, I turned down two out of four with no negative vote anywhere down the line.
>
> *This was still under the contract policy?*
>
> Yes, it was this "critical review." ... [The president and I concluded that] we wouldn't be able to deny reappointment to somebody after the first five-year contract. You might threaten them, so five years later you might be able to do something, but that assumes continuity in administration. It was hard enough to turn someone down who's been a part of the community for five years, let alone ten or 15 years. ...
>
> *Your sense was not only was there de facto tenure under the contract system, but that the evaluation during critical review was not that rigorous?*
>
> That's right. That first year happened to be a bad year. I struggled with which two I was going to "tenure."

Faculty who were hired under the contract system had mixed feelings about the lack of tenure. One professor said, "I came here not having gotten tenure at my previous institution, and the contract system was very attractive to me." A colleague saw both strengths and weaknesses: "I felt that it may have been more generous than a tenure system. On the other hand, I thought that the disadvantage was that it might be more capricious and subject to the whims of the administration." Others remarked that the faculty employment system was not a significant criterion in accepting Accomac's job offer:

> *When you first arrived, was it a concern that you were on a non-traditional employment arrangement?*
> I thought about it, but I guess I was naïve enough and excited enough to be getting an academic position that it wasn't a critical thing.

A colleague said, "I did not think the [lack of a traditional tenure system] was a concern. I frankly thought that I wouldn't stay very long. I had discussions with colleagues here who saw the good points of a contract system—that it had played in the faculty's favor in terms of retention and security."

The Signal for a Move Back to Tenure

Despite some professors' ambivalence about the contract system early in their careers at Accomac, the faculty as a whole was unhappy with the lack of tenure. "While no one's academic freedom was transgressed," said one professor, "there wasn't the commitment [to faculty] with contracts." Another said, "After we had the de facto system [critical review], people began to be concerned that we were half-way and we were caught in limbo." Yet another commented,

> There were always rumblings about re-establishing tenure. But it wasn't until the late 1980s that it began to get serious discussion. . . . There were other problems that needed to be addressed first. The school was in the red, and we had to address the questions of recruiting and retaining better students, and hiring faculty. There were a lot of problems that took an enormous amount of attention. Tenure was more on the back burner.

After Hopper departed in 1981, faculty leaders approached Duane Robinson early in his presidency about reintroducing tenure. At that point, however, the president said that he "was not about to take on the issue, especially without having a good feel for where the board stood." Several years later, the faculty senate president approached him again about considering a proposal for tenure, but he "dismissed the issue out of hand" because he didn't trust the senate leader. In 1989, when a different faculty leader broached the subject, Robinson signaled his willingness to move back to tenure. Robinson's reasons for his decision were complex:

[The lack of tenure] eroded faculty leadership. All academic initiatives in the first 10 years of my presidency came from the top. There was almost nothing from the faculty. The faculty were not willing to take on the administration. There was no dialogue taking place on academic matters.

Second, by the 9th or 10th year [of my presidency], we had accomplished a lot as an institution. The faculty had worked very, very hard. I thought the institution had to make a commitment to the faculty. Tenure was something they deserved. It was also appropriate because Accomac was an emerging institution. In 1983, it was just another public college. But year-by-year, we were competing more and more with the best liberal arts colleges in the country.

The fact that we did not have tenure hurt at the margins with young faculty. Now in my experience, most young faculty don't consider things like tenure when they are interviewing for jobs. But they could point to our employment arrangement as being a little uncertain, since other colleges had tenure and we did not.

Robinson did not make the decision to discuss a tenure proposal in isolation. He consulted with other administrators at the college as well as Board Chairman Connallon, who indicated he was open to the notion. "But," Robinson noted, "it wouldn't have gone forward if I hadn't wanted it to." A faculty member agreed with that assessment: "The faculty had been talking about [tenure] every year in some way or another. It probably wasn't a fight the faculty would have wanted to take on if there wasn't some signal that the president was willing to entertain a proposal."

The Ad-Hoc Committee on Tenure and Negotiations with the Provost

The faculty approved the formation of an ad-hoc Committee on Tenure at its monthly meeting in November 1990. That December, the faculty elected six members of the committee: one from each of the four divisions and two at-large members. All four division members had to have passed critical review or hold tenure; at least one at-large member had to be pre-critical review.[2] Michael DeMarco, the chair of the ad-hoc committee, explained that they had "a free-hand" to develop a proposal: "The faculty trusted us."

The faculty committee worked during the 1990–91 academic year to write a tenure proposal. When Provost Longo came to Accomac in January 1991, he realized that "faculty already expected that we would make at least an honest effort to return to tenure." In April 1991, the faculty voted to "receive the draft tenure document with the recommendation that the Ad Hoc Committee carry on conversations with the Faculty,

---

2. In 1990 there were 79 members of the full-time continuing faculty: nine were tenured (11 percent), 37 were past the critical review under the contract system (47 percent), and 33 (42 percent) were pre-critical review (i.e. junior faculty).

Administration, and other relevant interested parties." The faculty committee began a process of discussion, debate, and negotiation with the provost. "I was negotiating with them myself," Longo recalled. "It's kind of hard to deal with [the committee] when you're also trying to establish yourself as their leader. I didn't want to be too confrontational."

The ad-hoc committee and the provost spent the 1991–92 academic year in a process that committee members described as "acrimonious," "grueling," "lengthy, and "difficult." Committee Chairman DeMarco explained,

> The administration wanted certain things that the faculty did not find acceptable. We wanted a tenure system as close to the AAUP tenure guidelines as possible. The administration, of course, wanted clauses that would have made it easier to get rid of people with tenure and things like that.
>
> *How did those negotiations play out?*
>
> I would say both sides gave and both sides conceded to the other. I think, on balance, the faculty won.
>
> *How so?*
>
> We started out with a draft that I wrote and that was countered by a draft that the provost wrote. Then I wrote another compromise draft, and he objected to some things. So, we must have written at least a dozen drafts. We would have a meeting, we decided to make some changes, we came up with a new draft, there would be changes to that. It was very, very tedious.
>
> *In summary, though, you said that the faculty got more of what they were asking for?*
>
> In my judgment, that's correct.

Many committee members reported frustration with the provost in the negotiations. Said one, "We would all agree. The provost would agree. The faculty would agree. Then we would meet the next week to take on the next issue and the provost would say, 'I've been thinking it over, and I don't want to go along with what we agreed to last week.' And we would start from the bottom again."

The faculty and Provost Longo mentioned several areas in which there was considerable disagreement. Faculty and administration clashed over the amount of flexibility the college needed to adjust its programs in a changing environment. The administration wanted to include language in the document providing leeway for the college to convert tenured positions to term (non-tenured) positions in case of "serious financial or enrollment shortfalls, changing educational or curricular needs, or developments that create an undesirable tenure ratio." The faculty committee was skeptical about language that sounded like a tenure quota. Additionally, Longo wanted to make the tenure evaluation process more "comprehensive." One

Accomac College

of the ways he sought to do that was by using external commentators to review a tenure candidate's scholarship. Committee members adamantly opposed the idea, worried about the usefulness of external assessments at a college where tenure files are not confidential.[3]

The provost concurred with DeMarco's assessment that the administration conceded more than the faculty: "There was compromise, probably more so in the final stages on our part, because I don't think the president wanted to set back morale at that point." Later in the interview, he elaborated:

> We wondered [at the time] if we compromised too much.
> *Did the administration compromise too much?*
> Certainly in terms of getting some kind of outside look at scholarship. . . .
> *Why did you give in on that?*
> . . . We thought we had gone far enough down this road [that] for it to come to naught would have been a real downer for the faculty and a sign of divisiveness between administration and faculty that this place could ill-afford. We had gotten out on a limb in a sense.

By November 1992, the ad-hoc committee and the provost had reached consensus so that the tenure proposal could be presented to the whole faculty. Faculty accepted the document "in principle" by a vote of 47 to 1 (with four abstentions).

Negotiations with the Board of Trustees

During the early stages of the tenure discussions in 1991, President Robinson kept the board abreast of the negotiations. A trustee said that "there were misgivings [about tenure] on the part of some" trustees but "I wouldn't call it dissent. . . . [There were] concerns such as 'Can we do this?' 'Can we handle this?' 'Is there going to be ossification of the faculty with this?'" In fall 1992, as the ad-hoc committee and provost drafted their compromise proposal, the academic affairs committee of the board met twice with the faculty committee. The board committee was concerned about two areas: post-tenure review and merit pay. The chair of the board's academic affairs committee, James Bush, noted that trustees "did not want

---

3. These disagreements were eventually resolved in the following ways: The Faculty Handbook states that tenurable appointments will be made when institutional projections "show that it is *probable* that the appointment can lead to tenure primarily on the basis of meritorious performance. Occasionally, the institutional interest may require that a tenurable appointment be made if there is a reasonable *possibility*, rather than probability, that the appointment can lead to tenure" (p. 19. Emphasis added). Outside evaluations were made voluntary. The Faculty Handbook states, "The Faculty member may solicit written evaluations from other Faculty members at or outside the College" (p. 28).

to do anything that would tend to stultify or cause the faculty to lose their dynamic quality . . . Yes, we would move to tenure, but along with that would come a merit [pay] program." A faculty member recalled, "We had gotten to a particular point in the discussion where most things had been decided, but there were some sticking points, like post-tenure review. [The board and faculty committees] needed to get together as a conference to see if we could come to consensus."

After the tenure proposal was revised based on the faculty-trustee meetings, the faculty approved the document by a 50-to-6 margin in February 1993. The board gave final approval to the tenure policy in its June meeting. All faculty on five-year contracts were automatically given tenure, whether or not they had gone through a critical review.[4] Those faculty who were on two- or three-year contracts (i.e. junior faculty), were placed on a tenure-track. With the grandfathering provision, 65 percent of all faculty were tenured once the policy went into effect.

Both faculty and administrators noted that such a move was less than ideal. One professor remarked,

> We had to grandfather 50 faculty into tenure. They received no review. It was discussed briefly, but not very strongly, that everyone would have to go through a review. A large portion of the faculty hadn't even had a critical review. . . . It's dangerous to suddenly take a whole lump of people and create a tenure system, when they might be here another 30 or 40 years. So you create a division. Junior faculty feel like they're carrying the institution on their backs.

President Robinson agreed: "We had to tenure a number of people that we wouldn't have otherwise . . . I can think of three or four faculty members who got tenure who shouldn't have." But participants noted that granting tenure to long-time faculty was necessary for the proposal to be accepted. One faculty member of the ad-hoc tenure committee said: "It would have been highly unlikely that the proposal for tenure would pass the faculty if [a provision for an up-or-out review of all post-critical review faculty] had been part of it." Said another, "I don't know the solution to the [grandfathering] problem. It was the price we had to pay."

---

4. When the critical review process was implemented in 1987, those faculty who had been at the college eight or more years (i.e. those who had already received their second five-year contract) were considered to have automatically passed their critical review. Therefore, faculty who were hired without tenure prior to 1980 were grandfathered twice: first into the critical review process in 1987 and then into tenure in 1993.

REASONS FOR THE OVERHAUL IN POLICY

Interviewees consistently referred to several problems that the reinstatement of tenure was intended to solve:

Faculty Recruitment

By far, the most cited reason for shifting to a tenure policy was to improve faculty recruitment. Board Chairman Connallon said, "For some people that the college wanted to hire, the absence of a tenure system was discouraging." A professor posited, "Tenure is a good recruiting tool. I think we found that many good faculty didn't want to come to a place that didn't have tenure." A colleague emphatically agreed: "When we had a contract system, we really couldn't compete with the institutions we would have liked to compete with for the same faculty."

Interviewees said that the college did not have hard data to support the assertion that recruitment suffered under the contract system. "From my point of view," said a professor, "it's more anecdotal." Another concluded that "I'm sure that [the belief that the lack of tenure hurt recruitment] was impressionistic, but we also went though a number of hiring processes, and we would lose people. . . . You watch your candidates go to institutions with tenure and you draw some conclusions about that." A former department chair recalled, "It used to be a real turn-off when you would tell people that you don't have tenure. . . . You could noticeably see the faces drop when you'd say [that]." Provost Longo was more skeptical about the ability of tenure to improve recruitment:

> My sense is that there are other things on prospective faculty members' minds [during the hiring process]. . . . I'm not sure [tenure] would have changed the minds of a large percentage of the people we hired. It probably played a minor role in many people's minds and maybe a major one in a few. But, I wasn't convinced that it would make a major difference in our hiring ability. . . . To the extent that [prospective faculty members] are interviewing here and at Hamilton or Davidson, I'm not sure that the lack of tenure would have been the major factor [in their choice to go to a different college.]

Faculty Evaluation

Participants asserted that tenure would make the faculty evaluation process more rigorous. A professor maintained, "It's easier to say yes to someone under a contract system than a tenure system in those early contracts. . . . I think there was a shift in the psychology of the institution in how carefully those reviews were done, and how seriously they were taken. . . . People believe that the bar has been raised." According to the president,

"There was the understanding that the board would be tougher in their evaluation of faculty up for tenure and promotion."

Tenure did lead to a more rigorous evaluation system for new faculty members. The evaluation standards for junior faculty under the tenure policy were stricter than under the contract policy. Acceptable "professional activities" prior to 1993 included endeavors such as publications (without any stipulation of type or scope), "actively participating in professional conferences or conventions," "taking new coursework or training in one's field to remain current and competent," and public speeches. In the new evaluation standards for tenure, "professional activities and achievements" included areas such as *scholarly* publications, "presentations of papers at professional meetings" (simple participation was no longer sufficient), "articles on intellectual topics in journals, magazines, or newspapers," "publications of textbooks or other books of an intellectual character," and "studying or training that expands the competence of the person *into new areas*" (emphasis added. 1994 Faculty Handbook, pp. 23, 44).

However, 65 percent of senior faculty were grandfathered into the new tenure system. So while the faculty handbook indicated that new faculty must produce scholarly publications to earn tenure, a feat to which their senior colleagues were not held, tenure was also awarded *en masse* to senior faculty, many of whom never underwent any type of performance review.

Quality of Faculty

Several interviewees postulated an indirect relationship between tenure and higher quality faculty. *If* tenure was an incentive to attract faculty with better credentials, and *if* the new tenure evaluation process induced faculty to produce higher quality scholarship and better teaching, *then* tenure would improve the overall quality of the faculty. Board Chairman Connallon stated that the board thought tenure would help attract better faculty and "at the trustee level, the desirability of tenure came from the desire to have the highest possible quality of faculty." President Robinson, who was intent on improving Accomac's reputation as a premier liberal arts institution, said, "The tenure policy was a way to strengthen the quality of the faculty [through tougher expectations for faculty performance]."

Quid Pro Quo

With the expectation for faculty to improve the quality of their output—most notably, the quality of research—several interviewees saw tenure as a "quid pro quo." As previously noted, the president thought that "the institution had to make a commitment to the faculty. Tenure was something that the faculty deserved." A faculty member said that, with the greater expectation for research and scholarship, tenure was a way for the president "to challenge the faculty." He continued:

> It was a quid pro quo in some ways, for what they would give back to the college. . . . If the college wanted this kind of commitment from the faculty, it certainly would require more work and more real dedication to the institution. The institution was going to have to step up and say back to the faculty that "we will support you in some kind of special way." The special way that I thought was tenure. . . . Restoring tenure showed the institution's vestedness to the person and a reciprocal relationship of the faculty back to the institution.

Status and Stature

Observers believed that tenure would improve the institution's stature within the higher education community by eliminating the vestiges of counter-culture that had permitted tenure to be removed in the first place. "The administration and board put forth the argument that it was 'regularizing' the institution and getting it out of the counter-culture and making it as comparable as it could be to our so-called peer institutions," said the provost. "The argument was that we needed to be similar to them in our policies. There's something funky about an institution that doesn't have tenure." A faculty member noted that "the college wanted to be more traditional and more mainstream."

While it was argued that tenure would bring status to the *college*, far fewer interviewees mentioned that tenure would also improve the status of *individual faculty*. Unlike Lakeview College, where faculty wanted tenure to gain respect among their peers at other institutions, only one Accomac faculty member offered a similar line of reasoning: "There is something in saying, 'I have tenure.' . . . I think there's a status element: 'I've made it. I'm no longer an apprentice. I'm a master in the guild. I passed the test.'"

Security to Participate in Campus Governance

Interviewees argued that tenure provided protection for faculty to more fully participate in decision making. Some faculty, but not all, saw tenure as a means for extra protection against administrators. One professor maintained,

> The health of the institution depends on senior faculty who can express their views and advise the administration. Under the contract system, you don't have security—however you want to define it—you're always looking over your shoulder and . . . you're doing the things that you think are going to

keep you safe. . . . [Now,] faculty can make an appeal to the administration and stick our necks out in ways in which we just couldn't before."

Others were less sure that tenure provided more protection for faculty participation in governance. Said a faculty member, "The seasons of caution here, in terms of what we can say about criticizing the administration, wax and wane. It has more to do with the personalities of the president and the provost than with tenure or lack thereof. Under President Hopper, people were afraid to speak out against him, and we had [both tenured and untenured faculty] at that time. Even people with tenure were cautious."

AN ANALYSIS OF THE PROCESS OF CHANGE

The process of change in faculty employment policies at Lakeview and Scott colleges involved clear shifts in the balance of power. Tenure was a mechanism that transferred power in decision making and governance from one constituency to another—President Kelly at Scott College abolished tenure, in part, to reduce the faculty's influence, while the president and faculty leaders at Lakeview used tenure to solidify shared governance. Shifting lines of power and influence are not overt at Accomac. While political maneuverings around the *details* of the tenure policy were present, there was little disagreement on the outcomes—the various organizational actors wanted to reinstate tenure for the same fundamental reasons. The process of change was primarily collegial. Faculty, administrators, and trustees formulated a policy through deliberation and consensus rather than through power and politics. A collegial model is predicated on shared meaning and norms—it is possible only if there is a mutual understanding of organizational culture, expectations, and behavior. Therefore, one must ask the question, "how did different groups at Accomac arrive at the consensus that tenure was a beneficial attribute for the institution?" The answer lies in the powerful agreement on meaning and symbol.

The Collegial Model of Change

The process of change at Accomac was an example of divergent groups (faculty, administration, and board), with common beliefs about participation and deliberation, affecting the outcome of a policy change. Collegial decision making focuses on "consensus, shared power, common commitments and aspirations, and leadership that emphasizes consultation and collective responsibilities" (Birnbaum, 1988, p. 86). The components of collegial systems serve as a framework for the analysis of Accomac. Collegial decision making (1) is egalitarian and democratic, (2) is formed by consensus, with an emphasis on thoroughness and deliberation, (3) respects different groups, (4) lacks procedures for implementation and evaluation of decisions, and (5) relies on shared meaning and symbols. (Birnbaum, 1988).

Democratic Decision Making

A collegial model of organizational change characterizes Accomac because, at the time that tenure was implemented, power and influence were shared among faculty, administrators, and trustees. However, this participatory style emerged as a reaction to years of autocracy, as at Lakeview. Faculty had strong residual mistrust for the administration resulting from the autocratic president, Roderick Hopper. Because of Hopper's mercurial, "even vicious" management, faculty remained "very suspicious of administrators acting in an arbitrary way," observed Provost Longo. The Hopper "legend" was an important part of the faculty ethos—every faculty member interviewed for this study, including those who came to Accomac after Hopper had departed, mentioned him without prompting. In the aftermath of Hopper's term in office, faculty fortified their position in campus governance through a revision to the college bylaws, which made it more difficult for administrators to unilaterally institute policy changes. By the time the tenure proposal was negotiated in the late 1980s and early 1990s, shared governance with faculty participation had become the norm.

The leadership style of the new president, Duane Robinson, influenced the ethos of egalitarianism. He espoused shared governance as a positive force for both Accomac and the higher education community in general. Accomac, however, did not transform from an autocracy one day to a democracy the next. Instead, the college's move to consultative decision-making was evolutionary because Robinson only slowly came to believe in the strengths of faculty participation. He recalled that, "in my first few years, I was told a number of times by some board members and faculty that the institution was run by the president and vice presidents—that all decisions were made by a few people. As I became more comfortable in my position, I became more open to consultation. And probably to tenure, too. I believe the best form of decision making is to involve key people—faculty, administrators, the board—trying to bring people together to consensus. As president, I learned increasingly to listen to many voices on campus."

Both the codification of a shared governance system and Robinson's shift in management style contributed to the democratic social context in which different groups voiced their opinions and attempted to influence the tenure initiative. As a result, one group did not dominate the process of change to tenure at Accomac. Moreover, the various constituencies—faculty, administrators, and trustees—expected participation from all sides. In collegial institutions, "members of the administration and faculty consider each other as equals, all of whom have the right and opportunity for discussion and influence as issues come up" (Birnbaum, 1988, p. 88). Such a view applied to trustees as well. James Bush, the chair of the board's academic affairs committee, emphasized that the board respected the norms of collegiality and insisted on a partnership with the faculty: "We wanted to have a sense of participation on the part of the faculty—that they were really being heard and that their views were being considered, and that they heard what we had to say. . . . We felt we were on a constructive move, and it was best to have participation. I have a very strong commitment to that. It's best to lay it all out on the table. No backroom conniving or anything."

Consensus and Deliberation

A second characteristic of collegial systems is an emphasis on consensus, achieved sometimes through painstaking deliberation (Birnbaum, 1988). Accomac's decision-making norm was for committees representing different groups to discuss a proposal and come to agreement on the specifics. One professor declared, "The system of governance fosters talking. We're not a Quaker institution, but we do try to reach consensus through elaborate discussion." The move to tenure embraced that norm. As a result, faculty and administrators describe the process of instituting a tenure policy as "compromising," "difficult," and "mediating." Another faculty member commented, "[The process of reinstating tenure] followed acceptable practices here, in which you have a joint committee and then hammer it out."

The primary deliberations occurred between the faculty committee and the provost. Members of the faculty committee described the process of forging a tenure document with the provost in collegial terms. Said one, "I think the process was typical. It goes through channels; it takes a long time." Another expounded on the complexities of consensus-building:

> *Can you characterize the committee's work?*
> It seemed like it went on forever.
> *What adjectives would you use to describe the process?*
> Lengthy, meticulous, and grueling.
> *Why grueling?*
> Because . . . any time you work on committees, it's hard. You're always trying to compromise and adjust and get consensus. It was a committee that worked by consensus. That's grueling, in my experience.

This deliberative give-and-take and emphasis on consensus does not mean, however, that a collegial model of decision making ignores conflict, as some have suggested (Baldridge, et al, 1978). Conflicts arose in the process of moving back to tenure, but as one professor noted, "We both wanted the same thing." In other words, the disagreements were not over *whether* to return to tenure, but *how* the policy should be written. Participants observed that faculty and administration had divergent ideas about how the new tenure system should be conceived. One faculty member believed those disagreements were normal and expected, because "there is a legitimate difference in view between faculty and administration. Administration wanted as much flexibility as possible [in the tenure policy] . . . and faculty wanted to keep it in their hands as much as possible."

The key to resolving disagreement in Accomac's collegial system was how consensus was achieved. In a political environment, different players make threats and promises, form coalitions, and offer tradeoffs (Baldridge, et al, 1978). The use of threats and promises was absent in the deliberations at Accomac. Rather, in a collegial environment, real consensus "arises when open discussion is possible and expected, participants feel that they have had a fair chance to state their position and to influence the outcome, and when people are comfortable about supporting the chosen alternative even if it was not their first view (Schein, 1969)" (Birnbaum, 1988, pp. 88–89). These characteristics were more apparent at Accomac. For example, the provost stated that, in hindsight, he thought the compromise he reached with faculty on the use of outside reviewers in the tenure-evaluation process "was the wisest thing to do," even though it was not his first view.

Consensus and deliberation also occurred between the faculty committee and the board of trustees. Here, too, the different groups compromised on various points to ensure that the policy was enacted. One trustee said that the board was willing to "bite the bullet" and approve a tenure policy but only with a post-tenure review process and merit-pay scheme. The faculty committee agreed to that compromise. As noted earlier, a committee member said, "We needed to get together as a conference to see if we could come to consensus. I think we did. I think that meeting went very well."

Cordiality and Respect

Participants in the change process were respectful cordial, and decorous. "Tenure was a major change," said Trustee Connallon, "but it was never divisive." A professor noted that while negotiations between Provost Longo and faculty were sometimes difficult, the atmosphere was always productive. "People were talking to each other. No one ever shouted at Paul." Trustee Bush made similar comments about the faculty/board relationship. Speaking of this collegial environment, he said:

> Many of us were on the board because we saw a certain character there, a certain ethos.
> *So, is there respect for faculty among the board?*

Absolutely.
Was there antagonism between the board and faculty?
No. . . . We [the trustees] weren't muscled into [accepting tenure]. It wasn't that kind of approach.
Was it the right decision to make?
Oh, yes. We supported it genuinely. As the cliché goes, it was a win-win situation.

This norm of civility was demonstrated in a last-minute compromise between the board and faculty committee. The full faculty approved the new tenure policy in February 1993. At the board meeting in March, trustees broadened the reasons for dismissal for cause by including the phrase, "seriously disruptive and insubordinate behavior." Faculty objected to the language, believing that it "could be interpreted in many ways . . . . An administration less benevolent than the present one may well use [the broadened dismissal for cause] to restrict academic freedom or to enforce conformist behavior." At a more politicized campus, faculty might have re-voted and rejected the proposal, staged a protest, or contacted the media to denounce the trustees' "underhanded," after-the-fact alteration. None of this occurred at Accomac. Instead, at its next meeting, the faculty voted to adopt the following statement:

> The faculty approves the tenure document with the changes made by the Board of Trustees at the meeting of March 6, 1993. We have, however, reservations about some of the modifications and believe they may have an adverse effect on the college. We therefore urge the Board of Trustees to reconsider these changes and, *if possible,* return to the language which was approved by us earlier. . . . (Faculty meeting minutes, April 13, 1993. Emphasis added.)

The faculty's choice of language is important because it highlights the amicable relationship between faculty and trustees. Despite their reservations, the faculty *still* approved the altered policy and requested (not demanded) a reconsideration, *"if possible."* The faculty's statement to the trustees was civil, cordial, and respectful. Even though the faculty adopted the trustees' version, the board agreed to rethink their changes, and the two groups struck another compromise about wording that was acceptable to both.[5]

---

5. The objectionable "seriously disruptive or insubordinate behavior" was changed to "serious and sustained disruptive behavior."

No Procedures for Implementation of Decisions

Because collegial institutions rely on informal norms rather than bureaucratic rules, a decision made is not necessarily a decision enacted. "Procedures to follow up and assess the consequences of decisions are often lacking, so that once decisions have been reached, they may not be implemented, or, if implemented, they may not be evaluated" (Birnbaum, 1988, p. 99). This is not to say that decision making is an empty façade; if nothing else, the decision-making process is important symbolically for its demonstration of inclusiveness. Nor do collegial institutions fail to enact all policies they approve. However, especially around issues where there is disagreement, the organization may not implement what it intended.

At Accomac, this collegial characteristic was evident in the post-tenure review policy. The faculty and the board agreed that PTR would be part of the new tenure system and placed responsibility for the reviews on the provost. From 1993 to the time of this research in 1999, however, post-tenure review has never occurred. The acting provost at the time of this research who previously had been a faculty member commented, "Post-tenure review hasn't happened because we're too busy." There are two other possible explanations for why PTR was not enacted. First, the debate among faculty, administration, and trustees over post-tenure review may have been more important for what it symbolized than for what it produced (Bolman & Deal, 1991). By simply raising the issue, trustees signaled to faculty their concern with the potential for unproductive faculty members. Post-tenure review also gave trustees a voice in the specifics of the deliberations; because they had a cause to champion, they had a legitimate role in the collegial process.

A second possibility why post-tenure review has not occurred involves an incongruity in the nature of a collegium or "community of scholars." This phrase "contains a contradiction. Actions that strengthen the community weaken the scholarship. And actions that strengthen the scholarship weaken the community" (Weick, 1983, p. 15). This tension between scholarship and community can be envisioned if a post-tenure review process had been implemented. Senior faculty members would have had to make a critical assessment of a colleague's scholarship (which they never had to do previously, since the majority of faculty were grandfathered into tenure). A negative judgment could very easily cause hurt feelings and divisiveness, which would be harmful to the institution's sense of community, especially among long-time faculty members who were integral to the coherence and traditions of the faculty. Therefore, since organizational participants highly value community and harmony with their peers, it is possible that PTR has not been enacted because faculty would be unlikely to voluntarily engage in behavior that threatens that norm. This may also shed light on why the faculty rejected Provost Longo's attempt to include outside reviews as part of the tenure-evaluation process. While external assessment of scholarship may have provided another avenue to make a judgment on a tenure candidate's work, such critical appraisals could have added a degree of competitiveness and confrontation that would have weakened Accomac's sense of equality and collegiality.

The Importance of Symbols

A collegial institution "develop[s] a strong and coherent culture with distinctive symbols, rites, and myths" (Birnbaum, 1988, p. 91). Participants at Accomac College developed a very strong culture with a shared meaning about tenure. In this regard, Accomac is similar to Lakeview, where tenure was viewed as a symbol of achievement, growth, and status. Lakeview constituents wanted to be part of the mainstream generally. For them, tenure delineated who they were *not*: "We are no longer part of the counter-culture." But they did not necessarily hope that tenure would put them on par with other *specific* institutions. Accomac, however, had a very definite aspirant group in mind: the small, prestigious liberal arts college, the "Little Ivies." For Accomac, tenure demonstrated who they *were* (or wanted to be): We are like Swarthmore, Hamilton, William and Mary, and Davidson.

Accomac was fortunate because it was endowed with many of the symbols of these traditional private colleges: the bucolic setting and verdant lawns; the imagery of the wise don instructing a small coterie of students, in this case, along the riverfront; even the semi-autonomy from the state contributed to the "myth" of exclusivity. But something was missing. As a professor noted, "A lot of the institutions with whom we were competing for faculty had tenure systems." In order for Accomac to be recognized as part of that group—a prominent, selective institution with name recognition—Accomac wanted to, and probably had to, imitate those other places. As noted earlier, an administrator said, "If you're going to become a first-rate liberal arts institution . . . you probably ought to be like them in most respects." Trustees accepted that tenure was a symbol that the college could not do without. Trustee Bush said, "The consideration of tenure really went with the territory. . . . We supported it genuinely." Board Chairman Connallon acknowledged, "We were trying to move a good institution to become a superb institution. It if took tenure to do that, then so be it."

Participants at Accomac shared the belief that tenure would help the institution reach its goals. That belief was shared, in part, because many of the institution's leaders came from similar backgrounds. Unlike both institutions that abandoned tenure, Accomac had leaders who hailed from academe. Board Chairman Connallon was a former president of a large, nationally known research university (with tenure). President Robinson

Accomac College

had been an administrator at an Ivy League institution (with tenure). Provost Longo served as academic dean at college very much like those to which Accomac aspired. Based on their previous learning and socialization, many members of the Accomac community shared a similar expectation, ethos, and aura of tenure.

SUMMARY

At the level of the negotiation of details, the process of change from tenure to contracts was politicized. Divergent groups attempted to exert their self-interest, arguing over the fine points of the new tenure policy. Accomac College is like many higher education institutions that have an autonomous faculty, codified policies about decision-making norms, and—at least since the 1980s—an ethos and expectation of shared governance. Under these conditions, the formation and execution of policy initiatives are often marked by negotiation and compromise. It is certainly possible to examine the process of change using a political framework—one would find instances of disagreement and compromise between the faculty and the administration.

This political interpretation, however, would miss the big picture by focusing on the minute details. Overall, the process of change at Accomac was more collegial than political. Interviewees noted that every constituency wanted the same thing—tenure—and only disagreed about the particulars of policy and procedure. They described the interactions among the various groups as "open" and "professional." The process had a "win-win" outcome. When the tenure policy was finally approved, President Robinson recalled "the moment as a time for celebration for the institution." Everyone was happy.

CHAPTER 7

How Did These Colleges Move in Opposite Directions?

IN EXPLORING HOW FOUR COLLEGES UNDERWENT THE PROCESS OF REVISING their faculty employment policies, the underlying assumption was that fundamental differences would be evident between the two sets of institutions—that colleges that eliminated tenure would undergo a process of change markedly different than those that instituted tenure. This assumption rested on the idea that academic tenure is a bedrock principle of mainstream American higher education. To eliminate tenure, a college, by necessity, would have to do so in a top-down, exclusionary fashion. Furthermore, colleges instituting tenure would exhibit qualities that are more typical of the standard, conventional American colleges and universities—highly professionalized faculty, an emphasis on participatory decision making and shared governance, and incremental and decentralized change. Therefore, their change processes would embrace these ideals.

The case studies of Accomac, Lakeview, Rowlette, and Scott colleges demonstrate that, in fact, these colleges varied in the process of organizational change. Scott College was the most centralized, leader-centered, and authoritarian of the four sites. All action was directed by the president with the support of the board, and faculty were excluded from decision making. At Rowlette, the process of instituting multi-year contracts took a convoluted path, marked by fits and starts, multiple and changing participants, and an elongated timeframe. Lakeview moved to tenure through the coalescence of the new president, faculty leaders, and an activist board chair into a dominant coalition. Accomac's change process was the most collegial of the four. The faculty, administration, and board worked by consensus to reinstate traditional tenure.

Table 7.1. Summary Characteristics of Change Processes at the Four Colleges

College	Year of Change	Participants: President	Participants: Faculty	Participants: Board	Governance	Dominant Organizational Theory
Scott	1993	Dominant actor, Authoritarian, "Dictator."	Majority had shared belief in strong management. "Alternative" group of faculty left institution.	Shared disdain for tenure. Mostly business people. Waited for strong leader to eliminate tenure.	Administration-directed. No shared governance. Most top-down system of the four sites.	Power. Strong-leader model
Rowlette	1973–1986	"Revolving door." Inconsistent leadership.	Majority uninterested in formal tenure policy because they had tenure in practice.	Majority business people. Not sympathetic toward tenure. Consumed with financial crises.	History of crises-management and strong administrative control in 1970s, but shared governance since 1980s.	Loose coupling, organized anarchy.
Lakeview	1997	Traditional academic leader, former college president and provost at institutions with tenure.	Older faculty from industry, not interested in tenure and rank. Newer faculty hailed from academe, interested in "trappings" of higher education.	Activist board chair. Most trustees against tenure at beginning of process, but embraced the policy shift after being "educated."	History of strong administrative control and additional layer of power in department chairs. Shared governance had been recently introduced.	Power; Organizational growth
Accomac	1993	Well-liked president. Believer in shared governance.	Since early 1980s, faculty strong participants in governance.	Highly supportive of president. Board chair was former university president.	Strongest system of participatory management at the four sites.	Collegiality

Table 7.1 provides a graphic summary of the primary characteristics of each college's participants, governance style, and the dominant organizational theory used in each case analysis.

In addition to exploring the cases individually, it is important to compare and contrast the change processes across the four sites to determine the similarities and differences in how tenure was implemented or eliminated. While the descriptive differences in the change processes among the four colleges are a necessary part of this study, it is also important to provide an understanding of the reasons for these differences. What organizational characteristics or patterns are found among the colleges? What are the differences in these patterns between the two sets of institutions? Are there any pattern similarities among all four colleges? The first section of this chapter explores three patterns: (1) institutional growth and maturity, (2) presidential leadership and learning, and (3) the symbolic purposes of organizational change. The process of change at each college cannot be wholly explained by any one of these comparisons. Rather, these three themes, taken together, offer an interpretation of why the two sets of colleges differed in the processes of change.

INSTITUTIONAL GROWTH AND MATURITY

These four colleges share an interesting pattern of growth, even though the sites were chosen without regard to their history or origins. A quick glance at institutional characteristics did not indicate much similarity in historical roots: the oldest college, Accomac, began operation in 1840, while the youngest, Rowlette, was founded in 1946. Two interesting facts emerged. First, three of the four colleges were started as secondary schools or women's colleges and only later evolved into four-year coeducational baccalaureate institutions. The fourth, Rowlette College, began with a three-year curriculum for returning World War II veterans, so it, too, had a nontraditional background. Second, as illustrated in Table 7.2, all four institutions received full accreditation as four-year baccalaureate colleges within a seven-year time span (1967 to 1974), despite the 106–year variance in the dates they were founded.

Table 7.2. Date of Founding, Original Institutional Status, and Date of Accreditation for the Institutions in the Study

Institution	Year Founded	Founded as	Year accredited as four-year baccalaureate college
Accomac	1840	Women's high school	1968
Lakeview	1890	Women's college	1974
Rowlette	1946	Three-year college for veterans	1967
Scott	1909	High school	1971

These data points emphasize how "young" these institutions are compared to the larger higher education community; they do not have long track records as full-fledged colleges. As a result, they share several common points of development. Many observers noted that original faculty members did not come from traditional academic paths. At Scott College, for example, a professor noted that "even by the late 1970s, many faculty had been hired out of a secondary education mode." Similarly, a Rowlette professor called early faculty hires "amateurish." Lakeview faculty members were, for a long time, part-timers who were practitioners, not academics. Furthermore, many Lakeview faculty and administrators considered themselves "revolutionaries" who purposefully and proudly eschewed traditional symbols of academe such as rank, accreditation, and tenure. At Accomac, many faculty hired in the late 1960s promoted the idea of the college becoming, in the words of one long-time professor, a "hippie place" that did away with conventions like tenure and grading.

Without a large cadre of faculty socialized to the prevailing norms of higher education, these colleges developed without strong systems of shared governance, with solid emphases on teaching but little interest in research and publication, and with atmospheres in which the quality of life was decisively important to faculty. Many long-time faculty at these campuses talked about the importance of the small campus atmosphere, the absence of the publish-or-perish criterion of research universities, the ability to interact with colleagues and students in their homes and other informal settings, recreational activities in the region, and safe environments for raising families. Moreover, they were willing to trade certain faculty prerogatives for these types of environments. For example, one Scott professor said she was willing to forego an active voice in campus governance for the Christian, family-friendly atmosphere. ("People can tell me what to do.")

Contract-to-Tenure Institutions: Craving the Mainstream

While the two sets of institutions had similar histories of evolution into four-year baccalaureate colleges and common nontraditional backgrounds, they differed in their patterns of growth and aspirations. Participants at Accomac and Lakeview colleges noted that their institutions "grew up" in various ways—by increasing the number of faculty with doctorates, encouraging scholarship and research rather than just teaching, and implementing faculty committees and other structures of shared governance. Additionally, faculty, administrators, and trustees asserted that moving to a tenure system was a mark of institutional maturity. Constituents at these two institutions envisioned tenure as a vehicle to demonstrate to internal and external constituencies that the college had matured, moved into the mainstream, and shed its counter-cultural image. Faculty members and administrators said that tenure was intended to "make the college come of age, to take the college into a mature stage of academic life" (Lakeview professor) and that "a tenure system would be a good sign of the maturity of the college" (Lakeview president). For these colleges, then, tenure was both a mechanism for promoting a coming-of-age and an outward symbol of achieving it.

This "move to maturity" raises the question of why these two colleges came to resemble other institutions. After all, as any strip mall in American suburbia demonstrates, a certain amount of institutional distinction and individuality is lost by modeling an organization after the dominant institutional archetype. The tenets of institutional isomorphism theory (DiMaggio and Powell, 1991) suggest that tenure is widespread in American higher education for three reasons: (1) External organizations like the AAUP and cultural expectations within academe *pressure* colleges and universities to offer tenure; (2) Colleges *mimic* well-known, established, and successful higher education institutions, all of which offer tenure; and (3) Many faculty and administrators in higher education are socialized during their training to believe that tenure is *normative*. Accomac and Lakeview embraced tenure for the second and third reasons.

These colleges emulated more prestigious higher education institutions. The Accomac president wanted the college to be recognized as a premier liberal arts college. To attain that goal, he began a "Campaign for National Prominence." College constituents, especially the president and the board of trustees, believed that, in order to be perceived as a first-rate liberal arts institution, Accomac would have to demonstrate the attributes of the "Little Ivies," including a low student-faculty ratio, a selective student admissions profile, and an academic tenure system. Furthermore, faculty and administrators believed that tenure would improve the institution's stature within the higher education community. As the Accomac provost said, "There's something funky about an institution that doesn't have tenure." Accomac did not want to be perceived as "funky." Similarly, Lakeview wanted to cast aside its reputation as a revolutionary outlier.

Another isomorphic tendency at play involved norms of professionalization. At both institutions, an increasing number of new faculty members hailed from traditional paths—Ph.D.s minted from programs at research universities. Faculty members believed that tenure was the common currency by which professional legitimacy was recognized and through which entry into the "priesthood" was conferred. Tenure solved the problem of professional recognition and ended a self-image of illegitimacy. A Lakeview professor stated that tenure "would give us recognition outside the institution. It was a clear and consistent system that provided credibility to the outside." The lack of tenure was a "glaring omission in the faculty's status among their peers."

Tenure-to-Contract Institutions: Anti-Isomorphism at Play

Institutional growth and maturity did not resonate at Rowlette and Scott colleges. Instead, these colleges exhibited tendencies that might appropriately be called anti-isomorphism, the force of resistance that insures an institution does not resemble others in the environment. Evidence in the two cases suggests that there are several types of anti-isomorphism:

Mission Socialization—We don't want to be like them.

Scott College, but not Rowlette, exhibited the anti-isomorphic tendency of mission socialization. Because of Scott's religious and cultural mission, the college did not want to mimic secular institutions that the president regarded as elitist and aloof. The board of trustees and the president prevented the college from adopting trends or values that the greater higher education community might take for granted—co-educational residence halls, for example. Also, the president disdained faculty prerogatives, such as shared governance and tenure, considered sacrosanct on other campuses. He remarked, "I resent people who see it as their duty to get inside a college with a special mission and make it like everybody else." College officials also felt little coercive pressure from the AAUP. In fact, when the AAUP considered an investigation after the college abolished tenure, the board passed a resolution censuring the association for "inappropriately intervening in the internal affairs of the college."

Furthermore, the president and trustees wanted to demonstrate that they were capable of bold, aggressive leadership, steadfastly at odds with the established norms of higher education. There is arguably no better way to make a statement of iconoclastic leadership in higher education than the removal of tenure.

Financial Distraction—We can't afford to be like them.

A family in severe financial hardship focuses on basic necessities, not on keeping up with the Joneses. Rowlette College, but not Scott, experienced a similar anti-isomorphic tendency. Rowlette suffered constant and repeated financial setbacks. Faculty and administrators reported being driven to distraction and desperation by these fiscal crises, so that the institution's focus was on survival rather than "luxury items" like tenure. Furthermore, trustees originally stopped awarding tenure because they were fearful of long-term financial commitments; faculty did not react to the unofficial tenure moratorium because they were distracted by more pressing problems, like low salaries.

Faculty Zones of Indifference—We don't care if we are like them.

Another isomorphic inclination of these two colleges—more an enabler of change that a reason for the policy shift—was that the faculties *as a whole* were indifferent to tenure. Observers noted that most faculty at these institutions were uninterested in the national "scene" of higher education. They were not professionally competitive—they welcomed life at small colleges centered on teaching, not research. Tenure, therefore, meant little to them when their institutions awarded it; they were nonchalant when it was taken away. At Rowlette, a professor declared, "Call us demented, but there were a number of us on the faculty who just couldn't have cared less about tenure. . . . The faculty on the whole has remained consistently indifferent to this matter."

Summary: Institutional Growth and Maturity

These two sets of colleges shared similar institutional histories but "grew up" in different ways. In one manner of speaking, these colleges were in the awkward age of adolescence, two sets of teenagers with different aspirations. Accomac and Lakeview colleges were like teenagers yearning to be recognized as adults. The move to tenure was their formal debut, a ceremony that demonstrated they were mature members of the club and no longer "pseudo-academics." Rowlette and Scott colleges were like other teenagers for whom membership in the club had little utility or import. They knew that the club existed but did not value membership. When they lost it, they were unconcerned. Like adolescent nonconformists, they preferred to be different.

PRESIDENTIAL LEARNING AND LEADERSHIP

A second important theme in the analysis of the four colleges is presidential learning and leadership. An interesting pattern emerged from an examination of the presidents' previous jobs: those at the two institutions that moved to tenure came from large universities with tenure while those at the tenure-to-contract sites came from less traditional professional backgrounds. The presidents' previous on-the-job learning may have influenced the direction and nature of the change process in faculty employment policy. This section will also explore the role of presidential leadership in the overhaul of employment policies at the four sites.

Presidential Learning

As Table 7.3 illustrates, the two presidents at each set of institutions shared similar career backgrounds. At the two institutions that moved to tenure, both executives came from four-year institutions with tenure. At the two institutions that moved to contracts, one president previously served at another institution without tenure, and the other worked at an association of two-year colleges—neither the association itself nor most two-year colleges offer tenure.

Table 7.3. Backgrounds of Presidents at the Four Institutions in the Study

Institution	President's previous post
Accomac	Dean at Ivy League institution
Lakeview	Chancellor of state higher education system; university president; provost
Rowlette	Position at association of junior colleges
Scott	President of small, private college without tenure

While it is not possible to determine cause-effect relationships between the presidents' previous posts and the move toward or away from tenure, it is noteworthy that the relationships exist because they underscore the importance of presidential learning. These individuals were subject to the experiences they had in their prior positions. Cohen and March (1986) have speculated that "college presidents attempt to learn from their experience. They observe the consequences of actions and infer the structure of the world from those observations. They use the resulting inferences in attempt to improve their future actions" (p. 199). In other words, presidents, like all people, make judgments based on what they have encountered in the past. It is likely that previous learning, where each president nominally succeeded, contributed to his preference for one system over the other. President Kelly at Scott College, for example, inferred that the contract system at his previous institution did not pose any significant disadvantages and, in fact, made his job easier. He said, "I came from a college that did not have tenure . . . so I was comfortable with the [Scott] trustees' attitude [of wanting to eliminate tenure.]" Therefore, he "learned" that a contract system was a preferable alternative to tenure. President Potrowski at Rowlette became familiar with non-tenure systems while at an association of junior colleges, so it is possible that he was comfortable when the board of trustees imposed a moratorium on tenure. President Murin at Lakeview came to the college having "learned" of tenure's importance to high-quality institutions. While he noted some of tenure's shortcomings, he also observed: "Having served as a president and as a chancellor in both public and private higher education for twenty years, I am more committed to tenure than ever." In his prior post as dean at an Ivy League college, President Robinson of Accomac had a similar learning experience about tenure, including, he asserted, its positive effect on faculty recruiting. Academic tenure was inextricably linked to his concept of elite, high-quality institutions. Unlike his counterparts at Scott and Lakeview who immediately supported the change in policy upon their arrival at the institution, however, Robinson's thinking evolved during the first eight years of his presidency: "As I became more comfortable in my position, I became more open to consultation. And probably to tenure, too."

Each of these individuals came to his presidency with prior attitudes about tenure and contracts. The executives at the two sets of institutions differed in their socialization to the norms and expectations of traditional higher education. Presidents Murin and Robinson came from universities that engaged in typical organizational practices of mainstream higher education, while Presidents Kelly and Potrowski did not share an affinity for those practices.

Presidential Leadership at Contract-to-Tenure Institutions

Both of the contract-to-tenure institutions share a history of domineering presidents with contempt for academic tenure. Accomac faculty and administrators described the previous president, Roderick Hopper, as confrontational and oppressive. President Lynch at Lakeview was the "founding father" of the institution, known for running the college "out of his back pocket." While he was not the subject of scathing opprobrium from the college community as Hopper was at Accomac, Lynch was known for his disdain for shared governance, planning, and participatory management. The new presidents—Murin at Lakeview and Robinson at Accomac—hailed from more conventional academic backgrounds and, as a result, were more predisposed to the idea of academic tenure. Their role in the process of change was that of gatekeeper. While the tenure movements did not originate with them (at both colleges, faculty had tried to mobilize support prior to their arrival), they provided important assistance in advancing the movement for tenure. President Robinson and President Murin engaged in three similar strategies: (1) they publicly supported a move to tenure; (2) they championed the cause of tenure with the board of trustees; and (3) they removed themselves from the specific negotiations of the tenure policy, letting faculty and administration representatives control the process.

Public support for the tenure movement.

Presidential endorsement of tenure was vitally important. Accomac's provost recalled that President Robinson "in a fairly public way had signaled his determination to see if we could return to tenure." Similarly, a Lakeview professor recalled that, during a faculty association presentation, President Murin "spoke and came out for tenure. He was very clear." At both colleges, constituents noted that the tenure proposals would not have been successful without the president's support. Accomac's president bluntly declared, "It wouldn't have gone forward if I hadn't wanted it to," a sentiment echoed by a faculty member: "if [Robinson] hadn't supported it, I don't think it would have happened."

Champion tenure with the board.

Once he had given faculty committees his backing for the establishment of tenure, the president on each campus worked to garner support and enthusiasm for the idea with the board. Accomac trustee Connallon maintained that the board was willing to go along with the move to tenure *because* Robinson persuaded them to do so. He wryly commented, "The board said collectively, 'Oh, what the hell, let's go with Duane.'" The Lakeview board was strongly opposed to the tenure when President Murin first proposed it to them. However, the president and board chairman pushed on despite these objections. Murin said, "We began a process of trying to educate [trustees] about tenure," which was eventually successful.

Absent from negotiations.

Both Murin and Robinson did not take part in the nitty-gritty of negotiations between faculty and administration and faculty and the board. Members of the faculty committee at Accomac noted that they never once met with Robinson; instead, they dealt exclusively with Provost Longo. President Murin appointed an aide to represent him on the Committee on Faculty Status. There are several reasons why the presidents may have removed themselves from this level of involvement. First, presidents are busy people and their time and attention for any one committee, event, or situation is limited. Second, both presidents believed in participatory governance and decision making. By involving others in the process of change, these presidents encouraged faculty, administrators, and trustees to "own" the process and to feel vested in its import and outcome. Third, by staying above the fray, each president was able to remain focused on the larger principles. Fourth, they could preserve their options and mediate between various proposals, if needed.

Presidential Leadership at Tenure-to-Contract Institutions

Unlike Accomac and Lakeview, the two tenure-to-contract institutions share fewer commonalities in presidential leadership. Presidential leadership at Rowlette is difficult to encapsulate because the process of change occurred over the course of three presidencies. The president's influence at Scott College is easier to capture.

President Kelly epitomized the aloof, strong-willed, authoritative leader endorsed by Fisher (1984) and decried by other commentators in higher education (e.g. Emmert, 1998; Green, 1997). Kelly's decision-making and leadership style contradicts Cohen and March's assertion that college presidents have "modest control" over their institutions (1986, p. 2). In fact, Kelly had *total* control of the institution once his changes in governance and academic tenure were completed. A proposition in chapter one hypothesized that the change process at tenure-to-contract institutions would be directed and controlled by a limited number of participants "from the top;" the president would have a clear line of authority to implement the policy shift; and faculty would be excluded from the decision-making and organizational change process. In the case of Scott College, this is largely what occurred. Kelly's leadership role in the shift to term contracts can be characterized in three stages. In a mirror image of the two contract-to-tenure colleges, he (1) publicly acknowledged his disdain for academic tenure; (2) championed the removal of tenure with the board; and (3) did not involve faculty in the decision-making process.

Public statements against tenure.

As a candidate for the presidency in 1987, Kelly stated to the presidential search committee that he was philosophically opposed to tenure. A faculty member on that committee recalled that Kelly "had been very up-front when he interviewed for the presidency: he didn't like tenure." Despite some faculty members' assertions that the announcement was unexpected, most professors "knew it was going to happen; it was just a matter of when. We knew for several years that it was coming."

Championed the cause with the board.

Unlike Lakeview and, to a lesser extent, Accomac, the board of trustees at Scott College did not need much convincing to change the type of faculty employment policy. Scott's board was already united in its dislike for the tenure system. Trustees had not dismantled tenure on their own, said Kelly, because they were lacking a leader to actually do it. "I was that person—I was the catalyst." During the board meeting at which the vote took place, Kelly armed himself with "books I had read on the subject and [articles] on tenure by others in prominent positions. I had plenty of ammunition."

Exclusionary decision making.

Kelly strongly professed that the faculty should not be involved in management decisions at the college. As a result, faculty members were not consulted about the change process; rather, they were informed a month after the board had voted on the policy shift. The president said, "I was harshly criticized because I didn't *ask* the faculty. Well, I don't *report* to the faculty for one thing. My duty is to recommend what's in the interest of the college. So I just did it."

There are more similarities in presidential leadership among Scott, Accomac, and Lakeview colleges than between Scott and Rowlette. This is not to say that the presidents at Accomac and Lakeview acted as autocratically as President Kelly, but at the very least, all three presidents had an active hand in moving the policy agenda forward and promoting the intended change. All three used the same levers—public statements, influence on the board, and faculty governance—but for different goals. The president's role at Rowlette is more ambiguous. Part of this ambiguity results from the long timeframe during which the change in policy occurred. The policy change did not happen in a one-year period in 1986, as originally anticipated, but rather took place over a period of 13 years. Three presidents served at Rowlette during this history. Nevertheless, one primary theme is evident from the case: the presidents never focused on the change in faculty employment policy. Because the college was in dire financial straits during much of the 1970s, and even into the 1980s, there is little evidence of any constituency—the president, the board, or the faculty—paying much attention to the problems of faculty employment policy. The story at Rowlette is about an absence of presidential leadership in this realm rather than one dominant voice. Decisions about faculty employment policies were not made because of more pressing issues.

Summary of Presidential Learning and Leadership

These four colleges can be compared in the dimension of presidential influence. First, there is an interesting distinction between the two sets of institutions based on prior presidential experience. The presidents presided over a change process that made their institution more similar to the ones from which they came. While this conclusion does not imply that the shift to tenure or contracts occurred because of this phenomenon, it nevertheless suggests that presidential "learning" may have a role in why the presidents supported and endorsed that change. Second, along a continuum from most to least influential presidents in the process of change in faculty employment policies, President Kelly at Scott had the most decisive role because shared governance and participatory management were anathema to him. The two contract-to-tenure institutions, conversely, had a shared process where the president played an important, but not singular, role in the shift in policy, consistent with the norms of shared governance in American higher education. Rowlette College falls last in the continuum of presidential influence in terms of change to faculty employment policy because President Potrowski, and other constituents at the college, were consumed by ongoing fiscal difficulties.

SIMILAR SYMBOLIC PURPOSES

A third theme in the analysis of these four institutions is the symbolic purposes of the shifts in policy. The colleges' constituents articulated various substantive reasons for the move toward or away from tenure. In addition to these various explanations, the two sets of colleges also shifted policies because the addition or abolition of tenure was an easily identifiable symbolic solution for larger, more ambiguous problems. Participants at Accomac and Lakeview asked, "How do we improve quality and prestige?" At Rowlette, trustees wondered, "How do we ensure financial stability in a tumultuous environment?" At Scott, the president pondered, "How can we achieve a proper balance of power?" The implementation or discontinuance of tenure became the answer to each of these questions. Why? Because "faced with uncertainty and ambiguity, human beings create symbols to resolve confusions, increase predictability, and provide direction" (Bolman and Deal, 1991, p. 244). These colleges used the elimination or implementation of tenure as a means to communicate that they were attending to and solving problems, even though they had a host of alternative solutions and were unsure that the shift in tenure policy could substantively solve the problems they had identified.

Interviewees at Scott College, for example, asserted that tenure was a problem because, once tenured, some professors became "deadwood." The college may very well have addressed this problem by stringently reviewing candidates before granting tenure. But, in the act of abolishing tenure, the president also wanted to convey to faculty that he was in charge, to the board that he was a bold leader, and to the external community that Scott College was marching to its own drummer. For Scott College, the abolition of tenure was a ceremony of power and distinctiveness as much as it was an act to improve evaluation. Likewise, fundamental improvements to the faculty evaluation process at Rowlette may have addressed the trustees' concerns that the tenure-granting process lacked rigor. However, trustees also wanted a visible signal that the board was attending to its grave fiscal situation. By putting a moratorium on tenure, they were able to convince themselves—and faculty, too—that they were doing *something* to address the crisis that afflicted the college, even if abandoning tenure did not actually benefit the college's bottom line.

Many college constituents at Lakeview wanted tenure to demonstrate that Lakeview faculty were as good as those at other institutions. Accomac College also wanted to signal its seriousness about faculty quality, not only through the substantive process of evaluation but through the symbolic act of tenure. By putting faculty through a *tenure* evaluation rather than a *contract*-renewal evaluation, the college could credibly claim that its faculty quality was better, even though most of the faculty, who were grandfathered, never underwent a tenure review. Tenure was, simply put, a proxy for quality. When participants at Accomac maintained that tenure helped increase faculty quality because it addressed their problem of poor evaluation, no doubt they referred to the increased standards to which junior faculty were held. But, significantly, for the majority of faculty, the standards were *not* changed. Instead, the faculty's and administration's *beliefs* about quality and rigor changed to a far greater extent than their *behavior* (Cohen and March, 1986).

Rituals and ceremonies—the traditional acts and routines that give meaning to human activity—are important in organizations. Bolman and Deal (1991) explained that rituals and ceremonies serve four purposes: "to socialize, to stabilize, to reduce anxieties and ambiguities, and to convey messages to external constituencies" (p. 262). The ceremony of establishing or discontinuing tenure at each of the sites served one or more of these purposes. Participants at Accomac and Lakeview asserted that tenure would move the college into the mainstream. The ceremony of adopting tenure would convey to the external higher education community that they were joining "the club" and would socialize new faculty to believe that the college was "normal." For Rowlette, trustees espoused flexibility and nimbleness through the removal of tenure. The ceremony of discontinuing tenure was an attempt to reduce anxiety about the college's precarious financial position and sent a message to outside groups (such as creditors and donors) that the college was taking action to protect its fiscal health. For Scott, the president believed that the act of abolishing tenure would send a message to faculty that he was in charge and compel them to be accountable to him. That act socialized both long-time and new faculty to this hierarchical decision-making norm.

Summary of Symbolic Purposes

Despite the differences in the shifts to academic employment policy between the two groups of colleges, there is an interesting similarity in the symbolic purposes for the changes. These college did have important substantive reasons for the change in policy. Notably, all four colleges had the same goal of improved faculty accountability (a finding that will be explored further in chapter eight). However, all four colleges used the addition or discontinuance of tenure to signal to various constituents that they were attending to large, hard-to-define problems. Despite the colleges' substantive goals for altering their faculty employment policies, they also used the shift toward and away from tenure symbolically, to send a message about institutional identity—about "who we are."

LOOSE COUPLING AND CHANGE IN FACULTY EMPLOYMENT POLICY

The theories of loosely coupled systems (Weick, 1976, 1984) and organized anarchy (Cohen & March, 1974, 1986) suggest a model for organizational change with the following characteristics. First, Cohen and March (1986) asserted that "the president's role [in decision-making is] more commonly sporadic and symbolic than significant. . . . The president has modest control over the events of college life" (p. 2). If leaders promote organizational change, they tend to focus on incremental changes that are confined to subsystems (Weick, 1976). Second, many constituencies are involved in decision making. Because faculty are involved in campus governance, "the authority of various constituencies to participate in or make decisions is often unclear and frequently contested" (Birnbaum, 1988, p. 28). Third, the reasons and processes of change are not always rational or tied to clear objectives and goals. Individual and organizational choice determine preferences rather than preferences guiding choice; people do not know what they want until after they have made a decision (Cohen & March, 1974). Fourth, loosely coupled systems focus on continuous adaptation but have less tolerance for fundamental overhaul. Broad-scale change is difficult to coordinate and diffuse (Weick, 1982).

This loosely coupled model is often assumed to be the normative framework of organizations in higher education. Whether purposefully or unconsciously, researchers and practitioners sometimes make blanket assertions that all colleges and universities "are loosely coupled organizations" (Richardson & Skinner, 1990, p. 492), despite studies that come to contradictory conclusions on whether and, if so, how the loosely coupled model applies to different types of higher education institutions under different circumstances. Some research has found that loose coupling is an appropriate model for colleges and universities (Cannon & Lonsdale, 1987; Cohen & March, 1974; DiBiasio & Ecker, 1982; Lutz & Lutz, 1988); other studies concluded that the loose coupling/organized anarchy model is not an applicable organizational model for the sites or circumstances under study (Clugston, 1986; Lutz, 1982; McCarty & Reyes, 1987; Trow, 1983).

This study proposed that the theories of loosely coupled systems would apply more readily to the institutions that introduced tenure because, in effect, they would be embracing higher education's traditional arrangement. Because higher education prizes incremental change, decentralized authority, and shared decision-making, a change to tenure would support a loosely coupled interpretation: a president with sporadic influence, multicephalous leadership, nonrational reasons for change, and a change process that is slow and time-consuming.. Conversely, I speculated that the loosely coupled model of change would not apply to the colleges that moved from tenure to contracts. They would display fewer elements of loose couplings in their decision-making and change processes because diffuse, fluid, decentralized decision-making processes would be antithetical to how term contracts were *imposed* upon the institution in a hierarchical fashion. Instead, the proposition was that other theories would apply more forcefully to the change process. For example, would Fisher's theory of the strong president (1984) would be more appropriate if the president forced the college to dismantle tenure?

The analyses of the four case studies indicate that some of these original hunches are supported while others are disconfirmed. This section will consider the ways in which loose coupling is a helpful lens to analyze the two sets of institutions. It is not the intent in this section to repeat the analyses already presented in the individual case studies. Instead, this section will focus on the parts of the loosely coupled model that most strongly illuminated the change process at each set of institutions.

Tenure-to-Contract Institutions

Loose coupling does *not* apply similarly to Scott and Rowlette colleges. Scott College exhibited the characteristics in the original proposition: a top-down exclusionary decision-making process imposed by the president. Rowlette College, however, disconfirmed the proposition about tenure-to-contract institutions; it was the most loosely coupled of the four colleges in the study—a place of ambiguous goals and undefined preferences. Three tenets of the loosely coupled model highlight the differences between the process of change at these two colleges: (1) leaders and participants, (2) slack resources, and (3) intentionality.

Leaders and Participants

One of the principles of an organized anarchy is that many organizational constituents can participate in decision making if they want, but the time and energy that any one person has for participation is limited. "The concept of the larger-than-life heroic leader whose wise decisions and forceful administration solve institutional problems and advance the institution's fortunes appears out of place in the organized anarchy" (Birnbaum, 1988, p. 167). Scott College did not display these properties of an organized anarchy. While some would disagree that President Kelly's decisions were "wise," it is irrefutable that his was a *forceful* administration that was able to solve problems (as he defined them). Moreover, the ability of other constituents to be involved in the decision-making process was tightly circumscribed by the president; the faculty had no say in the decision to alter employment policy.

Conversely, at Rowlette, no one person dominated the process of change. Participation was much more fluid. A number of different presidents and chief academic officers presided in the 15 years during which the changes in faculty employment policies were considered. When asked to identify the most influential person in moving from tenure to term contracts, interviewees cited a number of different individuals, including a faculty member, a trustee, and several administrators, but never the president.

Slack Resources

Organizational slack is a component of the organized anarchy framework. Cohen, March, and Olsen (1972) defined organizational slack as "the difference between the resources of the organization and the combination of demands made on it. Thus, it is sensitive to two major factors: (a) money and other resources provided to the organization by the external environment, and (b) the internal consistency of the demands made on the organization by participants" (p. 12). Organizations with slack resources will be more loosely coupled, require more time to make decisions, and be less efficient at solving problems.

Scott College had 50 times more financial resources than Rowlette (as measured by their respective $200 million and $4 million endowments). The organized anarchy model would suggest that, because of slack resources, decision making at Scott College would be much more loosely coupled than Rowlette. One might have expected Rowlette to have a tightly controlled process of shifting to contracts because of its catastrophic fiscal crises. Of course, the actual experiences of the two institutions demonstrated the opposite—Scott was top-down and hierarchical while Rowlette was loose and ambiguous. As Cohen, March, and Olsen (1972) noted, however, organizational slack is also dependent upon "the internal consistency of the demands made on the organization by participants" (p. 12). This element is a more interesting basis for comparison of the two institutions.

Participants at Rowlette were wildly inconsistent in when and how they attended to the problems with the college's tenure and contract policies. Trustees, administrators, and faculty were often distracted by the ongoing fiscal difficulties and did not regularly or consistently deal with academic tenure. Presidents came and went. Trustees issued directives but did not follow up on them. Faculty did not demand resolution to the inconsistencies in the policy. In terms of "the internal consistency of the demands" participants made on the organization, Rowlette suffered from an abundance of organizational slack. Scott College had none of this slack because of the president's singular voice in dictating organizational policies. Faculty members at Scott were socialized into the college's mission-driven environment. Regardless of whether professors agreed with or merely tolerated this management style, there was little faculty dissent with the various changes the president imposed. In terms of consistency of organizational demands, Scott displayed little or no slack whatsoever—President Kelly would not permit it.

Intentionality

A third element of the loosely coupled/organized anarchy model in which Rowlette and Scott colleges differed is that of intentionality or purposefulness. "The key concept in diagnosing whether or not the organization is an organized anarchy . . . is that of intention. Not only are there presumed to be no overarching organizational goals, but presumably intention is problematic even at the level of sub-units and groups within the organization. Action occurs, but it is not primarily motivated by conscious choice and planning" (Pfeffer, 1981, p. 27). This component of the organized anarchy model is probably the most difficult for members of an organization to accept because it suggests a high degree of randomness, inconsistency, and unpredictability on the part of organizational actors. The case of Rowlette College demonstrates, however, that unintentional actions can occur in one arena because constituents are driven to distraction in another arena. The college suffered from problematic preferences in its faculty employment policies because it was overloaded with fiscal emergencies. For example, it appeared that trustees' *actions* of discontinuing tenure in 1973, nominally for financial reasons, dictated their *preference* for an alternative system of faculty employment, rather than their preferences for contracts determining their action to end tenure.

Scott College, on the other hand, was guided by a much more intentional strategy. The president knew in advance of the decision that his preference was to eliminate tenure. While the *outcome* of the change may have been as much a symbolic act as a substantive one, the change *process* was driven by purposefulness and strategic intention.

Summary of Tenure-to-Contract Institutions

The loosely coupled model of organizations does not appear to apply equally at both institutions that eliminated tenure. While the original conjecture about the process of change at these institutions was applicable to

Scott College, the change process at Rowlette was instead dominated by fluid participation, problematic goals, and slack human resources in terms of "the consistency of the demands made on the organization by participants" (Cohen, March, and Olsen, 1972, p. 12). Scott College had a narrow field of organizational decision-makers (limited to President Kelly and several trustees); Rowlette College had a history of faculty participation (to varying degrees). While shared governance and participatory management were not tenets of the loosely coupled model, per se, it is one of the most unique characteristics of higher education (Birnbaum, 1988). There may be a relationship between the hierarchical nature of governance at Scott College (lack of shared governance) and its intentionality of actions in shifting its academic employment policy.

Contract-to-Tenure Institutions

Both Accomac and Lakeview colleges display some characteristics of loosely coupled systems, but the case studies suggest it would be inaccurate to label their processes of change as "loosely coupled." Part of the original proposition about the change process at contract-to-tenure institutions is confirmed by the case studies, while other elements do not apply. There are two areas in which the loosely coupled model is particularly robust: (1) leaders and participants, and (2) the element of time. However, these colleges did not exhibit the randomness that the organized anarchy model would suggest.

Leaders and participants

The two contract-to-tenure colleges were similar with respect to the roles played by various organizational actors. In both cases, faculty made tenure an important organizational issue and were involved in negotiating the details of the policy. Trustees also played a significant role, not in imposing their will on other constituents, but by acting as one voice in a group process. Presidents Murin and Robinson were both influential in signaling support, championing the cause for tenure, and encouraging a participatory style of implementation.

So, at both colleges, the process of change to tenure was open, shared, inclusive, and participatory—a shared style of governance that one might expect to find at most American colleges and universities, given that participatory management is the norm (AAUP, 1995). The multi-participant change processes at these campuses, however, resulted in several outcomes, all characteristic of a loosely coupled system. First, the influence of any one individual was diminished. When asked to identify the most influential person in the change process at Scott College, respondents unanimously named the president. When interviewees were asked the same question at

Accomac and Lakeview, the replies were more varied—some named the president while others mentioned faculty members, other administrators, and trustees. Second, participation was sometimes fluid. Not every committee member attended every meeting, producing an outcome best illustrated in a Lakeview professor's exasperation with the Committee on Faculty Status: "The academic dean was not particularly helpful—she didn't come to very many meetings, and when she did, she rehashed issues that had been settled months before to the obvious satisfaction of everyone involved."

The Element of Time

If change needs to be introduced into an organization, "that change is more likely to occur quickly when the system is tight than when it is loose" (Weick, 1982, p. 674). Pfeffer (1981) noted that organized anarchies are not sensitive to deadlines. Decisions are made eventually rather than immediately. Accomac and Lakeview displayed this long-term decision-making style. At Accomac, the faculty formed its tenure committee in 1990; the policy was implemented three years later. At Lakeview, faculty leaders began researching tenure and rank in 1993; the tenure policy was approved four years later in 1997. These long decision-making timelines fall in the middle of the four sites. Rowlette's process of change, identified as quite loosely coupled, took 13 years; Scott's shift in tenure policy took several months.

These differences in "decision time" are illustrative of other elements of organized anarchies. It took Accomac and Lakeview a long time to make decisions because many people were involved and their participation was fluid. It is also important to note that long decision-making timelines are not unique to the loosely coupled model. The same tenet is part of the collegial framework, for instance, because of its attention to deliberation and consensus.

Intentionality

The theory of organized anarchies posits that institutions have few or no overarching goals or intentions. Action occurs because of an unplanned confluence of different problems, solutions, actors and choice situations. Accomac and Lakeview vary in the degree to which they exhibit this unintentional behavior. On the one hand, the rationales and reasons for change were symbolic as well as substantive. These two colleges marshaled tenure as a proxy for quality, a signal of prestige, and a talisman of acceptance into the mainstream of higher education. In this sense, any rational organizational intentions were supplanted by more powerful symbolic goals. For example, at Lakeview, different constituents offered a plethora of reasons for moving to tenure. There was not one central goal; faculty wanted power, the trustees wanted better evaluation, the president wanted institutional prestige and normality.

However, the *process* by which these two colleges instituted the policy shift was much more intentional. Regardless of reason, organizational actors moved with purposefulness and intentionality in instituting tenure. Unlike Rowlette, where the discontinuance of tenure just *happened* by the actions of the board of trustees and only later became an official policy, the two contract-to-tenure colleges underwent a thoughtful, intentional process whereby a goal (tenure) was set and then achieved. The intervention of the two presidents was an important catalyst for making the change possible.

SUMMARY

I chose the framework of loose coupling to explore the process of change in faculty employment policies because it has been invoked so often to describe colleges and universities. But does it in fact apply to all types of higher education institutions under all kinds of circumstances? Or does it only apply when both the organization and the type of activity is close to the norm of American higher education? Or will it not be a helpful framework for any situation, a *theory* that has little usefulness in *practice*?

The theory of loosely coupled systems/organized anarchy was the dominant and most obvious framework for Rowlette College. It was far less illustrative of the Scott College case. Instead, models of power and politics (Pfeffer, 1981; Fisher, 1984) seemed to be more appropriate choices. While other organizational theories such as collegiality and organizational growth applied more readily *in toto* to the cases of Accomac and Lakeview colleges, they did exhibit some of the tendencies of loose coupling as well. Why did these institutions change in the ways they did? What might these observations reveal about the theories of loose coupling and organized anarchies?

The experiences of the four colleges suggest that there is a relationship between the loosely coupled nature of organizations and the ideals of shared governance and participatory decision making. While all types of organizations will at times exhibit characteristics where one element is loosely coupled to another, higher education institutions that embrace shared governance may be more loosely coupled because of the multiple people involved in a decision, the participants' ability to change the amount of attention they devote to an issue, and the length of time it takes to agree upon a course of action and to implement decisions. Scott College, which had a hierarchical, top-down, exclusionary decision-making style, had a tightly coupled process of change from tenure to contracts. The other three colleges were more loosely coupled.

Another interesting relationship exists between organized anarchy theory and the shared understanding and meaning of symbols. Earlier in this chapter, it was argued that tenure had an important symbolic purpose at all four sites. At the most tightly coupled of the institutions—Scott College—constituents uniformly agreed upon the meaning and symbol of tenure. They asserted that tenure was a crutch that allowed some faculty members to hide from accountability. The absence of tenure also was an important symbol at Scott—it signaled that the college was different than its peers. Even faculty members supported these common refrains. At Scott College, then, where there was little disagreement about what tenure meant, there was little ambiguity in the process of change. The shift in policy was tightly coupled, in part, because of a common understanding of the symbol.

Such tight coupling stands in stark contrast to Rowlette, the most loosely coupled college. Faculty members professed little interest in formal academic tenure because they had "tenure" regardless of official policy. Most faculty members said their work lives did not change after the discontinuance of tenure. There was very little agreed-upon meaning of tenure among faculty, administrators, and trustees. Since there was little interest in or agreement on the meaning of the presence or absence of a formal academic tenure policy, the shift away from traditional tenure was unintentional and ambiguous. There appears to be a correlation between the degree of shared meaning and interest in the organizational element undergoing change (in this case, tenure policy) and the degree to which the process is loosely coupled.

Accomac and Lakeview colleges had symbolic *reasons* for the shift in policy, but the *process* of change was more tightly controlled and intentional. The move to tenure might be inherently symbolic because a cause-effect relationship cannot be empirically demonstrable. For example, did the addition of tenure improve faculty recruiting at Accomac? Perhaps, but so might have the college's inclusion in *U.S. News* rankings, higher SAT scores of entering students, lower student-faculty ratios, or a number of other factors. "Many organizational events and processes are important more for what they express than for what they produce" (Bolman and Deal, 1991, p. 244). For Accomac and Lakeview, tenure served as a proxy for quality, prestige, and normalcy. So, while a direct cause-effect relationship between tenure and improved faculty recruitment may be difficult to establish, an indirect substitution effect may be more evident. Because tenure *expresses* (rather than produces) certain institutional characteristics, it served as an important signaling mechanism to prospective faculty members.

CHAPTER 8
Conclusions

STUDY OVERVIEW

LET ME BRIEFLY REVIEW WHAT HAS BEEN DEMONSTRATED THUS FAR IN this book. There were differences in the process of organizational change at the four sites. At Scott College, which abolished tenure, the president tightly controlled the governance and management of the college; faculty were excluded from decision making. The two institutions that embraced tenure used a process of shared decision-making and consultation. Faculty, administrators, and trustees all had an active role in determining the outcome of the new tenure policy. Rowlette College was an anomaly. Because of a history of financial emergencies, constituents at Rowlette only gave sporadic attention to the issue of faculty employment. Most constituents, including faculty members, did not show much concern for tenure. It is also important to acknowledge that Rowlette was an anomaly because, unlike the other three sites, its policy change did not occur within the term of one president. Rather, the 13-year gradual shift to long-term contracts involved three presidents. This inconsistent leadership contributed to the sporadic nature of the change process.

For Accomac and Lakeview colleges, the process of change to a tenure system was part of a larger context of moving into the mainstream of higher education. Tenure was both a mechanism for achieving, and a visible sign of having attained, institutional maturity. For Scott and Rowlette, the process of change to contracts was driven by anti-isomorphic pressures to be different from the norm. Factors such as faculty zones of indifference (both colleges), financial distraction (Rowlette College), and mission socialization (Scott College) made these institutions less likely to be attracted to the mainstream employment model in higher education.

Each college president embraced the change in faculty employment policy based in part on the "learning" of his previous successful job experiences. The presidents at Accomac and Lakeview both hailed from large universities with tenure. The presidents at Rowlette and Scott both worked for organizations without tenure. Each president relied on past learning to guide his endorsement of the shifts in policy.

All four colleges used the addition or discontinuance of tenure as a symbolic solution to various problems. The shift to or away from tenure was a signal about institutional identity to constituencies on and off campus. Accomac and Lakeview used tenure to indicate normalcy, quality, and prestige. Scott used the removal of tenure to signal presidential power, bold leadership, and a rejection of academic orthodoxy. Rowlette's trustees used the discontinuance of tenure to signal that they were attending to the college's financial problems.

This book suggests that there is a tenuous relationship between the loosely coupled nature of organizational change in higher education and shared governance. Scott College, which rejected the shared governance model, had the most tightly coupled process of the four institutions. Accomac and Lakeview colleges, which embraced participatory management, displayed some characteristics of the loosely coupled/organized anarchy model. Rowlette College, which displayed the most loosely coupled process of change, had an exaggerated model of participation, in which multiple leaders and many participants moved in and out of the decision-making arena over the course of 13 years.

This study also suggests there is an inverse relationship between loose coupling and shared meaning of symbols among organizational participants. As more people agree on the meaning of a particular symbol, the change process surrounding that symbol will be more tightly coupled. At Scott College, most constituents viewed tenure in the same negative light, and the decision-making process was highly controlled. At the other end of the continuum, constituents at Rowlette could not muster much interest in, let alone shared meaning of, academic tenure. Tenure was not an agreed-upon rite, and the change process was loosely coordinated.

ADDITIONAL FINDINGS

In the process of conducting the research for this book, other important findings emerged. These findings are as follows:

Conclusions

All four colleges wanted to improve faculty evaluation

Paradoxically, the two sets of colleges moved in *opposite* directions in an attempt to accomplish the *same* goal: to improve the way by which faculty are evaluated for long-term, protected employment status. For the vast majority of faculty, employment security at these colleges has never been in jeopardy. Table 8.1 provides a comparison of dismissal rates at the four colleges under both old and new employment policies. Under both policies, faculty were rarely dismissed for performance-related reasons. Prior to the policy changes at Accomac and Lakeview colleges, contracts were regularly renewed for all faculty, so much so that the faculty referred to the system as de facto or virtual tenure. These colleges moved to a tenure system because they wanted to intensify the scrutiny of faculty performance. Consistent with the arguments of tenure's proponents, they believed that a one-time tenure decision would bear greater weight and impose more rigor than periodic contract reviews.

Table 8.1 Turnover Rates for Performance-Related Reasons at Research Sites

	Contract-to-Tenure Colleges	
	Under Contracts (before change)	*Under Tenure (after change)*
Accomac	Between 1983 and 1993, contracts for five faculty members not renewed	Between 1994 and 1999, of 21 tenure candidates, three professors denied tenure and four others counseled to resign.
Lakeview	Data unavailable, but the provost reported, "I think we've terminated three people in 15 years."	In 1999 (first year of new policy), all eight candidates successfully earned tenure. All nine professors who underwent post-tenure review received positive results.
	Tenure-to-Contracts Colleges	
	Under Tenure (before change)	*Under Contracts (after change)*
Rowlette	Data unavailable, but interviews suggest that, prior to moratorium, tenure was rarely denied.	From 1988 to 1999, the college hired 67 new faculty members, five of whom did not have contracts renewed for cause.
Scott	Data unavailable, but interviews suggest that tenure was rarely denied.	Between 1994 and 1999, 10 of 12 junior faculty members awarded long-term contracts; the other two remained on annual contracts. Of 42 post-tenure or contract-renewal reviews, 39 successful and three counseled to resign.

Similarly, Scott and Rowlette colleges—prior to their policy changes—offered tenure to nearly all candidates, often without *any* type of review. Two examples are worth repeating:

- After my fourth year, I went to the dean's office to pick up my new contract. I told the dean, "I'm supposed to get tenure this year." So, the dean picked up the phone and told his secretary, "Sandra, Steve gets tenure this year." (Scott College)
- The contract I had to sign [gave] a rank and a salary, and then there was a section that said "comments." And under "comments," it said "tenure." That's all. Just one word. (Rowlette College)

The tenure-granting process did not entail a rigorous examination of teaching ability or scholarship. Instead, faculty, administrators, and trustees viewed tenure as a mechanism that guaranteed job security regardless of qualifications, rather than a system that ensured selectivity and quality control.

Did the change in policy produce the desired effect of more rigor in the evaluation process? At Accomac and Lakeview, the new evaluation policy led to increased rigor for some faculty, but not for all. On one hand, the standards for new faculty members were raised. At Accomac, for example, junior faculty on the tenure track were expected to produce more scholarship of higher quality than peers at the college ten years earlier. An analysis of the Accomac faculty handbooks (see Table 8.2) indicates that evaluation standards were indeed stricter under the new tenure policy than under term contracts. Furthermore, as Table 8.1 demonstrates, a slightly higher number of junior faculty members were forced or counseled to resign once the new tenure policy was implemented.

Table 8.2. Differences in Acceptable Forms of Scholarship in Accomac's Faculty handbook under Contract Policy (prior to 1993) and Tenure Policy (after 1993)

Accepted "Professional Activities" Under Contract Policy	Accepted "Professional Activities" Under Tenure Policy
Publications (without any stipulation of type or scope).	Scholarly publications. "Articles on intellectual topics in journals, magazines, or newspapers."
"Actively participating in professional conferences or conventions."	Presentations of papers at professional meetings.
"Taking new coursework or training in one's field to remain current and competent."	"Studying or training that expands competence... *into new areas*." (Emphasis added)

On the other hand, the move to tenure contributed to the very problem that it was supposed to solve—lack of rigor in faculty evaluation—because large numbers of faculty were grandfathered into the new tenure

Conclusions

systems without any type of review. Sixty-seven percent of Accomac full-time faculty and 83 percent of Lakeview full-time faculty were automatically awarded tenure without having to undergo performance evaluations, an unsettling practice for some faculty members at the colleges. An Accomac professor remarked:

> We had to grandfather 50 faculty into tenure. They received no review.
>
> Q: *Was there concern that some of your colleagues were getting tenure without really earning it?*
>
> Yes. . . . It's dangerous to suddenly take a whole lump of people and create a tenure system, when they might be here another 30 or 40 years. So you create a division. Junior faculty feel like they're carrying the institution on their backs.

The automatic tenuring process was politically necessary at both institutions because, for all intents and purposes, faculty already had employment security under contracts. Senior faculty would not have agreed to the new tenure systems without a guarantee of their own job security. After many years under the contract system—in which they were not held to stringent standards, especially for scholarship and publication—these professors did not want to face the possibility of being denied tenure. While politically expedient, the grandfathering of large numbers of faculty created a glaring irony for these two institutions. In order to improve the rigor of the evaluation process for future junior faculty, the colleges had to first forego increased rigor for the majority of current faculty. While the post-tenure review process written into the policies at both institutions theoretically might mitigate this concern, the actual track record of post-tenure review at each institution suggests otherwise. Accomac has never implemented its review of tenured faculty members, and Lakeview has granted positive reviews to all PTR candidates in its first year of operation.

The outcomes of the policy changes are also mixed at Scott and Rowlette. Faculty members at Rowlette and Scott colleges observed that the evaluation process became more rigorous under the new policy of term contracts, an unsurprising finding given the complete lack of standards under the former tenure policy. But, interviews and faculty-employment data also suggest that faculty members were not terminated at significantly higher rates than under the prior tenure system. Scott College has a five-year track record since tenure was abolished (1994–1999). As indicated in Table 8.1, of the 54 faculty members who have undergone contract-renewal or post-tenure review, none has been dismissed, although three departed voluntarily after receiving negative evaluations. Similarly, in a ten-year period (1988–1999) following the implementation of multi-year contracts, Rowlette College did not renew five of 67 faculty members' contracts for performance-related reasons. These data are consistent with Chait and Trower's research (1997), which found that "contract systems, *in practice*, mirror tenure systems on the dimension of economic security" (p. 6. Emphasis in original).

On one hand, the solution to abolish tenure did not fit the problem of faculty evaluation. While the faculty evaluation process at Scott College led to three voluntary separations, 94 percent of faculty members reviewed under the new contract system remained. If the goal were to induce some modest turnover, the college could have simply tightened its standards for tenure. On the other hand, the abolition of tenure at Scott College was an important ceremonial event that prompted faculty to be more attentive to their performance. The president stated:

> I think [the elimination of tenure] had a halo effect. . . . It showed our seriousness. It caused people to think, "Well, if they can get rid of tenure, they can get rid of me." . . . If discontinuing tenure doesn't send a signal that accountability is taken seriously, I don't know what does.

The elimination of tenure sent a powerful symbolic message that the college was attending to the problem of faculty accountability, even though the shift in policy may not have produced much faculty turnover in practice. The mere change in policy signaled that the college was willing to make radical strides to address issues of faculty performance.

All four colleges could have improved the effectiveness of their faculty evaluation process without revamping the employment system. But as discussed in chapter seven, the addition or removal of tenure signaled something "big." The policy shifts sent messages about institutional identity to various constituencies that simple improvements to faculty evaluation could not. A complete overhaul to faculty employment policy was necessary to catch people's attention. So, while the two sets of colleges moved in *opposite directions*, they undertook the same action—a fundamental and complete shift in existing policy—for the *same purpose*. The very act of overhaul, irrespective of direction, had greater impact than the substance of the change per se.

The colleges that instituted tenure did not do so as a matter of principle.

Faculty members at the two colleges that adopted tenure rarely talked about the basic principles of tenure: academic freedom or economic security. Many commentators have asserted that academic freedom cannot exist in the absence of tenure (e.g., Adams, 1974; Benjamin, 1995; Chemerinsky, 1998; Commission on Academic Tenure, 1973). Therefore, one might have expected faculty at Accomac and Lakeview to claim that academic freedom prompted their advocacy for the adoption of tenure. Participants at these

Conclusions

colleges, however, did not offer this argument. This is not to say that academic freedom was unimportant or irrelevant, but interviewees did not assert that it was a primary reason to shift policy. Instead, the chief benefits of a tenure system in the eyes of faculty were largely symbolic.

As discussed in chapter seven, tenure was a sign of maturation, prominence, personal and institutional honor, and entry into the guild. At the institutional level, constituents at Accomac and Lakeview asserted that their colleges would gain prestige if they offered tenure. At a personal level, faculty on contracts felt like second-class citizens. They felt that faculty at institutions without tenure did not have the appropriate vestments to signify entry into the "priesthood." In this sense, faculty members' preoccupation with having tenure seems not too different than the preoccupation of high school seniors (and their parents) gaining admission to "name-brand" colleges. While they may (or may not) be able to discern a substantive difference in the quality of teaching and learning between an Ivy League school and other less selective institutions, students are more likely to be concerned with the non-educational benefits, such as name recognition and attribution that accrue from attending the former rather than the latter. Tenure has similar benefits. Does tenure ensure procedural safeguards against infringements to academic freedom? Yes. Is this reason why the faculty members in this study wanted tenure? No. Tenure was more important for what it communicated than for what it stipulated.

At some small college campuses, academic freedom is not dependent on tenure; at others, the definition of academic freedom is circumscribed.

The Commission on Academic Tenure in Higher Education (1973) maintained that "academic freedom is not adequately protected" under contract systems (p. 19). By contrast, this research found that academic freedom can and does exist at some institutions without tenure, supporting the findings of Trower (1996a) and Chait and Trower (1997). At Rowlette and Lakeview colleges, most participants maintained that academic freedom has always been protected regardless of employment policy. While one Lakeview professor maintained that junior faculty members were sometimes reluctant to speak against the powerful chairs under the contract system, a colleague expressed the majority opinion that, both before and after tenure was introduced, "this [has been] a very open place, a rather liberal place. Nobody's threatened because of what they say or do." In fact, interviewees at both campuses took pride in their institutions' steadfast commitment to openness, freedom, and truth. A Rowlette professor bluntly declared, "There has never been a loss of academic freedom." The Lakeview provost stated, "If you can find anybody on campus to say, 'I'm glad we got [tenure] because I thought my academic freedom was at risk,'

I would fall out of my chair. And I'm not being cute. I really have never, ever heard that."

Academic freedom at these colleges depended on the interplay of personalities. As one professor maintained, "The seasons of caution here... wax and wane. It has more to do with the personalities of the president and the provost than with tenure or lack thereof." This finding, too, is consistent with Chait and Trower's (1997) conclusion that academic freedom at contract colleges depend upon "a mix of procedural safeguards, policy statements, *and* tradition, trust, and goodwill" (p. 24. Emphasis in original).

This finding does not imply that academic freedom exists equally robustly on *all* campuses without tenure. Some faculty members at Scott College diverged in their interpretation of academic freedom. Many faculty members claimed that their academic freedom was not diminished after tenure was eliminated because they narrowly defined the concept. One professor interpreted academic freedom to mean only "the ability to teach in your field things that have been found in research, regardless of whether the administration agrees with it or not." Using this definition, he asserted, "I don't feel any threat that I'm going to lose my job if I do that." The Scott faculty handbook also defined academic freedom more narrowly than the norm: "Teachers should at all times seek accuracy, should exercise appropriate restraint, should show respect for others, should make explicit they are not an institutional spokesman [sic], and should not make statements which are detrimental to the mission and/or operation of the College" (1996, p.14).[1] Many Scott faculty did not define their loss of voice in campus governance as an abridgement of academic freedom because they believed the president had a right and responsibility to make management decisions. Those who believed the faculty should participate in governance felt differently about the impact on academic freedom in the move away from tenure. Said one long-time professor, "I feel that people are reluctant to rock the boat too much. I think that is unfortunate because everyone needs to be able to express their opinion. I do feel that has changed [with the removal of tenure]."

---

1. This is in contrast to the AAUP's definition of academic freedom, which encompasses three areas for college and university faculty members: (1) "full freedom in research and in the publications of the results . . ." (2) "freedom in the classroom in discussing their subject . . ." and (3) "when they speak or write as citizens," freedom "from institutional censorship or discipline." (AAUP, 1995, pp. 3-4).

Conclusions

In terms of job security, contracts are, in effect, de facto tenure.

One of the key rationales for tenure is that it provides "a sufficient degree of economic security to make the profession attractive to men and women of ability" (AAUP, 1940, p. 49). Because term contracts provide institutions with the flexibility to more easily increase or decrease the size of their faculty, advocates of tenure have argued that contracts offer faculty less job security than academic tenure (Commission on Academic Tenure, 1973). In practice, there was little difference in job security between tenure and contract systems at these four colleges. In the five years since the onset of contracts, only three faculty members at Scott College have left the institution as a result of negative performance reviews. At Rowlette College, in the ten years from 1988 to 1999, only five faculty members have been denied contract renewals.

Furthermore, interviewees at these two tenure-to-contract sites did not associate job security more with one employment policy than the other. When asked why faculty were not upset when tenure was discontinued at Rowlette College, a tenured professor replied, "It wasn't a gut issue. You didn't need tenure; you could stay here forever." For some faculty members, a contract system was just as good as tenure. An untenured Rowlette professor asserted, "Faculty just [didn't] feel that tenure would enhance security in any way."

IMPLICATIONS FOR PRACTICE

The research for this book was conducted to infuse the literature on faculty employment policies with evidence about how and why colleges abolish or institute tenure. This book concludes with some practical advice. These findings have implications for faculty, administrators, and trustees on campuses that are considering or are in the process of altering their faculty employment policies. Policy makers should consider the following:

1. Before embarking on any alteration to policy, faculty and administrators should be diligent in assessing and improving performance evaluation processes, regardless of the type of employment policy. Scott College faculty and administrators noted that if they had been more rigorous in awarding tenure so that unqualified people did not assume tenured positions, then the grave problems with "deadwood" might not have occurred down the line. Proponents of tenure have argued that, in theory, only the most qualified people survive the strenuous up-or-out review process, so that tenure ensures a high-quality faculty (Commission on Academic Tenure, 1973; Finkin, 1996; Machlup, 1964). In practice, not all colleges are so disciplined. Advocates who want to insure that their faculty employment systems are effective and functional should heed the reminiscence of a Scott professor: "I really believe if we could have implemented

this evaluation system 15 or 10 years ago, then maybe the tenure issue would not have been a problem."

2. Do not underestimate the symbolic, nonrational reasons for change in employment policy. Those who view the academy in a rational, bureaucratic way ignore the significant isomorphic pressures on colleges to offer tenure systems. For example, in a December 1999 article, the former chairman of the Massachusetts Board of Higher Education denounced tenure because, in his view, it protects mediocre or incompetent professors from accountability; if colleges would abolish tenure, he asserted, then they could cut away their faculty deadwood (Carlin, 1999). This argument, however, is not likely to convince policy makers to reform academic employment policy. In addition to being an element of faculty employment policies, tenure is a magical token, a proxy, a badge, and a metaphor. For mainstream colleges and universities to relinquish tenure, an adequate substitute for those symbolic attributes would need to be offered. This book does not identify what that substitute might be.

Policy makers would be better off to stress the argument that the change is inextricably tied to symbolic benefits. For example, trustees at both Accomac and Lakeview were willing to adopt tenure because they were convinced that it was a vehicle to transport the college to a higher level of prestige and quality. According to the Accomac board chair, trustees "were persuaded by President Robinson that the quality of the faculty was so closely linked to tenure that it would be sabotage by the board not to do it."

Furthermore, policy makers should not expect much substantive change in practice. For example, the elimination of tenure is not likely to produce greater institutional flexibility and more faculty turnover. If the goal of the elimination of tenure is to remove "deadwood" or gain institutional nimbleness through labor force adjustment, policy makers are likely to be disappointed. The experiences of Rowlette and Scott colleges indicate that faculty turnover did not significantly change.

3. Do not assume that all faculty will support the shift. This almost goes without saying for colleges considering a modification to or elimination of tenure. At Scott, the change in policy elicited protests from a small group of faculty and left others feeling uneasy about their future. Before creating a divisive situation by discontinuing tenure, decision-makers should first consider other options, such as an early retirement plan or a post-tenure review process. Academic leaders could avoid much rancor by considering changes that stop short of the abolition of tenure. Commentators at Rowlette and Scott noted that early retirement programs spurred more faculty turnover than the changes in employment policy. Furthermore, Scott College could have improved its faculty evaluation system in less drastic ways than the discontinuation of tenure. If Scott simply

wanted to identify and remediate marginal or mediocre professors, it could have considered a post-tenure review process, which serves the same policy objectives.

Likewise, campuses considering a shift toward tenure also should not assume faculty will be on board. Some faculty members intentionally choose to work at institutions without tenure. The experiences of Lakeview College indicated that, for some professors, tenure was a symbol of stagnancy and an obstacle of hierarchy between junior and senior faculty members. They came to Lakeview to avoid, as one professor described, "the political elements of tenure." Proponents of tenure need to make a clear and compelling case to all constituencies.

Furthermore, campus leaders should expect that many current faculty members will want to be automatically granted tenure. Under the contract system, long-time faculty members at both Accomac and Lakeview considered themselves tenured for all practical purposes. Therefore, they demanded to be grandfathered into the new policy. This expectation operated on two levels. First, there was an emotional level. Senior faculty members felt a high amount of personal investment in the school, a place to which they had devoted their lives. Being forced to go through a formal evaluation—in essence, a process to prove their worth—would have been an affront to their long-time loyalty and, in their view, their long record of competent performance. Second, there was a concern about economic security. Both colleges moved to tenure to increase expectations for scholarly output. Senior faculty did not want to be subject to these higher standards.

Administrators of other institutions contemplating a move to tenure should be cognizant of this expectation. Research at another college attempting to move to tenure (Mallon, 1999) revealed that the process has stalled for years because, in part, faculty have resisted the president's insistence that *all* faculty members undergo an up-or-out review if a tenure policy is to be installed.

4. Advocates of change should seek a president who comes from an institution with an employment policy similar to the desired change. This study indicates that presidents are likely to support the move to tenure if they previously succeeded at an institution with tenure. Both presidents at the contract-to-tenure institutions brought their sympathies for and strong belief in academic tenure to their new posts. Conversely, a leader who has been on a campus with contracts and has resisted the strong isomorphic pressures to offer tenure will be more apt to stay that course. A leader who has experienced success at a college without tenure will be more likely to try to replicate that environment.

Supporters of the change in policy also should be cognizant of the importance of the backgrounds of the governing board. While the majority of trustees at all four colleges were corporate leaders, the boards at the two institutions that abolished tenure were almost exclusively business people. The colleges that instituted tenure had board members with more diverse professional backgrounds, including several academics. The board chair at Accomac was a retired university president.

College presidents should consider the following:

1. They should make public statements early and often in favor of initiatives they support. The presidents in this study who overcame resistance to the change in employment policy did so by publicly advocating for change. Their visible, public support provided legitimacy to and momentum for the movement, and also gave confidence to core supporters. Many sources on these campuses professed that the change would not have occurred without the president's outward support.

2. With complex and controversial issues, presidents should develop a small coterie of like-minded influential people to diffuse support for the issue. President Murin at Lakeview faced an initial outcry against tenure from the majority of trustees. However, with the aid of the board chair and several knowledgeable consultants, he was able to win over board members. President Robinson at Accomac also insured he had the support of the two most influential trustees for the tenure proposal.

Faculty leaders should consider the following:

1. Position changes as beneficial to the institution. Faculty leaders at Accomac and Lakeview successfully argued that tenure would bring prestige to the institution as well as to the individual. They argued that tenure was an important step in achieving broader institutional goals. Other controversial proposals might gain support from administrators, board members, students, alumni, and other constituencies if the case can be made that the institution would benefit from the policy change.

2. First present a proposal privately and informally and allow the idea to percolate. Big changes, such as those to faculty employment policy, may be initially hard to swallow for presidents and other leaders. President Robinson took several years before he warmed up to the idea for moving back to a tenure system. Additionally, change agents who raise a proposal privately and informally give leaders time to carefully consider the idea. Faculty leaders at Lakeview discussed their tenure and rank proposal with President Murin in a private meeting during the presidential selection process. By the time Murin officially assumed the president, he was aware of and prepared to engage in the discussions.

3. Continue to apply pressure. Large-scale change does not happen overnight. Proposals for change may need time to gather momentum. Faculty leaders at Accomac had to approach the president several times during his first years in the president before he was prepared to undertake the tenure issue. Other large-scale changes in higher education will take similar persistence.

Appendix
Research Design and Methodology

THIS STUDY ON CHANGE IN FACULTY EMPLOYMENT POLICIES WAS GUIDed by a rigorous qualitative research design and methodology. This appendix describes guiding research questions, research design and rationale, methods, data analysis procedures, trustworthiness and ethics, and limitations of the study.

RESEARCH QUESTIONS AND PROPOSITIONS

The following research questions guided this study:

1. Does the organizational change process differ between the institutions that changed faculty appointment policies from term contracts to tenure and the institutions that shifted from tenure to term contracts? If so, how?

2. Does the theory of loosely coupled systems apply similarly to the process of organizational change at the two sets of institutions (colleges that moved from contracts to tenure and colleges that moved from tenure to contracts)?

As noted in chapter one, I developed the following propositions based on the literature as well as my own hunches about academic tenure and higher education administration. These were hunches, not hypotheses:

For colleges that instituted tenure, the process of organizational change is marked by the involvement of many participants in the decision-making and change process. Because tenure is the standard of faculty employment, I expected faculty to be active and supportive in the change process. The president is one voice among many who contributes to the change in policy. "Who's in charge" of the organizational change process is unclear and, at times, contested. Participants do not agree upon the goals and outcomes of the change in faculty appointment policy.

Second, for colleges that dismantled tenure and implemented term contracts, the process of organizational change is tightly coupled. The literature on tenure implies that faculty would never agree to relinquish what they view as an "inviolable principle" of the academy (Adams, 1974). Therefore, these institutions operated under a different organizational change model than loose coupling's decentralized decision making and limited presidential authority. Instead, the change process is directed and controlled by a limited number of participants "from the top," including the board of trustees and the president. The president has a clear line of authority to implement the policy shift. Faculty are largely excluded from the decision-making and organizational change process. The change leaders tie the results of the shift in policy to intended goals.

Third, the theories of loosely coupled systems apply to the process of organizational change when institutions embrace tenure. Institutions that embrace tenure are, in effect, embracing higher education's values and traditions. Because higher education prizes incremental change, decentralized authority, and shared decision-making, a change to tenure supports a loosely coupled interpretation: a president with sporadic influence (Cohen & March, 1986); multicephalous leadership (Scott, 1992); nonrational reasons for change (Cohen & March, 1986); and a change process that is slow and time-consuming (Weick, 1982).

Conversely, the loosely coupled model of change does not apply to colleges that moved from tenure to contracts. Colleges that eliminate tenure display fewer of the elements of loose couplings in their decision-making and change processes. The diffuse, fluid, decentralized decision-making processes of loose coupling (Cohen & March, 1974, 1986; Weick, 1976, 1984) are antithetical to how change to term contracts is *imposed* upon the institution in a hierarchical fashion. Instead, other theories apply more forcefully to the change process. For example, Fisher's theory of the strong president (1984) may be appropriate when the president forces the college to dismantle tenure.

RESEARCH DESIGN AND RATIONALE
Qualitative Methods

The purpose of this study was to examine the process of organizational change at two institutions that instituted academic tenure and at two institutions that relinquished tenure for term contracts. I wanted to understand (a) the process by which each college instituted a new faculty employment policy, (b) each college's historical and sociological context surrounding the change process so that I could fully understand each case, and (c) the applicability, if any, of the loosely coupled model of organizational change to the actual experiences of each college. I used qualitative research methods because I raised questions about how "existing theories, models, and concepts apply to [a] new and different population or setting" (Marshall and Rossman, 1989, p. 22). Qualitative research

> assumes that there are multiple realities—that the world is not an objective thing out there but a function of personal interaction and perception. It is a highly subjective phenomenon in need of interpreting rather than measuring. Beliefs rather than facts form the basis of perception. Research is exploratory, inductive, and emphasizes processes rather than ends. (Merriam, 1988, p.17)

It was appropriate to use a qualitative research design for this study because I wanted to investigate a complex organizational process (Marshall and Rossman, 1989) of change, specifically change in faculty appointment policies. I assumed at the beginning of this study that participants would have multiple views of why and how the changes in policy occurred. Because there was scant research on this topic, my study was exploratory and required in-depth analysis (Merriam, 1988; Patton, 1990).

The Case Study Method

The case study method is used to investigate bounded systems (Stake, 1995). Patton (1990) wrote:

> Case studies . . . become particularly useful where one needs to understand some special people, particular problem, or unique situation in great depth, and where one can identify cases rich in information—rich in the sense that a great deal can be learned from a few exemplars of the phenomenon in question. . . . Case studies are particularly valuable when the evaluation aims to capture individual differences or unique variations from one program setting to another, or from one program experience to another. . . . [A] qualitative case study seeks to describe that unit in depth and detail, in context, and holistically. (Patton, 1990, p. 54)

I used case study methods to address the research questions because this study focused on complex, contemporary processes that are hard to control and quantify (Merriam, 1988). My study met Yin's guidelines (1994) for adopting case study methods:

1. The research questions are "how" and "why" questions. My research questions, in essence, asked, "how did change in faculty appoint-

ment policy occur on each campus?" and "how did the change processes differ among campuses?"

2. Little control exists over events. I could not control and manipulate variables, such as institutional history, participants in the change process, or order of events.

3. Context is important because of contemporary, real-life problems. I focused on an applied problem of organizational change in which contemporary campus constituents took part.

I analyzed the four cases of organizational change through the lens of loosely coupled systems (Cohen & March, 1974, 1986; Weick, 1976, 1984). Such an analysis called for a case study method because "interpretative case studies . . . are used . . . to illustrate, support, or challenge theoretical assumptions held prior to data gathering" (Merriam, 1988, pp. 27-28).

Multiple Case Methods

More specifically, I used multiple case study methods by investigating change at four sites. Miles and Huberman (1994) offered two reasons for using multiple cases:

> One aim of studying multiple cases is to increase generalizability, reassuring yourself that the events and processes in one well-described setting are not wholly idiosyncratic. At a deeper level, the aim is to see processes and outcomes across many cases, to understand how they are qualified by local conditions, and thus to develop more sophisticated descriptions and more powerful explanations. (p. 172)

In this study, I searched for comparisons of the change process between and among groups of institutions that shifted in opposite directions. While a single case study on an institution that either instituted or abolished tenure would have added to the literature on faculty employment policy, a multiple case study of colleges that enacted decisions in opposite directions is essentially richer and more interesting. Furthermore, by including two colleges that executed each policy shift, I transcended the "radical particularism" of single site studies (Firestone & Herriott, 1983).

Yin (1994) instructed that multiple case studies must have "replication logic" so that each case "(a) predicts similar results (a *literal replication*) or (b) produces contrasting results for predictable reasons (a *theoretical replication*)" (p. 46. Emphasis in original.) My study was predicated on theoretical replication logic. I expected that the two colleges that instituted tenure would display similar patterns of loose coupling in their process of change, but the change process at colleges that eliminated tenure would not be loosely coupled. I expected predictable reasons for these contrasting results: institutions moving to tenure would be embracing the traditions of higher education, including decentralized decision making and multicephalous leadership, whereas leaders at institutions eliminating tenure would impose the change on faculty without their input.

Unit Of Analysis

The unit of analysis—"what my case is and where my case leaves off" (Miles & Huberman, 1994)—can be a program, event, process, group, organization, or concept (Merriam, 1988). In this study, the unit of analysis was the process of change in faculty appointment policy at each institution. I was not studying the nature of *all* decision-making processes at each institution but rather just the bounded territory of this one, albeit dramatic, change in faculty employment practices.

Nevertheless, I realized that institutional context would be an important factor in this research. Each campus's governance and decision-making norms influenced how the college undertook the process of change in faculty employment policy. For that reason, I included several questions in the interview protocol that addressed issues of context and history. While governance provided an important context, it was not itself the focus of the study.

RESEARCH METHODS
Sample

I investigated four sites—two institutions that moved to tenure and two institutions that moved to contracts. Two sites from each category was appropriate because the total universe of colleges that have changed faculty appointment policies is small and access may have been difficult at a larger number, especially those that made the alteration in policy many years ago.

I relied on several sources to identify institutions that changed faculty employment policies.

1. I conducted a search of the *Chronicle of Higher Education*'s online database archive, with the assumption that, in some cases, such fundamental policy changes would have generated press coverage.

2. I researched articles in the AAUP's magazine, *Academe*, which publishes results of the association's investigations of alleged abridgements of academic freedom. I expected that the magazine would have reported on some instances when colleges abolished or reinstated tenure.

3. I accessed the files of the Project on Faculty Appointments at the Harvard Graduate School of Education, a national research project on fac-

ulty appointment issues. The Project had records on several colleges that shifted policies that I had not identified through the first two approaches. Through each of these sources, I identified a number of institutions that had changed policy. In total, I found eight institutions that moved from contracts to tenure and 15 institutions that shifted from tenure to contracts.

Next, I attempted to contact by phone the chief academic officer (CAO) at each institution to confirm that the college had in fact changed policy, to inquire if the new policy was still in effect, and to request a copy of the faculty handbook. Seven of 8 colleges that moved to tenure and 11 of 15 colleges that moved to contracts responded to my inquiry and sent me the requested information. I attempted to re-contact each CAO at the five non-responding institutions. At three of the non-responding colleges without tenure, the CAO did not reply to repeated phone messages nor would the staff disclose information to me. At one of the contract institutions and at the tenure institution, the CAO referred me to the president's office. Both presidents requested a letter in writing explaining the purpose of the study but still did not respond when that request was filled. I was not able to determine in any of the five cases the reasons for their lack of response.

Based on the review of responding institutions, I developed the following criteria of importance (Patton, 1990):

(1) The change occurred at a single institution.

One of the institutions that embraced tenure did so as a result of a merger with another institution. I felt that combination of campuses would complicate my research design, so I eliminated this institution from consideration.

(2) The institution fundamentally changed its faculty appointment policy "recently."

I was cognizant that key informants' retrospective stories of important actors, events, and processes in the organizational change process would be subject to errors of recall (Glick, et al., 1995), which would most likely increase with the passage of time. Therefore, my priority was to recruit those sites in which the change process occurred most recently. I listed each group of institutions in descending chronological order. I first contacted those institutions that overhauled their policy most recently.

For the contract-to-tenure colleges, I sent an inquiry letter to the presidents of Lakeview College, which changed in 1997, and Accomac College, which changed in 1993 (see Exhibit 1 for a sample inquiry letter). The pres-

Appendix: Research Design and Methodology

idents of the two institutions called me after receiving my letter and enthusiastically agreed to participate.

I initially contacted three tenure-to-contract sites based on the year in which their policy shift occurred. One of the institutions, Scott College, which moved to contracts in 1993, agreed to participate, while the other two declined. I sent another letter to the president at a fourth tenure-to-contracts institution, Rowlette College, which changed in 1986. The president agreed to participate.

(3) The institution granted access for my study.

The presidents at two of the first three tenure-to-contract institutions that I contacted declined participation in the study. Both stated that they didn't want to rekindle difficult and contentious issues that the shift to contracts apparently engendered.

(4) The presidents and most institutional leaders (e.g. vice president for academic affairs, faculty leaders, and board of trustees leaders) were accessible to be interviewed;

In my initial conversation with each president, I requested access to administrators, faculty, and board leaders who participated in the change process. At Lakeview and Scott colleges, numerous participants in each category were still employed with the college, and the president assured me accessibility to them. At Accomac and Rowlette colleges, the former presidents and board leaders involved in the change had retired from the institution, but I was told that these individuals could be contacted. Therefore, I felt comfortable with each site that I could access those people integral to the story of how the institution changes its faculty employment policy.

Selecting Informants

In order to understand an organizational change process, "it [is] necessary that the research methodology slice vertically through the organization, obtaining data from multiple levels and perspectives" (Leonard-Barton, 1995, p. 40). I used several methods to identify key informants who held various positions at each campus.

First, during my initial contact with the president of each institution, I asked for the name of a primary informant (Merriam, 1988), someone who was knowledgeable about the process and could inform me about other people with whom I should speak. At the four sites, the primary informants, respectively, held positions of dean of the college (Scott College), assistant to the vice president for academic affairs (Rowlette College), special assistant to the president (Accomac College), and consultant to the president (Lakeview College). I asked this primary informant to identify other key informants, such as the chief academic officer, deans, key faculty members, and board of trustees members who were instrumental in the change process. To further expand the informant base, I used a snowballing or chain technique (Patton, 1990; Bogdan and Bilken, 1992) for locating "information-rich key informants" by asking these secondary informants, "Who knows a lot about this process? Who should I talk to?" (Patton, 1990, p. 176). By asking these questions to interviewees, I identified at least one additional person on each campus who had an important perspective on the change process.

Finally, to eliminate key informant biases (Maxwell, 1996), I reviewed institutional documents (faculty senate minutes, student newspaper articles, and other documents) and external sources (newspapers and accreditation reports) to identify other informants, particularly those who opposed the change in policy or who had left the institution. Through this strategy, I identified two additional informants, one at Scott College and one at Rowlette College.

Data Collection

I used three data collection techniques to investigate the research questions: in-depth interviews, institutional documents, and external written material related to the change in faculty appointment policy.

Interviews

Interviews from key informants were the primary method for attaining information on the events and processes of organizational change that have already occurred (Glick, et al, 1995). Because it is important to portray differing views in a case study, "the interview is the main road to multiple realities" (Stake, 1995, p. 64). Interviews are useful to gather large amounts of data and to immediately pose follow-up questions (Marshall & Rossman, 1989).

I compiled a set of potential interviewees at each site. (See Exhibit 2 for a list of interviewees at each college.) I sent letters to the individuals informing them about the study and asking them to participate. (See sample request letter in Exhibit 3.) After I mailed the letters, I telephoned each person. Most people replied affirmatively to the request when reached by phone. I re-contacted those individuals who had not responded to my initial phone call. These individuals also agreed to participate. During the phone conversations, I scheduled a one-hour block of time for the interview during my time on campus.

In each interview, I wanted to obtain the informant's story of how the institution changed its faculty appointment policy. I used a focused inter-

Appendix: Research Design and Methodology

view approach, which uses a set of structured, open-ended questions to elicit comments on particular topics (Yin, 1994). The focused interview protocol was the same for both sets of colleges that moved in opposite policy directions (see Exhibit 4). The interview protocol began with broad questions that allowed the informant to tell his or her story about the change process. Follow-up questions allowed me to focus on issues of presidential involvement, faculty and trustee participation, and the decision-making process—influential factors of change identified in the loosely coupled model. The focused interview design allowed me to probe additional issues and concerns that each interviewee raised. In this way, the open-ended questions permitted me to gather the informant's point of view without predetermining important elements of the organizational change process (Patton, 1990). The answers to these questions illuminated the role that various actors had in the organizational change process and the ways in which the change process unfolded.

I interviewed ten individuals at Scott College, ten at Accomac, nine at Lakeview, and seven at Rowlette for this study (for a total of 36 interviews). Thirty-one interviews were conducted in person when I was on each campus and five interviews were conducted by phone. In three of these five cases, the interviewee was no longer affiliated with the college and, therefore, was not on campus; one faculty member was away during my visit; and one trustee lived in a different state. With each of these individuals, I conducted a phone interview after my site visit, a less-than-perfect but sometimes necessary way of reaching people (Rubin & Rubin, 1995). The one main difference between in-person and phone interviews was length: the in-person interviews generally lasted between 45 minutes and one hour; the phone interviews generally lasted 30–45 minutes. I attributed the difference in length to two factors: (1) It is more difficult to maintain long conversations by phone than in person; and (2) I conducted the phone interviews after the on-campus interviews were completed; therefore, I was already aware of the basics of the process and eliminated some introductory questions, which decreased the interview time. Otherwise, I did not detect differences in the substance and quality of phone interviews and in-persons interviews.

Prior to the start of each interview, I explained the purpose of my research and discussed confidentiality issues, reminding informants that no names—individually or institutionally—would be used in the study. (See Exhibit 5 for a sample consent script.) I requested permission to audio-tape the interview, informing participants that I would turn off the tape recorder at their request at any time during the interview, although no one exercised that option. I audiotaped 29 of the in-person interviews; two interviews were not recorded because of equipment failure. In addition, I did not have recording equipment to tape the five phone interviews. On these seven occasions, I recorded notes of the conversation.[1] In four of these instances, I forwarded a paraphrased transcript to the informant for review to insure that my notes properly captured the meaning and interpretation of the interview.

Written Documentation

"One particularly rich source of information about many programs is program records and documents" (Patton, 1990, p. 233). I collected both institutional and external documents for three primary reasons.

1. I searched for additional informants not identified by other people.
2. I looked in records for additional events, processes, and relationships that informants did not mention during the interviews. At Rowlette College, minutes of the board of trustees' meetings referenced a Tenure Task Force that interviewees did not discuss. The Accomac faculty meeting minutes provided information on the sequencing of events. In these cases, documentation provided an additional source of information.
3. I used written documents to triangulate interviews (Patton, 1990). Because written documentation often provides a contemporaneous official record of events, participants, and processes, they can verify the accuracy of statements about the past (Marshall & Rossman, 1989).

I obtained documentation from the primary informants identified by the college presidents, from interviewees, and from public sources. These written data included:

Internal documents:
- Faculty handbook prior to the change in faculty appointment policy
- Faculty handbook after the change in faculty appointment policy
- Presidential speeches and memoranda/letters relating to the change in policy
- Strategic planning documents
- Minutes from faculty senate meetings and other faculty groups
- Minutes from board of trustees meetings
- Accreditation self-study reports

External documents
- Local newspaper articles

---

1. Case study methodologists seem impartial towards audio recording versus hand recording interviews. Yin (1994) stated that the use of tape recorders is a matter of personal preference.

- Accreditation reports
- Letters to the editor from student newspapers, local newspapers, and *The Chronicle of Higher Education*
- AAUP reports in *Academe*
- Consultants' reports

See Exhibit 6 for a specific list of documentation obtained at each institution.

Data Analysis Procedures

"Data analysis is the process of bringing order, structure, and meaning to the mass of collected data. It is a messy, ambiguous, time-consuming, and fascinating process" (Marshall & Rossman, 1989, p. 112). I undertook this process in several ways.

Data management and organization

I managed the data in a systematic way. After each site visit, I filed all written documentation and transcribed the audio-recorded interviews via word-processing. I maintained both electronic and hard copies of each interview.

Generating categories, themes, and patterns

To bring order to and make sense of the plethora of data, I used several of the strategies suggested by qualitative methodologists (Maxwell, 1996; Miles and Huberman, 1993; Patton, 1990).

- I developed coding strategies for data across the research sites to develop categories and "recurring regularities" (Guba, 1978). As Maxwell (1996) noted, coding schemata may be developed from prior theory as well as inductively. Many of my coding categories and themes emerged from the ongoing data analysis process (Miles and Huberman, 1993). However, I developed some initial categories from the loosely coupled model of change.
- I read the interviews and written documentation at least twice (in some cases, three or four times) and coded the data separately after each read-through. This process enabled me to continually develop new codes and insights without being constrained by my previous work. Then, I compiled the various codes into "meta-codes," collapsing and combining categories. These codes and the meta-codes were entered into an Excel spreadsheet, in which I could sort and manipulate the codes by institution, interviewee position, and coding category.

- As outlined by Patton (1990), I developed a stand-alone case study for each institution that represents the "idiosyncratic manifestation" of the organizational change process (Patton, 1990, p. 387). This strategy permitted me to understand the data in context (Maxwell, 1996) so that I could analyze the organizational change process at each institution. I used the coding schemata to distill and organize the interview and written documentation data at each institution.

I used the coding schemata and stand-alone cases to develop a multi-case comparison, analyzing similarities and differences in the change processes at the four sites. This multi-case comparison is presented in chapter seven.

Testing emerging hypotheses against the data

I wrote regular memos to myself as I conducted the data analysis to capture analytic thinking and develop new insights (Maxwell, 1996). I compared the meaning I attributed to the data in these memos with the actual data to determine the plausibility (Miles & Huberman, 1994) of my propositions.

TRUSTWORTHINESS AND ETHICS

Maxwell (1996) cautioned, "validity is a goal rather than a product. It is never something that can be proven or taken for granted" (p. 86). I instituted a number of strategies to increase the trustworthiness of my study. Patton (1990) suggested several types of triangulation of which I made use. I collected data through a variety of techniques, including interviews, internal documentation, and external document gathering. I triangulated sources by interviewing people at varied levels of each institution. I also relied on ongoing feedback from various peers and colleagues. I shared my findings and analyses regularly with three different groups of colleagues.

In addition to triangulation strategies, I looked for discrepant evidence, negative cases, and rival explanations that would have contradicted my analyses and conclusions (Maxwell, 1996; Patton, 1990). I also primarily relied on "rich data" by audio-recording interviews when possible and using verbatim transcripts (Maxwell, 1996).

Based on these safeguards, I have confidence in producing extrapolations (Patton, 1990) from this study. Extrapolations are not generalizations, but "modest speculations on the likely applicability of findings to other situations under similar, but not identical, conditions. Extrapolations are logical, thoughtful, and problem oriented rather than statistical and probabilistic" (Patton, 1990, p. 489).

Appendix: Research Design and Methodology

I made every attempt to proceed ethically during the course of research. I acknowledge that my influence as a researcher was impossible to eliminate (Maxwell, 1996) and the interviews I conducted could have affected the interviewees (Patton, 1990). I attempted to interact with the people I interviewed in a natural, trustful manner (Bogdan & Bilken, 1992).

LIMITATIONS OF THE STUDY

Every study has imperfections. This study was limited by issues of methodology, researcher experience, and sample selection.

I chose case-study design because it was the best method for answering my research questions—its strengths outweighed its limitations (Merriam, 1988). Nevertheless, case method has its drawbacks. First, because case studies produce a plethora of data, researchers may oversimplify or exaggerate a situation (Guba & Lincoln, 1981). I have been sensitive to this concern. Second, "the researcher is the primary instrument of data collection and analysis" (Merriam, 1988, p. 34). Therefore, this study is subject to my personal biases. Of course, all investigative methods are subject to researcher bias and error.

Goetz and LeCompte (1984) highlighted another limitation of qualitative research: the researcher "may fail to recognize the implications of a study until sufficient time and distance permit data to be reexamined in less-immediate, more-dispassionate ways" (p. 196). These authors acknowledged, however, that it may be impractical to wait 3-4 years before writing a report. The findings in this study had a considerable gestation period; after further reflection, however, I may develop additional extrapolations on the data beyond those covered in this book.

I focused my research on institutions that changed their faculty employment policies in the past. Glick, et al. (1995) noted that "retrospective event histories" have disadvantages:

> Responses may be associated with errors of recall; for example, informants may selectively neglect some events that are important or focus on trends that are actually unimportant but are temporarily conspicuous to the informant. . . . Errors of recall can result from strong cognitive processes such as rationalization, self-presentation, simplification, attribution, and simple lapses of memory. (p. 139)

This concern was minimized in this study to some degree because (1) I focused on a "big" change in the life of the institution; important changes tend to be recalled more reliably (Glick, et al., 1995); (2) I interviewed numerous people at each institution, minimizing the impact of any one informant; (3) I collected and analyzed written documentation to corroborate informants' stories.

The process of site selection affected this study in three ways. First, because of the limited number of institutions that overhauled their faculty employment policies, access became an important selection criterion. Second, the policy change at one institution in the study, Rowlette College, evolved over a period of 20 years. While very good written documentation on the change process existed at this site, fewer informants were available to be interviewed, and the recollections of these informants might have been affected by the passage of time more than at the other sites. Third, two tenure-to-contract institutions declined to participate because of the fear of revisiting contentious issues. This may suggest that the process of change at the two tenure-to-contract institutions in the study is not representative of the process at those institutions that declined, or at the whole "universe" of institutions that abolished tenure.

EXHIBIT 1
Request Letter Sent to Presidents at Potential Sites

November 4, 1998

«FirstName» «LastName»
President
«Company»
«Address1»
«Address2»

Dear President «LastName»:

I am writing to request permission to include «Company» in my doctoral dissertation research at the Harvard Graduate School of Education. I am conducting case studies on four colleges that changed their faculty employment policies: two colleges that switched from tenure to contracts and two colleges that moved from contracts to tenure. Because «Company» changed to «Company» in «year», I would very much like to include your institution in my study.

The purpose of the research is to examine whether the change process unfolded in similar ways at all four sites. I would like to interview individuals who were involved in and affected by the change: the president, academic vice president or dean, faculty members, and trustees. The research will *not* attempt to assess the efficacy of the decision; that is, I am not studying the appropriateness of the decision nor I am marshalling evidence to support or criticize one personnel policy over another.

The study will make minimal demands on you and your colleagues. I would like to make a two- or three-day site visit in late spring 1999. Each institution in the study will be kept confidential (pseudonyms will be assigned) and those individuals interviewed for the study will not be identified by name. Each interview will last about one hour.

I hope you will agree to participate in this study, as it will help the academy better understand how change occurs. I will make a phone appointment with you in the next two weeks to further discuss this request. In the meantime, please do not hesitate to contact me if you have questions (work: 617-49x-xxxx, home: 781-6xx-xxxx, email: bill_mallon@harvard.edu).

Thank you in advance for your time and consideration.

Sincerely,

Bill Mallon
Harvard Graduate School of Education

EXHIBIT 2
List of Interviewees at Each College

Accomac College

Administration and board members:
    Former president
    Chairman of the board
    Former trustee
    Former provost
Six faculty members
Total of ten interviews

Lakeview College

Administration and board members
    President
    Provost
    Academic dean
    Chairman of the board of trustees
    Consultant to the president
Four faculty members
Total of nine interviews

Rowlette College

Administration and board members
    Former president
    Former academic vice president
    Current academic vice president
    Member of the board of trustees
Three faculty members
    Total of seven interviews

Scott College

Administration and board members
    President
    Academic dean
    Member of the board of trustees
Seven faculty members (including one former faculty member)
Total of ten interviews

Grand total of 36 interviews:
20 faculty members, 11 administrators, and 5 trustees

EXHIBIT 3
Sample Inquiry Letter to Faculty

March 3, 1999

«Greeting» «first_name» «last_name»
«title»
Lakeview College

Dear «Greeting» «last_name»:

President Murin has generously agreed to allow me to include Lakeview College in my doctoral dissertation research at the Harvard Graduate School of Education. I am conducting case studies on four colleges that changed their faculty employment policies: two colleges that switched from tenure to contracts and two colleges that moved from contracts to tenure. Since Lakeview College changed to tenure in 1997, it is an ideal site for my study.

I will be visiting Lakeview on May 24-26 to interview faculty, administrators, and board members who were involved in or affected by the decision to institute a tenure system in 1997. Your name has been suggested to me by the President's Office. Therefore, I write to you to request your participation in this study.

I would be grateful for about one hour of your time to learn about your involvement in and perspectives on this change process. Your individual comments will be kept confidential and not used for attribution. In addition, each institution in the study will be kept confidential (pseudonyms will be assigned).

The purpose of the research is to examine whether the change process unfolded in similar ways at all four sites. The research will *not* attempt to assess the efficacy of the decision; that is, I am not studying the appropriateness of the decision nor I am marshalling evidence to support or criticize one personnel policy over another.

I hope you will agree to participate in this study, as it will help the academy better understand how change occurs. I will make a phone appointment with you in the next few weeks to determine your interest in participating in the study. In the meantime, please do not hesitate to contact me if you have questions (work: 617-4xx-xxxx, home: 781-6xx-xxxx, email: bill_mallon@harvard.edu).

Thank you in advance for your time and consideration.

Sincerely,

Bill Mallon
Harvard Graduate School of Education

EXHIBIT 4
Interview Protocol

Grand Tour questions:

1. Please tell me the story of how [COLLEGE] changed its faculty employment policy from [tenure to contracts/contracts to tenure] as you experienced it. Who did what?

2. What must I know about the institutional context and history of [COLLEGE] to understand how the change in policy was made and implemented?

3. Can you describe how major decisions are typically made on campus? Did the change follow the normal governance or decision-making process at the college? Was there anything different about the decision-making approach to this issue?

4. What was your role in the process? What did you do?

Participation and influence of campus constituencies

5. In your opinion, who on campus had the most influence in the decision-making process and in the implementation process of changing from [tenure to contracts/contracts to tenure]?

6. What was the role of the president in the process of change from [tenure to contracts/contracts to tenure]?

7. What was the role of faculty in the process of change from [tenure to contracts/contracts to tenure]?

Relationship between cause and effect

8. What was the intention of the overhaul in faculty appointment policy? What was the intended result? What evidence exists that the intended result was realized?

Alternative phrasing for question 8:
What was the college trying to accomplish by the shift from . . . to . . . ? Did the shift solve these problems? Did the shift create new problems?

9. What criteria were used to make the decision to change from . . . to . . . ?

Appendix: Research Design and Methodology 205

Summary questions

10. What was expected, typical, or normal in the change process from [contract to tenure/tenure to contracts]? What was unexpected, unusual, or surprising?

11. If the colleges was to do it all over again, should [College] make the change? Is so, should they undertake the change process in a different way, or do it the same way?

EXHIBIT 5
Sample Consent Script

Thank you for agreeing to participate in this study. The purpose of this research is to explore the process of organizational change when [COLLEGE] changed its faculty appointment policy from [contracts to tenure/tenure to contracts]. Your participation is valuable to me to gain an understanding of how different people perceived that process to have occurred.

I would like to audio-tape this interview so that I can assure the accuracy of your comments. If you agree, I will turn on the tape when I begin the interview momentarily. If, at any time, you want to turn off the tape recorder, you are free to do so. Of course, you also may end the interview or decline to answer a particular question.

Confidentiality will occur at two different levels. First, each institution in the study will be assigned a pseudonym that will provide anonymity at the institutional level. Second, you will not be identified by name in this study and your comments will be kept confidential. I may use direct quotations from the interview to illustrate a point or illuminate findings, but quotations will not be attributed by name. If necessary, the study might identify your position in general terms (a faculty member, etc.)

Despite these precautions, confidentiality in research such as this study cannot be *guaranteed*. For example, it is possible that, if individuals from [COLLEGE] read the dissertation study, they may be able to identify you as a participant based on the content of the quotation or based on the general descriptor used to identify the source of the quotation.

Do you have any questions or concerns about these confidentiality issues?

The audio-tape will be erased once the interview has been transcribed. Do I have your permission to audio tape this interview? [YES/NO]

EXHIBIT 6
Written Documentation Gathered at Each Institution

Accomac College

Current faculty handbook
Faculty handbook under previous system
Correspondence from former vice president for academic affairs
Faculty meeting minutes (various)
Faculty senate meeting minutes (various)
Annual report of the provost, various years
Report from Tenure Committee, March 30, 1993
Correspondence from faculty senate president to faculty
Minutes from board of trustees meetings
Correspondence from former VPAA to faculty, March 1975
Consultant report, 1974
Reaccreditation Self-Study Report, 1994
College Catalog
Admissions marketing materials

Lakeview College

City newspaper article, 1997
Student newspaper: Sept. 29, 1997, article and editorial; Oct. 6, 1997, letter to editor
Two national newspaper articles, 1997
Draft tenure document written by faculty committee
Faculty evaluation policy prior to tenure
New tenure policy
Article by president, "The Adoption of Tenure at Lakeview College in 1997"
"Chronology of events leading to the adoption of tenure" (from President's Office)
"Background and summary, Board of Trustees Approval of Tenure, May 1997" (from President's Office)
Faculty Handbook, prior to tenure
Admissions materials
College Catalog

Rowlette College

Rowlette College alumni magazine
College Catalog
Admissions marketing materials

Current faculty handbook
Former faculty personnel policy (1967)
Correspondence from former vice president for academic affairs
Board policy for faculty compensation, 1969
Minutes from board of trustees meetings
Report of the president, 1974
Report of Retrenchment Committee, 1982

Scott College
Three newspaper articles, 1994, 1995, 1999
Board of Trustees meeting minutes
Faculty Senate meeting minutes
Correspondence from president to faculty
Academic Council meeting minutes
Faculty Handbook, prior to change
Faculty Handbook, current
Student Newspaper, Dec. 9, 1993; Feb. 10, 1994; and Feb. 24, 1994
Report of Accreditation Team visit, March 1991
College Self-Study for accreditation visit, Spring 1991
College Catalog
Promotional pamphlet
U.S. News & World Report materials, 1997 & 1999
Admissions marketing materials

References

Adams, W. (1974). The state of higher education: Myth and realities. *AAUP Bulletin, 60*(2), 119–125.

Aigner, D. J. (1998, April 5). Tenure is turning untenable. *Boston Globe*.

American Association of University Professors. (1995). *Policy Documents and Reports*. Washington, D.C.: AAUP.

American Association of University Professors. (1915). General report of the committee on academic freedom and academic tenure. *AAUP Bulletin, 1*(1), 17–43.

American Association of University Professors. (1940). Academic freedom and tenure. *AAUP Bulletin, 26,* 49–54.

Ashcraft, M. H. (1983). Post-tenure productivity: Academic freedom vs. "a good vita." *American Psychologist, 38,* 115–116.

Austin, A. E., & Rice, R. E. (1998). Making tenure viable. *American Behavioral Scientist, 41*(5), 736–754.

Baldridge, J. V. (1971). *Academic Governance*. Berkeley, CA: McCutchan.

Baldridge, J. V., Curtis, D. V., Ecker, G., & Riley, G. L. (1978). *Policy Making and Effective Leadership*. San Francisco: Jossey-Bass.

Baldridge, J. V., & Deal, T. (Eds.). (1983). *The Dynamics of Organizational Change in Education*. Berkeley: McCutchan.

Barber, J. D. (1966). *Power in Committees*. Chicago: Rand McNally.

Benjamin, E. (1995, January/February). Five misconceptions about tenure. *AGB Trusteeship, 3*(1), 16–21.

Benjamin, E. (1998). Declining faculty availability to students is the problem—but tenure is not the explanation. *American Behavioral Scientist, 41*(5), 716–735.

Birnbaum, R. (1988). *How Colleges Work: The Cybernetics of Academic Organization and Leadership*. San Francisco: Jossey-Bass.

Bogdan, R. C., & Biklen, S. K. (1992). *Qualitative Research for Education*. Boston: Allyn & Bacon.

Bok, D. C. (1992, July/August). Reclaiming the public trust. *Change*, 24, 13–19.

Bolman, L. G., & Deal, T. E. (1991). *Reframing Organizations: Artistry, Choice, and Leadership*. San Francisco: Jossey-Bass.

Bowen, H. R., & Schuster, J. H. (1986). *American Professors: A National Resource Imperiled*. New York: Oxford University Press.

Boyett, J. H., & Snyder, D. P. (1998, March/April). Twenty-first century workplace trends. *On the Horizon: The Strategic Planning Resource for Education Professionals*, 6(2), 1, 4–9.

Breneman, D. W. (1993). *Higher Education: On a collision course with new realities*. Washington, DC: Association of Governing Boards.

Breneman, D. W. (1997). *Alternatives to tenure for the next generation of academics*. Washington, D.C.: American Association for Higher Education.

Brewster, K., Jr. (1972). On tenure. *AAUP Bulletin*, 58(4), 381–383.

Brown, R. S., & Kurland, J. E. (1990). Academic tenure and academic freedom. *Law and Contemporary Problems*, 53, 325–355.

Butler, M., & Davis, H. (1992). Strategic planning as a catalyst for change in the 1990s. *College and Research Libraries*, 53(5), 393–403.

Cage, M. C. (1995, April 28). Report says Ph.D. students should prepare for off-campus jobs. *The Chronicle of Higher Education*, p. A47.

Cannon, R. A., & Lonsdale, A. J. (1987). A "muddled array of models": theoretical and organizational perspectives on change and development in higher education. *Higher Education*, 16, 21–32.

Cappelli, P., Bassi, L., Katz, H., Knoke, D., Osterman, P., & Useem, M. (1997). *Change at Work*. New York: Oxford University Press.

Carlin, J.F. (1999, November 5). Restoring sanity to an academic world gone mad. *Chronicle of Higher Education*, p. A76.

Carr, R. K. (1972). The uneasy future of academic tenure. *Educational Record*, 53(2), 119–127.

Carr, S. (1999, December 17). For-profit venture to market distance-education courses stirs concerns at Temple. *The Chronicle of Higher Education*, A46.

Carr, S. (2000, June 9). Faculty members at wary of distance-education ventures. *The Chronicle of Higher Education*, A41.

Chaffee, E. E. (1983). *Rational Decisionmaking in Higher Education*. Boudler, CO: National Center for Higher Education Management Systems.

References

Chait, R. P. (1995, Spring). *The Future of Academic Tenure.* Washington, D.C.: Association of Governing Boards.

Chait, R. P., & Ford, A. T. (1982). *Beyond Traditional Tenure.* San Francisco: Jossey-Bass.

Chait, R. P., & Trower, C. A. (1997). *Where Tenure Does Not Reign: Colleges with Contract Systems.* Washington, D.C.: American Association of Higher Education.

Chemerinsky, E. (1998). Is tenure necessary to protect academic freedom? *American Behavioral Scientist, 41*(5), 638–651.

Chronicle of Higher Education. (1994, February 16). Math society attacks hiring of part-time professors. *Chronicle of Higher Education,* p. A23.

Clugston, R. M. (1986, February 20–23, 1986). *Strategic planning in an organized anarchy: The emperor's new clothes?* Paper presented at the Annual Meeting of the Association for the Study of Higher Education, San Antonio, TX.

Coalition on the Academic Workforce (2000). *Who is Teaching in U.S. College Classrooms? A Collaborative Study of Undergraduate Faculty, Fall 1999.* Washington: American Historical Association. http://www.theaha.org/caw/index.htm. Accessed April 12, 2001.

Cohen, M. D., & March, J. G. (1974). *Leadership and Ambiguity: The American College President.* New York: McGraw-Hill.

Cohen, M. D., & March, J. G. (1986). *Leadership and Ambiguity: The American College President.* (2nd ed.). Boston: Harvard Business School Press.

Cohen, M. D., March, J. G., & Olsen, J. P. (1972, March). A garbage can model of organizational choice. *Administrative Science Quarterly, 17*(1), 1–25.

Commission on Academic Tenure in Higher Education. (1973). *Faculty Tenure.* San Francisco: Jossey-Bass.

Cotter, W. R. (1996, January-February). Why tenure works. *Academe,* 26–29.

Cottle, M. (1998, September). Too well endowed? Are top universities more concerned about money than about educating students? *Washington Monthly, 30.*

DiBiasio, D. A., & Ecker, G. (1982, March). *Academic program review in a loosely coupled system.* Paper presented at the Annual Meeting of the American Educational Research Association, New York.

DiMaggio, P. J., & Powell, W. W. (1991). The iron cage revisited: Institutional isomorphism and collective rationality in organizational fields. In W. W. Powell & P. J. DiMaggio (Eds.), *The New Institutionalism in Organizational Analysis* (pp. 63–82). Chicago: University of Chicago Press.

Eckel, P., Hill, B., and Green, M. (1998). *En Route to Transformation.* On Change Occasional Paper Series. Washington, D.C.: American Council on Education.

Emerson, R. M. (1962). Power-Dependence relations. *American Sociological Review, 27*, 31–41.

Emmert, M. A. (1998, July/August). The tyranny of our traditions. *AGB Trusteeship*, 6–10.

Finkel, S. W., & Olswang, S. G. (1994, November). *Impediments to tenure for female assistant professors*. Paper presented at the Annual Meeting of the Association for the Study of Higher Education, Tucson, AZ.

Finkin, M. W. (1996). *The Case for Tenure*. Ithaca, NY: Cornell University Press.

Firestone, W. A., & Herriott, R. E. (1983). The formalization of qualitative research: An adaptation of "soft" science to the policy world. *Evaluation Review, 7*, 437–466.

Fisher, J. L. (1984). *Power of the Presidency*. London: American Council on Education/Macmillan.

Fisher, J. L., Tack, M. W., & Wheeler, K. J. (1988). *The Effective College President*. New York: American Council on Education, Macmillan.

French, J. P. P., Jr., & Raven, B. (1959). The bases of social power. In D. Cartwright (Ed.), *Studies in Social Power*. Ann Arbor: Institute for Social Research, University of Michigan.

Friedrich, C. J. (1937). *Constitutional Government and Democracy*. New York: Harper and Brothers.

Gates, G. S. (1997). Isomorphism, homogeneity, and rationalism in university retrenchment. *Review of Higher Education, 20*(3), 253–275.

Gerber, L. G. (1997, September-October). Reaffirming the value of shared governance. *Academe*, 15–18.

Glick, W. H., Huber, G. P., Miller, C. C., Doty, D. H., & Sutcliffe, K. M. (1995). Studying changes in organizational design and effectiveness. In G. Huber & A. H. V. d. Ven (Eds.), *Longitudinal Field Research Methods* (pp. 126–154). Thousand Oaks, CA: Sage.

Goetz, J. P., & LeCompte, M. D. (1984). *Ethnography and Qualitative Design in Educational Research*. New York: Harcourt Brace Jovanovich.

Goodman, P. (1962). *The Community of Scholars*. New York: Random House.

Green, M. F. (1997, March/April). No time for heroes. *AGB Trusteeship*, 6–11.

Green, M.F, Eckel, P., and Hill, B. (1998, July/August). Core values and the road to change. *AGB Trusteeship*, 11–15.

Greenberg, M. (1997, Summer). What about tenure? Is tenure needed? *Metropolitan Universities*, 75–82.

Grunig, S. D. (1996). *Elimination, Modification, or Continuance of Tenure*. Unpublished paper: Arizona Board of Regents.

Guba, E. G. (1978). *Toward a Methodology of Naturalistic Inquiry in Educational Evaluation.* Los Angeles: Center for the Study of Evaluation, UCLA Graduate School of Education.

Guba, E. G. and Lincoln, Y.S. (1981). *Effective Evaluation.* San Francisco: Jossey-Bass.

Gumport, P. J. (1993). The contested terrain of academic program reduction. *Journal of Higher Education, 64*(3), 283–311.

Guskin, A. E. (1996, July/August). Facing the future: The change process in restructuring universities. *Change, 28,* 27–37.

Habecker, E.B. (1981, November). A systematic approach to the study of benefits and detriments of tenure in American higher education. An analysis of the evidence. ERIC Document Reproduction Service No. ED 212 208.

Hammond, M. F. (1981, March 3–4). *Organizational response for survival: a case study in higher education.* Paper presented at the Annual Meeting of the Association for the Study of Higher Education, Washington, D.C..

Hanna, C. (1988). The organizational context for affirmative action for women faculty. *Journal of Higher Education, 59*(4), 390–411.

Hardy, C. (1988). The rational approach to budget cuts: One university's experience. *Higher Education, 17,* 151–173.

Helfand, D. (1995, December 15). Tenure: thanks but no thanks. *Chronicle of Higher Education,* pp. B1.

Hofstadter, R., & Metzger, W. P. (1955). *The Development of Academic Freedom in the United States.* New York: Columbia University Press.

Holley, J. W. (1977). Tenure and research productivity. *Research in Higher Education, 6,* 181–192.

Hoverland, H., McInturff, P., & Rohm, C. E. (1986, Fall). Crisis management in higher education. *New Directions for Higher Education, No. 55, XIV*(3).

Iffland, J. (1998, April 12). Tenure essential to a diverse university. *Boston Globe.*

Immerwahr, J. (1999). *Taking responsibility: Leaders' expectations of higher education.* San Jose, CA: National Center for Public Policy and Higher Education. www.highereducation.org/reports/fs_responsibility.html

Indiana University Computer Science Department. (1993). *The Assistant Professor's Guide to the Galaxy,* [World Wide Web page]. Available: http://www.cs.indiana.edu/docproject/handbook/subsection1.9.0.6.8.html.

Jervis, J. (1995, January/February). The ideal academy. *AGB Trusteeship, 3*(1), 22–25.

Jones, S. (1977, Autumn). Faculty involvement in college and university decision making. *Managing Turbulence and Change, New Directions for Higher Education, V*(3), 81–90.

Keith, K. M. (1997, March). *Faculty attitudes toward tenure and academic freedom at private universities.* Paper presented at the Annual Meeting of the American Educational Research Association, Chicago, IL.

Kennedy, D. (1997). *Academic Duty.* Cambridge: Harvard University Press.

Kerr, C., & Glade, M. L. (1986). *The many lives of academic presidents: Time, place, and character.* Washington, D.C.: Association of Governing Boards of Universities and Colleges.

Kimball, R. (1990). *Tenured Radicals: How politics has corrupted our higher education.* New York: Harper & Row.

Kuh, G. D. (1993, July/August). Appraising the character of a college. *Journal of Counseling & Development, 71,* 661–668.

Kuhn, T. S. (1970). *The Structure of Scientific Revolutions.* (2nd ed.). Chicago: University of Chicago Press.

Leatherman C. (1998, October 16). U. of Phoenix's faculty members insist they offer high-quality education. *The Chronicle of Higher Education,* p. A14.

Leatherman, C., & Wilson, R. (1998, December 18). Embittered by a bleak job market, graduate students take on the MLA. *Chronicle of Higher Education,* p. A10.

Lehman Brothers. (1997). *Emerging Trends in the $670 Billion Education Market.* New York: Lehman Brothers.

Leonard-Barton, D. (1995). A dual methodology for case studies. In G. P. Huber & A. H. Van de Ven (Eds.), *Longitudinal Field Research Methods* (pp. 38–64). Thousand Oaks, CA: Sage.

Leslie, D. W. (1998). Redefining tenure. *American Behavioral Scientist, 41*(5), 652–679.

Lewis, L. S. (1980). Academic tenure: Its recipients and its effects. *The Annals of the American Academy, 448,* 86–101.

Levine, A. (1997a, January 31). Higher education's new status as a mature industry. *Chronicle of Higher Education,* pp. A48.

Levine, A. (1997b, Fall). How the academic profession is changing. *Daedalus, 126*(4), 1–20.

Levine, A. (2000, October 27). The future of colleges: 9 inevitable changes. *The Chronicle of Higher Education,* p. B10.

Licata, C. M. (1998, June). Post-tenure review: At the crossroads of accountability and opportunity. *AAHE Bulletin, 50,* 3–6.

Los Angeles Times. (1999, March 24). Beneath it all, the tenure issue. *Los Angeles Times,* B6.

Lutz, F. W. (1982). Tightening up loose coupling in organizations of higher education. *Administrative Science Quarterly, 27,* 653–669.

Lutz, F. W., & Lutz, S. B. (1988). Organizational structure and loose coupling in higher education. *Journal of Research and Development in Education, 21*(2), 36–44.

Machlup, F. (1964, Summer). In defense of academic tenure. *AAUP Bulletin, 50,* 112–124.

Mallon, W. T. (1999). *Olivet College.* [Teaching case study]. Cambridge, MA: Project on Faculty Appointments, Harvard Graduate School of Education.

Marshall, C., & Rossman, G. B. (1989). *Designing Qualitative Research.* Newbury Park, CA: Sage.

Maxwell, J. A. (1996). *Qualitative Research Design: An Interactive Approach.* Thousand Oaks, CA: Sage.

McCarty, D.J. and Reyes, P. (1987, September-October). Organizational models of governance: Academic deans' decision making styles. *Journal of Teacher Education,* 2–8.

McGrath, C. P. (1997, February 28). Eliminating tenure without destroying academic freedom. *Chronicle of Higher Education,* pp. A60.

McPherson, M. O. & Winston, G. C. (1993.) The economics of academic tenure: A relational perspective. In M. McPherson, M. O. Schapiro, & G. C. Winston (Eds). *Paying the Piper: Productivity, Incentives, and Financing in U.S. Higher Education* (pp. 109–131). Ann Arbor: University of Michigan Press.

Merriam, S. B. (1988). *Case Study Research in Education: A Qualitative Approach.* San Francisco: Jossey-Bass.

Meyer, J. W. (1975). *Notes on the Structure of Educational Organizations* (Occasional Paper No. 3. Eric Document Reproduction Service ED 109 768). Palo Alto: Stanford University

Meyer, J. W., & Rowan, B. (1978). The structure of educational organizations. In J. W. Meyer (Ed.), *Environments and Organizations* (pp. 78–109). San Francisco: Jossey-Bass.

Meyer, J. W., & Rowan, B. (1983). Institutionalized organizations: Formal structure as myth and ceremony. In J. W. Meyer & W. R. Scott (Eds.), *Organizational Environments: Ritual and Rationality* . Beverly Hills, CA: Sage.

Miles, M. B., & Huberman, A. M. (1994). *Qualitative Data Analysis.* (2nd ed.). Thousand Oaks, CA: Sage.

Millett, J. (1962). *The Academic Community.* New York: McGraw-Hill.

Mooney, C. J. (1994, December 7, December 7, 1994). Dismissals 'for cause.' *The Chronicle of Higher Education,* pp. A 17, A19–20.

National Center for Education Statistics. (1996). *Institutional Policies and Practices Regarding Faculty in Higher Education.* Washington, D.C.: U.S. Department of Education, Office of Educational Research and Improvement.

National Center for Education Statistics. (1998). *Fall Staff in Postsecondary Institutions, 1995.* Washington, D.C.: U.S. Department of Education.

O'Brien, G. (1998). *All the Essential Half-Truths about Higher Education.* Chicago: University of Chicago Press.

Orphen, C. (1982). Tenure and academic productivity: another look. *Improving College and University Teaching, 30*(2), 60–62.

Patton, M. Q. (1990). *Qualitative Evaluation and Research Methods.* (2nd ed.). Newbury Park, CA: Sage.

Penrod, J. I., & Dolence, M. G. (1991). Concepts for reengineering higher education. *Cause/Effect, 14*(2), 10–17.

Peterson, M. W. (1985). Emerging developments in postsecondary organization theory and research: Fragmentation or integration? *Educational Researcher,* 5–12.

Pew Higher Education Roundtable. (1994, April). To Dance with Change. *Policy Perspectives.* Philadelphia: Institute for Research on Higher Education, University of Pennsylvania.

Pew Higher Education Roundtable. (1996, November). Rumbling. *Policy Perspectives.* Philadelphia: Institute for Research on Higher Education, University of Pennsylvania.

Pfeffer, J. (1981). *Power in Organizations.* Cambridge, MA: Ballinger Publishing Company.

Premeaux, S. R., & Mondy, R. W. (1996, Spring). Tenure: administrative versus faculty perspectives. *CUPA Journal, 47*(1), 25–31.

Radner, R., & Kuh, C. V. (1977). *Market Conditions and Tenure in U. S. Higher Education, 1955–1973.* Cargenie Council on Policy Studies in Higher Education, Technical Report no. 2.

Richardson, R. C., & Skinner, E. F. (1990). Adapting to diversity. *Journal of Higher Education, 61*(5), 485–511.

Rowan, B. (1982). Organizational structure and the institutional environment: The case of public schools. *Administrative Science Quarterly, 27,* 259–279.

Rubin, H. J., & Rubin, I. S. (1995). *Qualitative Interviewing: The Art of Hearing Data.* Thousand Oaks, CA: Sage.

Rutherford, D., Fleming, W., & Mathias, H. (1985). Strategies for change in higher education: Three political models. *Higher Education, 14,* 433–445.

St. Louis Post-Dispatch. (1999, November 21). Post-tenure review is coming. *St. Louis Post-Dispatch,* B2.

Schuster, J. (1998, January/February). Reconfiguring the professoriate: An overview. *Change,* 49–53.

Scott, W. R. (1992). *Organizations: Rational, Natural, and Open Systems.* (3rd ed.). Englewood Cliffs, NJ: Prentice Hall.

Seymour, D. T. (1988). *Developing academic programs: The climate for innovation.* Washington, D.C.: Association for the Study of Higher Education.

Shulman, C. H. (1974). *Private Colleges: present conditions and future prospects.* Washington, D.C.: American Association of Higher Education.

Simsek, H., & Louis, K. S. (1994). Organizational change as paradigm shift. *Journal of Higher Education, 65*(6), 670–695.

Smith, P. (1990). *Killing the Spirit: Higher Education in America.* New York: Viking.

Sowell, T. (1998, September 7). An outbreak of sanity. *Forbes, 57.*

Stake, R. E. (1995). *The Art of Case Study Research.* Thousand Oaks, CA: Sage.

Sykes, C. J. (1988). *Profscam: Professors and the Demise of Higher Education.* New York: St. Martin's Press.

Taylor, F. W. (1911). *The Principles of Scientific Management.* New York: Harper & Row.

Tien, F., & Blackburn, R. T. (1993, April). *Faculty rank systems, research motivation, and research productivity.* Paper presented at the Annual Meeting of the American Educational Research Association, Atlanta, GA.

Tierney, W. G. (1998a). Leveling tenure. *American Behavioral Scientist, 41*(5), 627–637.

Tierney, W. G. (1998b). Tenure in the United States. *International Higher Education, 10,* 9–11.

Tierney, W. G. (1998c). Tenure is dead. Long live tenure. In W. G. Tierney (Ed.), *The Responsive University: Restructuring for High Performance* (pp. 38–59). Baltimore: Johns Hopkins University Press.

Tierney, W. G. (1998d). Tenure matters. *American Behavioral Scientist, 41*(5), 604–606.

Trachtenberg, S. J. (1996, January-February). What strategy should we adopt now to protect academic freedom? *Academe,* 23–25.

Trow, M.A. (1983, November/December). Reorganizing the biological sciences at Berkeley. *Change, 28,* 44–53.

Trower, C. A. (1996a). *Junior Faculty Behavior and Experiences: Work Life on the Tenure-track, Off the Tenure-track, and At Institutions Without Tenure.* Unpublished doctoral dissertation, University of Maryland, College Park, MD.

Trower, C. A. (1996b). *Tenure Snapshot.* Washington, D.C.: American Association of Higher Education.

Tully, S. (1995, May 1). Finally, colleges start to cut their crazy costs. *Fortune, 131,* 110.

Twombly, S. B. (1992). The process of choosing a dean. *Journal of Higher Education, 63*(6), 653–683.

Weber, M. (1947). *The Theory of Social and Economic Organizations* (T. Parsons, Trans.). New York: Free Press.

Weick, K. E. (1976). Educational organizations as loosely coupled systems. *Administrative Science Quarterly, 21*(1), 1–19.

Weick, K. E. (1982). Administering education in loosely coupled systems. *Phi Delta Kappan, 63*(10), 673–676.

Weick, K. E. (1983). Contradictions in a community of scholars: The cohesion-accuracy tradeoff. In J. L. Bess (Ed.), *College and University Organization* (pp. 15–29). New York: New York University Press.

Weick, K. E. (1984). Management of organizational change among loosely coupled elements. In Paul S. Goodman and associates (Ed.), *Change in Organizations: New Perspectives on Theory, Research, and Practice* (pp. 375–408). San Francisco: Jossey-Bass.

Wellman, J. (2001, March/April). Assessing state accountability systems. *Change, 33* (2), 46–52.

Whalen, J. J. (1995, December 4). *Seeking a model for change*. Paper presented at the KPMG Peat Marwick Conference on Higher Education in the 21st Century, Palm Beach, FL.

Wilke, A. S. (1979). *The Hidden Professoriate: Credentialism, Professionalism, and the Tenure Crisis*. Westport, CT: Greenwood Press.

Wolf, D. S. (1980). *The Union Plan: A Case Study of the Reform of a Traditional Tenure System*. Unpublished doctoral dissertation, University of Virginia, Charlottesville, Virginia.

Wolfe, R. A., Beyer, J. M., Blackburn, R. T., Greenhalgh, L., Nayyar, P. R., & Seth, A. (1996). Rethinking the tenure process. *Journal of Management Inquiry, 5*(3), 221–236.

Yin, R. K. (1994). *Case Study Research: Design and Methods*. (2nd ed.) Thousand Oaks, CA: Sage.

Index

abolishing academic tenure, 54–56, 76–82
    AAUP reaction to, 55
    alternatives to tenure, 79–80
    ambiguity of, 88–89
    analysis of, 61–68, 85–94
    board's role in, 54, 72, 77–82, 84–87, 95, 161–162
    effect on faculty, 59–60, 77
    faculty evaluation and, 56–57
    faculty reaction to, 55–56, 87–88, 157
    faculty resistance to, 59–60
    finances and, 84–85, 156–157
    governance and, 56–57
    job security and, 88–89
    loosely coupled theory and, 166–169
    marginalization of faculty, 65–66
    outcomes of, 93–94
    problems solved by, 90–91
    president's role in, 54–55, 87, 156, 160–162
    reasons for, 57–60, 77–80, 84–85, 156–157
    symbolism of, 58–59, 81–82, 178

academic freedom, 16, 18–21, 178–180
    at institutions without tenure, 178–180
    origins of, 16
academic rank
    See faculty rank
academic tenure
    academic freedom and, 18–20
    as quid pro quo, 140–141
    calls for reform to, 5–6
    changes to, 11–12
    characteristics of, 4
    compensating wage differential, 22
    cooperation among faculty and, 24
    deviations from AAUP policy, 107–109, 112
    differences with term contracts, 26, 83–84
    faculty dismissal and, 175–176
    faculty indifference to, 157, 182–183
    faculty productivity and, 29
    faculty quality and, 28–31
    faculty recruitment and, 139
    explanation of, 4

governance and, 27–28
grandfathering, 110–111, 138, 140, 176–178, 183
institutional flexibility and, 22
job security and, 21–27, 178–179, 181
lack of empirical study of, 3, 9–10, 17
meaning of, 83–84
mainstream higher education and, 26
norms of professionalization, 155–156
organizational growth and, 154–155
part-time faculty and, 7–8
perceived rigidity of, 22–23
post-tenure review, 108, 132, 147–148
power and, 110–111
pressures to change, 6–8
professional status of faculty and, 111, 141, 148–149, 154–156
public perception of, 24–25
similarities to term contracts, 107, 112, 163–164, 177–178
statistics about, 16
strengths and weaknesses of, 3, 17–33
symbolism of, 58–59, 83–84, 93–94, 120–121, 172–173, 179
teaching and, 30
See also abolishing academic tenure, instituting academic tenure
Accomac College, 125–149
analysis of change, 142–149
board of trustees, 127–129, 137–138
characteristics of, 126–128
change to tenure, 134–138
collegial model applied to, 142–149
faculty, 130–131
faculty evaluation, 139–140
faculty recruitment, 139
governance, 130–131, 141–144
growth in prominence, 128–129, 141
history, 125–126
president, 129–130
reasons for change in employment policy, 134–138
relationship to state, 127–128
term contract policy, 131–135
accountability, faculty, 57–58
Adams, Walter, 4, 17, 18, 178, 188
ambiguity, 85–94
American Association of University Professors (AAUP), 16, 18, 19, 22, 27, 55, 107, 112, 156, 169, 180, 181
anti-isomorphism, 156–157
Austin, Ann E., 5, 17, 19, 20, 28, 30
autocratic leadership, 49, 51, 56–57, 73, 98, 114–115, 126, 143

Baldridge, J. Victor, 10, 34–36, 144, 145
Benjamin, Ernst, 18, 178
Biklen, Sari, 13, 194
Birnbaum, Robert, 10, 36, 40, 61, 92, 93, 142–145, 147, 148, 165, 169
board of trustees
Accomac College, 127–129, 137–138
background of, 49, 72, 100, 129, 184
board chair, 100
Lakeview College, 100–101, 107–109
relationship with faculty, 75, 107–109, 145–146

Index

role in abolishing tenure, 54, 72, 77–82, 84–87, 95, 161–162
role in instituting tenure, 107–109, 118–119, 131, 137–138, 160
Rowlette College, 72
Scott College, 49
views on tenure, 107–108, 129, 137
Bogdan, Robert, 3, 194
Bolman, Lee G., 113, 119, 147, 163, 164, 172
Brewster, Kingman, 17, 18, 22

Campaign for National Prominence, 128
Cappelli, Peter, 7, 23
Carlin, James, 5, 182
Carr, Robert K. 7, 18, 19, 20, 22
case study methodology, 189–191
Chait, Richard P., 3, 4, 5, 10, 17, 21, 22, 23, 24, 25, 26, 27, 28, 29, 30, 31, 47, 84, 179, 180
Chaffee, Ellen, 10, 34
Cherminsky, Erwin, 18, 19, 20, 178
Cohen, Michael D., 10, 40, 41, 60, 85, 86, 88–93, 113, 116, 118, 121, 158, 161, 164–169, 188, 190
collegial model of organizations, 36, 74, 142–149
    consensus and, 144–145
    decision-making in, 143–144
    definition of, 142–143
Commission on Academic Tenure in Higher Education, 4, 18, 19, 20, 23, 24, 28, 178, 179
communication, as a barrier to faculty power, 65
competition and cooperation, 24
contract-renewal process, 80–81, 104–105, 131–134, 177–178
contracts
    See Term Contracts

Cotter, William R., 3, 4, 17, 18, 22, 29
"critical review" (Accomac College), 132–135

data analyses, 197–198
data collection, 13, 194–197
Deadwood, 23, 58
Deal, Terrence, 34, 113, 119, 147, 163, 164, 172
decision-making, 51, 65–66, 91–92
    importance of, 65–66
"de facto" tenure, 112, 133–134, 175, 181
department chairs, 101–102, 103–104, 109–110
differences between tenure and contracts, 26, 83–84
DiMaggio, Paul J., 36, 37, 120, 155

early career faculty
    See junior faculty
early retirement, 58, 82, 85
elimination of tenure, 10
    See also abolishing academic tenure
Evergreen State College, 29–30

faculty, characteristics of, 99, 117, 126
    non-traditional backgrounds, 100, 117, 154
faculty compensation, 71–72, 88
faculty dismissal, 175–176
faculty employment policy
    changes to, 54–56, 76–82, 105–113, 131–142, 178–179
    current status of, 5–8
    flexibility in, 24–25, 26
    institutions that have changed, 9
    introduction, 4
    poor institutions and, 24
    rationale for change to, 17–33
    types, 4

See also academic tenure, term contracts
faculty evaluation, 31, 53–54, 58, 76, 80–82, 85, 104–105, 109–110, 133, 139–140, 163–164, 175–178
    abolishing academic tenure and, 56–57
    board dissatisfaction with, 81–82, 85
    changes in, 53–54
    early retirement and, 82
faculty, growth of, 119–122
faculty homogeneity, 62–64, 99
faculty personnel policy
    See faculty employment policy
faculty power, 114–115
faculty productivity, 29
faculty professional status, 111, 141, 148–149, 154–156
faculty quality, 28–31
faculty rank, 105–107
faculty recruitment, 63, 113, 135, 139
faculty resistance to change in employment policy, 59–60, 132
faculty role in governance
    See governance
Faculty-trustee relationship, 75, 107–109, 145–146
Finances, effects on faculty employment policy, 84–85
Finkin, Matthew W., 3, 18, 22, 28, 181
First Amendment, 19
Fisher, James L., 10, 37, 38, 61, 161, 165, 171
flexibility in employment policies, 24–25, 26
fluid participation, 86–88, 91
Ford, Andrew, 4, 10, 22, 25, 26, 28, 29, 31
for-profit higher education, 6
"garbage can" theory, 40–43, 90–92
Glick, William H., 191, 194, 199

governance, 27–28, 50–52, 65–67, 73–75, 100, 101, 103–104, 114–117, 162, 171–172
    changes to, 51–52
    faculty role in, 28, 50–52, 65–67, 73–75, 100, 116–117, 130–131, 141–142,
    loosely coupled systems theory and, 171–172
    shared governance, 27–28
    term contracts and, 104–105
    tenure and, 109–110
grandfathering, 110–111, 138, 140, 176–178, 183
Green, Madeleine, 5, 41, 61, 161
Guba, Egon, 197, 199

higher education
    calls for reform to, 5
    changes to, 5
    for-profit, 6
organizational theories applied to, 33–44
homogeneity of faculty, 62–64, 99
"honorary" tenure, 80–82
Huberman, A. Michael, 12, 190, 191, 197, 198

implications for practice, 181–185
institutional maturity
    See organizational growth
institutional isomorphism, 36–37, 120
instituting academic tenure, 105–113, 131–142, 178–179
    academic freedom and, 178–179
    changes in governance, 109–110
    board's role in, 107–109, 118–119, 131, 137–138, 160
    faculty's role in, 106–109, 134–138, 155–156
    grandfathering, 110–111, 138, 140
    job security and, 178–179

Index

loosely coupled theory and, 169–172
outcomes of, 109–110
post-tenure review and, 132, 147–148
president's role in, 132, 134–138, 159–160
public support for, 159–160
reasons for, 110–113, 139–142, 178–179
rejected by faculty, 132
interviews, 194–196

Jervis, Jane, 21, 25, 28, 29
job security, 21–27, 88–89, 178–179, 181
Jones, Sherman, 10, 38, 62
junior faculty, 30–31
academic freedom and, 20
effect of tenure on, 30–31

Keith, Kent M., 17, 19, 20, 21

labor force adjustment, 24
Lakeview College, 97–124
analysis of change, 113–124
board of trustees, 100–101, 107–109
change in policy, 106–109
department chairs, 101–102
faculty, 99–100
faculty employment policies, 104–110
faculty rank, 105–106
governance, 103–104
growth, 102–103
history, 97–98
power, 113–119
president, 99
reasons for change in policy, 110–113
symbolism of change, 119–122
term contracts, 104–105

Lakeview College Faculty Association (LACFAC), 100, 101, 103, 106–107
leadership
See presidential leadership
Leslie, David W., 23, 28, 30
loosely coupled systems theory, 10, 40–43, 85–94, 165–172
application in higher education, 42
characteristics of, 165
effect on institutional decision-making, 171–172
focus on research universities, 42
governance and, 171–172
in abolishing tenure, 166–169
in instituting tenure, 169–172
limitations of, 10–11, 42–43
normative model in higher education, 165
symbols and, 172
Louis, Karen S., 10, 11, 38, 39
Lutz, Frank W., 11, 42, 165

Machlup, Fritz, 28, 29, 181
March, James G., 10, 40, 41, 60, 85, 86, 88–93, 113, 116, 118, 121, 158, 161, 164–169, 188, 190
market forces, 6
Marshall, Catherine, 189, 194, 196, 197
maturity
See organizational growth
Maxwell, Joseph A., 13, 194, 197–199
Merriam, Sharon B., 12, 189, 190, 191, 193, 197–199
Miles, Matthew B., 12, 190, 191, 197
mission, 47–49, 62, 98
moratorium on tenure, 77–80, 95

1940 Statement of Principles of Academic Freedom and Tenure (AAUP), 16, 18
non-probationary faculty, 104–105

non-tenure-track faculty, 21, 30
  increases in, 7–8
non-traditional faculty, 100, 117, 154

Olsen, Johan P., 85, 86, 88–91, 167, 169
organizational change in faculty employment policies, 61–68, 85–94, 113–124, 142–149
    ambiguities of, 85–94
    characteristics of, 152
    faculty evaluation and, 163–164, 175–178
    impact of institutional history on, 153–154
    outcomes of, 178
    reasons for, 57–60, 77–80, 84–85, 156–157
    symbolic nature of, 163–164, 182
    See also abolishing academic tenure, instituting academic tenure
organizational growth, 102–103, 115–118, 119–121, 128–129, 153–157
organizational theories in higher education, 10, 33–44
organized anarchy theory, 10, 40–43, 85–94
    application in higher education, 42
    focus on research universities, 42
    limitations of, 10–11, 42–43
    See also loosely coupled systems theory

paradigm-shifting model of organizations, 38–39
part-time faculty, increases in, 7–8
Patton, Michael Q., 12, 13, 189, 191, 193, 195–199
performance evaluation
    See faculty evaluation
Peterson, Marvin, 10, 11, 41
Pfeffer, Jeffrey, 61–67, 113–115, 117–118, 168, 170, 171
political model of organizations, 34–35
post-tenure review, 108, 132, 147–148
Powell, Walter W., 36, 37, 120, 155
power, 56–68
    centralized, 64–65
    faculty, 114–115
    instituting tenure and, 113–119
    presidential, 61–62
    reasons for tenure, 110–111
    sanctions and rewards, 64
    struggle between president and faculty, 56–57, 59, 60, 61–68
    types of, 61–62
power theory, 37–38, 62–68
presidential leadership, 51, 54–55, 61–62, 87, 99, 106–109, 115–116, 125–126, 129–130
    in abolishing tenure, 54–55, 61–62, 87, 156, 160–162
    governance and, 103–104, 114–115, 143–144
    instituting tenure, 106–109, 115–116
    Lakeview College, 99, 115–116
    personal characteristics, 61–62
    prevailing norms of, 61
    previous experience and, 51, 60, 99, 116, 143, 157–159, 183–184
    Rowlette College, 73–74
    Scott College, 54–55, 59, 61–62
presidential learning, 157–159
presidential turnover, 70
prestige, 31, 111
    faculty, 111
    institutional, 31
    affect of tenure and contracts on, 31
    See also faculty professional status

Index

political activity, 64–65
probationary period, 104–105
probationary faculty
    See junior faculty
problematic preferences, 88–89
productivity, faculty, 29
    affect of tenure on, 29
professional norms of tenure, 155–156
professional status of faculty
    See faculty professional status
public (state-supported) college, 126–128

quality of life, 50, 75–76, 154

rational model of organizations, 4, 33–34
research, lack of, 3, 9–10, 17
research design and methodology, 12–13, 187–203
research questions, 187–188
Rice, Eugene, 5, 17, 19, 20, 28, 30
rolling contracts
    See term contracts
Rossman, Gretchen B., 189, 194, 196, 197
Rowan, Brian, 37, 93
Rowlette College, 69–95
    analysis of change, 85–94
    board of trustees, 72, 77–78, 95
    early retirement, 82
    faculty, 74–76
    governance, 74–76
    financial position, 70–72, 77–78
    history of, 69–70
    "honorary" tenure, 81–82
    meaning of tenure, 83–84
    president, 73–74
    reasons for change in policy, 84–85
    tenure policy, 76–80
    term contracts, 80–84

sample of study, 12–13, 191–193
scope of book, 8–10
Scott College, 45–68
    abolishment of tenure, 54–56
    analysis of change, 61–68
    board of trustees, 49
    change in governance 51–52
    faculty, 50
    faculty evaluation, 53–54
    financial position, 47
    history, 45–47
    mission, 47–49, 62
    president, 49, 51, 54–55, 56, 59
    reasons for change in policy, 57–60
shared governance
    See governance
Simsek, Hasan, 10, 11, 38, 39
slack resources, 167–168
socialization of faculty, 63–64
Stake, Robert E., 189, 194
strong leader model of organizations, 37–38
study limitations, 199–200
study overview, 173–174
symbolic frame of organizations, 113, 119–122, 163–165
symbolism, 58, 81–82, 93–94, 113, 119–122, 178
    academic tenure and, 58, 59, 83–84, 93–94, 120–121, 172–173, 179
    rationalized myths and, 93–94

Tack, Martha W., 10, 37, 61
teaching
    effect of tenure on, 30
tenure
    See Academic Tenure
tenure-granting process, 52–53, 76, 80–82, 175–178
    development of, 53, 76
    "honorary" tenure, 8–82
    informality of, 52–53, 57–58, 76

term contracts
    academic freedom and, 18–20
    ambiguity of, 78
    arguments for and against, 17–33, 133–134
    characteristics of, 4, 17, 155
    description of, 77–82
    differences with tenure, 26, 83–84
    explanation of, 4, 17
    faculty dismissal and, 133, 175–176, 181
    faculty quality and, 28–31
    faculty perceptions of, 133–134, 155
    faculty recruitment and, 135
    governance and, 27–28
    grievances under, 105
    job security and, 181
    lack of turnover, 25–26
    one-year, 78
    perceived institutional flexibility of, 24–25
    performance evaluation and, 31, 133
    probationary period under, 80–81, 104–105, 131–132, 133
    similarities to tenure, 107, 112, 163–164, 177–178
    strengths of, 133–134
    weaknesses of, 104–105, 133–134
Tierney, William, 5, 6, 18, 19, 20, 22, 23, 28, 29, 30, 31
time, as a factor in decision-making, 170
transformation, institutional, 41
Trower, Cathy A., 4, 8, 10, 17, 21, 24, 25, 47, 84, 179, 180

unit of analysis, 191
up-or-out provision, 17, 28–29, 76–77, 79

Weick, Karl, 10, 34, 40, 41, 42, 86, 88, 89, 147, 165, 170, 188, 190
Wheeler, Karen J., 10, 37, 61
workforce, growth of contingent, 7
workplace transformation, 7

Yin, Robert K., 12, 13, 189, 190, 195

For Product Safety Concerns and Information please contact our EU representative GPSR@taylorandfrancis.com
Taylor & Francis Verlag GmbH, Kaufingerstraße 24, 80331 München, Germany

www.ingramcontent.com/pod-product-compliance
Lightning Source LLC
Chambersburg PA
CBHW060602230426

43670CB00011B/1940